Essential
Computer
Concepts

THE SHELLY CASHMAN SERIES

Essential Computer Concepts
Computer Concepts
Computer Concepts with BASIC
    ClassNotes and Study Guide to Accompany Computer Concepts and Computer Concepts with BASIC
Computer Concepts with Microcomputer Applications (Lotus® version)
Computer Concepts with Microcomputer Applications (VP-Planner Plus® version)
    ClassNotes and Study Guide to Accompany Computer Concepts with Microcomputer Applications
        (VP-Planner Plus® and Lotus® versions)
Learning to Use WordPerfect® (version 4.2), Lotus 1-2-3®, and dBASE III PLUS®
    ClassNotes and Study Guide to Accompany Learning to Use WordPerfect® (version 4.2), Lotus 1-2-3®,
        and dBASE III PLUS®
Learning to Use WordPerfect® 5.0/5.1, Lotus 1-2-3®, and dBASE III PLUS®
    ClassNotes and Study Guide to Accompany Learning to Use WordPerfect® 5.0/5.1, Lotus 1-2-3®,
        and dBASE III PLUS®
Learning to Use WordPerfect® 5.0/5.1, Lotus 1-2-3® Release 2.2, and dBASE III PLUS®
    ClassNotes and Study Guide to Accompany Learning to Use WordPerfect® 5.0/5.1, Lotus 1-2-3® Release 2.2,
        and dBASE III PLUS®
Learning to Use WordPerfect® (version 4.2), VP-Planner Plus®, and dBASE III PLUS®
    ClassNotes and Study Guide to Accompany Learning to Use WordPerfect® (version 4.2), VP-Planner Plus®,
        and dBASE III PLUS®
Learning to Use WordPerfect® (version 4.2)
    ClassNotes and Study Guide to Accompany Learning to Use WordPerfect® (version 4.2)
Learning to Use WordPerfect® 5.0/5.1
    ClassNotes and Study Guide to Accompany Learning to Use WordPerfect® 5.0/5.1
Learning to Use VP-Planner Plus®
    ClassNotes and Study Guide to Accompany Learning to Use VP-Planner Plus®
Learning to Use Lotus 1-2-3®
    ClassNotes and Study Guide to Accompany Learning to Use Lotus 1-2-3®
Learning to Use Lotus 1-2-3® Release 2.2
    ClassNotes and Study Guide to Accompany Learning to Use Lotus 1-2-3® Release 2.2
Learning to Use dBASE III PLUS®
    ClassNotes and Study Guide to Accompany Learning to Use dBASE III PLUS®
Learning to Use dBASE IV®
Computer Fundamentals with Application Software
    Workbook and Study Guide to Accompany Computer Fundamentals with Application Software
Learning to Use SuperCalc®3, dBASE III®, and WordStar® 3.3: An Introduction
Learning to Use SuperCalc®3: An Introduction
Learning to Use dBASE III®: An Introduction
Learning to Use WordStar® 3.3: An Introduction
BASIC Programming for the IBM Personal Computer
RPG II, RPG III, and RPG/400

Essential Computer Concepts

Gary B. Shelly
Thomas J. Cashman
James S. Quasney

Boyd & Fraser

The Shelly Cashman Series
Boyd & Fraser Publishing Company

© 1990 by boyd & fraser publishing company
A Division of South-Western Publishing Company
Boston, MA 02116

Developed by Susan Solomon Communications
Manufactured in the United States of America

Credits for photos and illustrations appear on page I-7, which constitutes a continuation of the copyright page.

Library of Congress Cataloging-in-Publication Data

```
Shelly, Gary B.
   Essential computer concepts / Gary B. Shelly, Thomas J. Cashman,
James S. Quasney.
      p.   cm. -- (The Shelly and Cashman series)
   ISBN 0-87835-456-5
   1. Electronic digital computers.   I. Cashman, Thomas J.
II. Quasney, James S.  III. Title.  IV. Series: Shelly, Gary B.
Shelly and Cashman series.
QA76.5.S458  1991
004--dc20                                   89-37347
                                               CIP
```

2 3 4 5 6 7 8 9 K 3 2 1 0

Contents in Brief

Contents

Chapter 3   Input to the Computer   3.1

Chapter 4   The Processor Unit   4.1

Chapter 5   Output from the Computer   5.1

Chapter 6   Auxiliary Storage   6.1

Chapter 7 File Organization and Databases **7.1**

Chapter 8 Data Communications **8.1**

Chapter 9 Operating Systems and System Software 9.1

Chapter 10 The System Development Life Cycle 10.1

Chapter 11 Program Development 11.1

Chapter 12   Trends, Issues, and Opportunities 12.1

Preface

Understanding the computer—how it works and how it can be used in the home, in school, and in business—is becoming more and more essential to be productive and successful in today's world. This textbook presents essential computer and information systems concepts from a user's perspective, with an emphasis on microcomputers. No previous experience with computers is required for this book.

This textbook is a derivative of earlier works by Shelly and Cashman. Great care has been taken to maintain the content and philosophy of the original works, as well as the Shelly Cashman pedagogy and teaching style — a style which has proven effective in educating millions of students.

Who Should Use This Book

Essential Computer Concepts provides the essential concepts of computers and information systems. The textbook is ideally suited for majors and nonmajors enrolled in an introductory computer course that combines computer concepts and programming or computer concepts and microcomputer applications software. The keynote of this book is clarity. It is written specifically for the introductory student, for whom continuity, simplicity, and practicality are characteristics we consider essential.

Organization and Scope of This Textbook

This book is divided into twelve chapters. The contents can be covered in 6 weeks, leaving the remainder of the semester to teach programming and/or microcomputer applications.

Chapter 1 presents the concept of the information system. The six elements of an information system—equipment, software, data, personnel, users, and procedures—are introduced in this chapter. Chapter 2 presents a unique overview of the most commonly used microcomputer applications—word processing, spreadsheet, database, graphics, data communications, desktop publishing, electronic mail, and project management. Chapters 3 through 6 describe in detail each aspect of the information processing cycle—input, processing, output, and storage.

Chapter 7 discusses file and database organization and emphasizes the significance and the advantages of relational database systems. Data communications, including networking, is discussed in Chapter 8.

Chapters 9 through 11 cover concepts relating to software, software acquisition, and software development: operating systems and systems software (Chapter 9), the systems development life cycle (Chapter 10), and program development and popular programming languages (Chapter 11).

The final chapter, Chapter 12, discusses current and future trends and issues in the information age and career opportunities in the computer field.

Supplements to Accompany This Text

Instructor's Materials

This manual includes four items to help improve instruction and learning. These items are Lesson Plans, Answers and Solutions, Test Bank, and Transparency Masters.

Lesson Plans—Each project lesson plan begins with chapter behavioral objectives. Next an overview of each chapter is included to help the instructor quickly review the purpose and key concepts. Detailed outlines of each chapter follow. These outlines are annotated with the page number of the textbook, on which the outlined material is covered; notes, teaching tips, and additional activities that the instructor might use to embellish the lesson; and a key for using the Transparency Masters.

Answers/Solutions—Complete answers and solutions for all exercises.

Test Bank—This is a hard copy version of the test questions. It is comprised of three types of questions—true/false, multiple choice, and fill-in. Each project has approximately 50 true/false, 25 multiple choice, and 35 fill-ins. Answers to all of these test questions are included.

Transparency Masters—A Transparency Master is included in *every* line drawing in the textbook.

Acknowledgments

We are grateful to the individuals whose efforts made the completion of this project possible and whose talents are reflected in the final results.

Thanks also to Jeanne Huntington, typesetter; Michael Broussard and Ken Russo, artists; Becky Herrington, production and art coordinator; Sheryl Rose and Elizabeth Judd, manuscript editors; Gerald Swaim, Debbie Moore, and Harriette Treadwell, research assistants; Martha Simmons, production assistant; and Marion Hansen, photo researcher.

We are especially grateful to Mary Douglas, director of production, and Susan Solomon, director of development, whose expertise in the field of publishing and commitment to quality is reflected on each page of the text. Our sincere thanks for your encouragement; you truly deserve your reputation as the ''best in the business.''

Finally we would like to thank Tom Walker, Vice President and Publisher of Boyd & Fraser. His belief in the project and commitment to excellence motivated us to do our best.

Research and Photo Acknowledgments

The following organizations donated materials used for research and photographs for use in this book. We thank them.

3Com Corp.; 3M Company; ACCO International, Inc.; Accurex Corp.; Acme Visible Records; ADAC Laboratories; Adage, Inc.; Addisk, Inc.; Adobe Systems, Inc.; Advanced Computer Communications; Advanced Matrix Technology, Inc.; Agricultural Software Consultants; Aim Technology; Aldus Corp.; All Easy Software Corp.; Allied Corp.; Amdahl Corp.; Amdek Corp.; American Laser Systems, Inc.; American Software; AMP, Inc.; Analog Devices; Anderson Jacobsen; Apollo Computer, Inc.; Apple Computer, Inc.; Applicon, Inc.; Applied Data Research, Inc.; Armor Systems, Inc.; Ashton-Tate; Ask Computer Systems, Inc.; AST Research, Inc.; AT&T Bell Laboratories; Atchison, Topeka and Santa Fe Railway Co.; Atek Information Services, Inc.; Auto-Trol Technology Corp.; Autodesk, Inc.; Automated Insurance Resource Systems, Inc.; Aydin Corp.; BancTec, Inc.; Bank of America; BASF Corp. Information Systems; Bates Manufacturing Co.; BBN Software Products; BDT Products, Inc.; Beagle Bros.; Beehive International; Bell & Howell Co.; Bishop Graphic, Inc.; BR Intec Corp.; Broderbund Software, Inc.; Brother International Corp.; Bruning Computer Graphics; Buttonware, Inc.; CADAM, Inc.; Cadlogic Systems Corp.; Career Corp.; CalComp; Camwil, Inc.; Canon USA, Inc.; Century Analysis, Inc.; Chrislin Industries, Inc.; Chromatics, Inc.; Chrysler Motors, Inc.; Cincinnati Milacron, Inc.; Cincom Systems, Inc.; Cipher Data Products, Inc.; Claris Corp.; Cognotronics Corp.; Coin Financial Systems, Inc.; Cole, Layer, Trumble Co.; Command Technology Corp.; Compaq Computer Corp.; CompuScan, Inc.; Computer Associates; Compute Methods Corp.; Computer Museum, Boston; Computer Power Products; Computer Power, Inc.; Computer Support Group; ComputerLand; Computervision Corp.; ComputerEdge Magazine; Control Applications; Control Data Corp.; Convergent Technologies, Inc.; Corning Glass Works; CPT Corp.; Cray Research, Inc.; Cullinet Softwear; Cummins-Allison Corp.; Cylix Communications Corporation; Dartmouth College News Service; Data General Corp.; Datacopy Corp.; Datagram Corp.; Datapoint Corp.; Dataproducts Corp.; Daytronic Corp.; DBX; Delco Associates, Inc.; Dest Corp.; Develcon, Inc.; Diebold, Inc.; Digital Equipment Corp.; Dorf & Stanton Communications, Inc.; Drexler Technology Corp.; Eastman Kodak Company; ElectroCom Automation, Inc.; Electrohome Ltd.; Electronic Arts; Electronic Form Systems; Emerson Electric Co.; Emulex Corp.; Engineered Data Products; Epson America, Inc.; Esprit Systems, Inc.; Evans & Sutherland; Everex Systems, Inc.; Eye Communication Systems, Inc.; Fellowes Manufacturing Co.; Firestone Tire & Rubber Co.; Forney Engineering Co.; Fortune Systems Corp.; Fujitsu of America, Inc.; Gandalf Technologies, Inc.; General Electric Co.; General Meters Corp.; General Motors Corp.; General Robotics Corp.; GenRad, Inc.; Geber Systems Technology, Inc.; Gould, Inc.; GRiD Systems Corp.; Harris Corp.; Harris/3M; Haworth, Inc.; Hayes Microcomputer Products, Inc.; HEI, Inc.; Heidelberg West; Hercules Computer Technology; Hewlett-Packard Co.; Hitachi America Ltd.; Honeywell Bull, Inc.; Hughes Aircraft Co.; Hunt Manufacturing Co.; ICS Computer Products; Imunelec, Inc.; Index Technology; Industrial Data Terminals Corp.; Information Builders; Information Design, Inc.; Infotron Systems Corp.; InfoWorld Publishing, Inc.; Intecolor Corp.; Integrated Marketing Corp.; Integrated Software Systems Corp.; Intel Corp.; Interface Group, Inc.; Intermec Corp.; Internal Revenue Service; International Business Machines Corp.; International Mailing Systems; International Power Machines; Intertec Diversified Systems, Inc.; Ioline Corp.; ITT Information Systems; Jax International; Jet Propulsion Laboratory/California Institute of Technology; John Fluke Manufacturing Co., Inc.; Kao Corp. of America; Kaypro Corp.; Krueger, Inc.; Kurta Corp.; L/F Technologies, Inc.; Lear Siegler, Inc.; Liberty Electronics; Lockheed Corp.; Logical Business Machines; Logitech, Inc.; Lotus Development Corp.; LXE Division of Electromagnetic Sciences, Inc.; Management Science America, Inc.; Maxell Corp. of America; Maxtor Corp.; MBI, Inc.; McDonnell Douglas Computer Systems, Inc.; MDS Qantel, Inc.; Mead Data Central; Memorex Corp.; Mentor Graphics Corp.; Message Processing Systems, Inc.; MICOM Systems, Inc.; Micro Display Systems, Inc.; Microcomputer Accessories, Inc.; Micrografx, Inc.; Micron Technology, Inc.; MicroPro International Corp.; Microsoft Corp.; Microtek; Mini-Computer Business Applications, Inc.; Minolta Corp.; Modular Computer Systems, Inc.; Moore Business Forms, Inc.; Motorola, Inc.; Mountain Computer, Inc.; MSI Data Corp.; NASA; National Semiconductor Corp.; NCR Corp.; NEC America, Inc.; NEC Home Electronics; NEC Information Systems, Inc.; Neuron Data, Inc.; Norman Magnetics, Inc.; Norsk Data; Northern Telecom, Inc.; Novation, Inc.; Okidata; Olivetti USA; Oracle Corp.; Packard Bell; Panafax Corp.; Panasonic Industrial Co.; Panel Concepts, Inc.; Paperback Software; Paradyne Corp.; Penril DataComm; Perception Technology; Pertec Peripherals Corp.; Photo & Sound Co.; Pitney Bowes; Plus Development Corp.; Polariod Corp.; Prentice Corp.; Princeton Graphics Systems; Princeton University; Printronix; Promethus Products, Inc.; Pyramid Technology; Quadram Corp.; Quality Micro Systems; Questronics, Inc.; Quicksoft, Inc.; Racal-Milgo; Racal-Vadic; Radio Shack, A Division of Tandy Corp.; RB Graphic Supply Co.; RCA; Reliance Plastics & Packaging Division; Ring King Visibles, Inc.; Rockwell International; Royal Seating Corp.; Sato Corp.; Schlage Electronics; Scientific Atlanta; Scientific Calculations, Inc.; Scotland Rack, Ltd.; Seagate Technology Shaffstall Corp.; Sharp Electronics Corp.; Siecor Corp. of America; Siemens Information Systems, Inc.; Silicon Graphics; Sony Corp. of America; Soricon Corp.; Spectra Physics; Spectragraphics Corp.; SRI International; STB Systems, Inc.; Steelcase, Inc.; Storage Technology Corp.; Summagraphics Corp.; Sun Microsystems, Inc.; Sunol Systems; Symbolics, Inc.; Synergistics, Inc.; Syntrex, Inc.; T/Maker Co.; TAB Products Co.; Talaris Systems, Inc.; Tallgrass Technologies; Tandem Computers, Inc.; Tandon Corp.; Tangent Technologies; TDA, Inc.; Tecmar, Inc.; Telematics; Telenet Communications Corp.; Telenova, Inc.; TeleVideo Systems, Inc.; Telex Communications, Inc.; Telex Computer Products, Inc.; Teltone Corp.; Texas Instruments, Inc.; Thomson Information Systems Corp.; Thunderware, Inc.; Toor Furniture Corp.; Topaz, Inc.; TOPS, a division of Sun Microsystems, Inc.; Toshiba America, Inc.; Totec Co. Ltd.; U.S. Department of the Navy; U.S. Postal Service; UIS, Inc.; Ungermann-Bass, Inc.; Unisys Corp.; Universal Data Systems; Varityper; Ven-Tel, Inc.; Vermont Microsystems; Versatec; Verticom, Inc.; Video-7, Inc.; Viking; Votan; Voxtron Systems, Inc.; Wandel & Goltermann, Inc.; Wang Laboratories, Inc.; Weber Marking Systems, Inc.; Western Digital Corp.; Western Graphtec, Inc.; Westinghouse Furniture Systems; WordPerfect Corp.; Wyse Technology; Xerox Corp.; Xtra Business Systems; Z-Soft Corp.; Zehntel, Inc.; Zenith Data Systems; Ziff-Davis Publishing Co.

ORDER INFORMATION AND FACULTY SUPPORT INFORMATION

For the quickest service, refer to the map below for the South-Western Regional Office serving your area.

1 ORDER INFORMATION
5101 Madison Road
Cincinnati, OH 45227-1490
General Telephone–513-527-6945
Telephone: 1-800-543-8440
FAX: 513-527-6979
Telex: 214371

FACULTY SUPPORT INFORMATION
5101 Madison Road
Cincinnati, OH 45227-1490
General Telephone–513-527-6950
Telephone: 1-800-543-8444

Alabama	Massachusetts	Ohio
Connecticut	Michigan	Pennsylvania
Delaware	Minnesota	Rhode Island
Florida	Mississippi	South Carolina
Georgia	Missouri	South Dakota
Illinois	Nebraska	Tennessee
Indiana	New Hampshire	Vermont
Iowa	New Jersey	Virginia
Kentucky	New York	West Virginia
Maine	North Carolina	Wisconsin
Maryland	North Dakota	District of Columbia

2 ORDER INFORMATION
13800 Senlac Drive
Suite 100
Dallas, TX 75234
General Telephone–214-241-8541
Telephone: 1-800-543-7972

FACULTY SUPPORT INFORMATION
5101 Madison Road
Cincinnati, OH 45227-1490
General Telephone–513-527-6950
Telephone: 1-800-543-8444

Arkansas	Louisiana	Texas
Colorado	New Mexico	Wyoming
Kansas	Oklahoma	

3 ORDER INFORMATION and FACULTY SUPPORT INFORMATION
6185 Industrial Way
Livermore, CA 94550
General Telephone–415-449-2280
Telephone: 1-800-543-7972

Alaska	Idaho	Oregon
Arizona	Montana	Utah
California	Nevada	Washington
Hawaii		

An Introduction to Computers

1

Objectives

- Explain what a computer is and how it processes data to produce information.
- Identify the four operations of the information processing cycle: input, process, output, and storage.
- Explain how the operations of the information processing cycle are performed by computer hardware and software.
- Identify the major categories of computers.
- Describe the six elements of an information system: equipment, software, data, personnel, users, and procedures.
- Identify the qualities of information.
- Describe the evolution of the computer industry.

Computers affect our lives every day: in businesses, schools, and government offices. If you buy groceries at a supermarket, use an automatic teller machine, or place a long-distance phone call, you are using a computer.

In recent years, the microcomputer or personal computer has had an increasing impact on our lives. Both at home and at work, these desktop computer systems help us to do our work faster, more accurately, and in some cases, in ways that previously would not have been possible.

As predicted in 1967 by Dr. John Kemeny of Dartmouth College, many people now believe that knowing how to use a computer is "as important as reading and writing," a basic skill necessary to function effectively in today's society. Given the increasing use and availability of computer systems, such knowledge will continue to be an important if not essential skill in the future. The purpose of this book is to present the material necessary for you to gain that knowledge.

What Is a Computer?

The most obvious question related to understanding computers and their impact on our lives is, "What is a computer?" A **computer** is an electronic device, operating under the control of instructions stored in its own memory unit, that can accept data (input), process data arithmetically and logically, produce output from the processing, and store the results for future use. An example of the devices that make up a computer is shown in Figure 1-1.

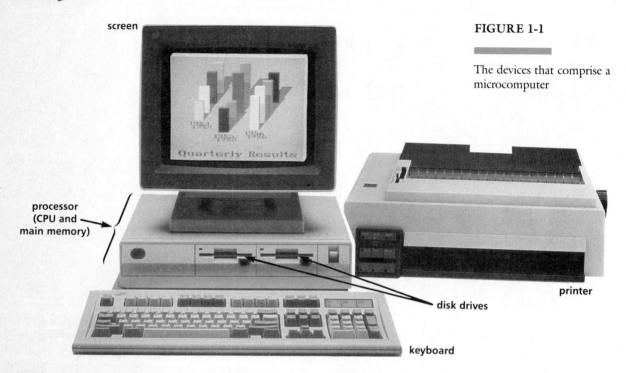

screen

processor
(CPU and
main memory)

disk drives

keyboard

printer

FIGURE 1-1

The devices that comprise a microcomputer

What Does a Computer Do?

Whether they are small or large, computers are capable of performing four general operations. These operations comprise the **information processing cycle**. They are input, process, output, and storage. The first three of these operations, **input**, **process**, and **output**, describe the procedures that a computer performs in order to generate information. The fourth operation, **storage**, describes a computer's electronic storage capability.

  Data is required for all computer processing. It refers to the raw facts, including numbers and words, given to a computer during the input operation. In the processing phase, the computer manipulates the data in a predetermined manner to create information. **Information** refers to data that has been processed into a form that has meaning and is useful. The production of information by processing data on a computer is called **information processing**, or sometimes **electronic data processing**. During the output operation, the information that has been created is put into some form, such as a printed report, that people can use. The information can also be stored in an electronic format for future use.

The people who either use the computer directly or utilize the information it provides are called **computer users**, **end users**, or sometimes just simply **users**. Figure 1-2 shows a computer user and demonstrates how the four operations of the information processing cycle can take place on a personal computer. (1) The user enters the data by pressing the keys on the keyboard. (2) The data is then processed or manipulated by the unit called the processor. (3) The output or results from the processing are displayed on the screen or printed on the printer, providing information to the user. (4) Finally, the output may be stored on a disk for future reference.

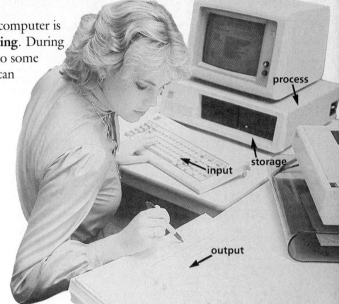

Why Is a Computer So Powerful?

The input, process, output, and storage operations that a computer performs may seem very basic and simple. However, the computer's power is derived from its ability to perform these operations very quickly, accurately, and reliably. In a computer, operations occur through the use of electronic circuits contained on small chips as shown in Figure 1-3. When data flows along these circuits it travels at close to the speed of light. This allows processing to be accomplished in billionths of a second. The electronic circuits in modern computers are very reliable and seldom fail.

Storage capability is another reason why computers are so powerful. They can store enormous amounts of data and keep that data readily available for processing. This capability combined with the factors of speed, accuracy, and reliability are why a computer is considered to be such a powerful tool for information processing.

How Does a Computer Know What to Do?

For a computer to perform the operations in the information processing cycle, it must be given a detailed set of instructions or steps that tell it exactly what to do. These instructions can be called a **computer program**, **program instructions**, or **software**.

FIGURE 1-2

The use of this personal computer illustrates the four operations of the information processing cycle: input, process, output, and storage.

FIGURE 1-3

A top view of the motherboard of an IBM PS/2

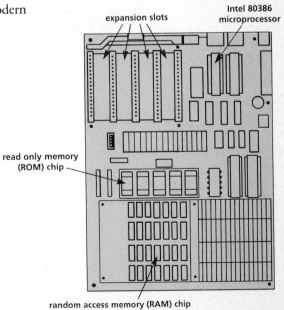

Before the information processing cycle for a specific job begins, the computer program corresponding to that job is stored in the computer. Once it is stored, the computer can begin to process data by executing the program's first instruction. The computer proceeds to execute one program instruction after another until the job is complete.

Information Processing: A Business Application

The example in Figure 1-4 illustrates the use of a computer to produce varied information from data contained on a sales invoice. Once the appropriate computer program has been loaded into the computer, processing occurs as described in the list at the top of the next page.

FIGURE 1-4

The data contained on the sales invoices is entered into the computer. After the data is processed, information in the form of a graph, a report, and a screen display is produced.

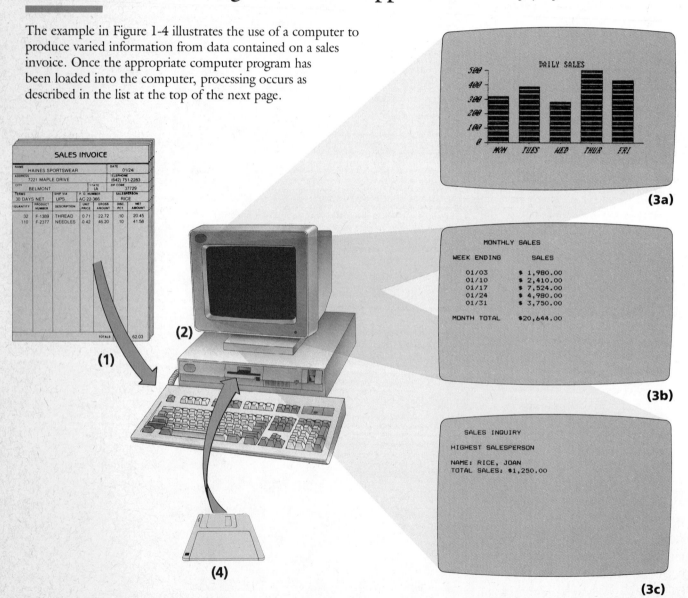

(1)

(2)

(3a)

(3b)

(3c)

(4)

1. The computer user enters data on the sales invoice into the computer via the keyboard.
2. The data entered into the computer is processed to create information.
3. Output from the processing is generated in three forms:
   a. A bar chart illustrates the daily sales, using a bar to represent each day of the week.
   b. A monthly sales report shows the monthly sales. The report displays the total sales for each week, together with the total sales for the month.
   c. The screen displays the name of the salesperson who generated the most sales during the month. In this example, Joan Rice had total sales of $1,250.00, which was the highest for the month.
4. The data entered and information created are stored for future use.

A key point of this example is that several different forms of information can be produced from a single set of data. Without the computer's ability to manipulate the data, the information would be difficult, costly, and time consuming to obtain.

What Are the Components of a Computer?

Processing data on a computer is performed by specific equipment that is often referred to as **hardware** (Figure 1-5). This equipment consists of: input devices, processor unit, output devices, and auxiliary storage units.

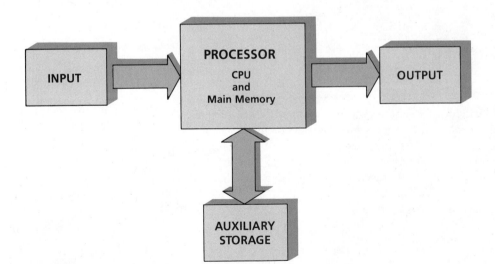

FIGURE 1-5

A computer is composed of input devices through which data is entered into the processor; the processor (central processing unit and main memory) that processes the data; output devices on which the results of the processing are made available; and auxiliary storage units that store data for future processing.

Input Devices

Input devices are used to enter data into a computer. A common input device is the **keyboard** (Figure 1-6a). As the data is entered, or **keyed**, it is displayed on a screen and stored in the computer.

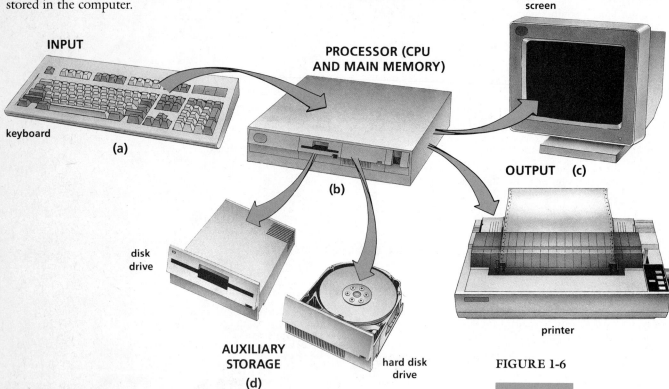

INPUT

keyboard

(a)

PROCESSOR (CPU AND MAIN MEMORY)

(b)

disk drive

AUXILIARY STORAGE

(d)

hard disk drive

screen

OUTPUT **(c)**

printer

FIGURE 1-6

A computer consists of (a) input devices, (b) the processor (CPU and main memory), (c) output devices, and (d) auxiliary storage units. This equipment or hardware is used to perform the operations of the information processing cycle.

Processor Unit

The **processor unit** (Figure 1-6b) includes the central processing unit (CPU) and main memory. The **CPU** controls and supervises the entire computer system and performs the actual arithmetic and logic operations on data, as specified by the program. Numeric calculations such as addition, subtraction, multiplication, and division are called **arithmetic operations**. Comparisons of data to see if one value is greater than, equal to, or less than another are called **logical operations**.

   Main memory, also called **primary storage**, electronically stores data and program instructions when they are being processed.

Output Devices

Output from a computer can be presented in many forms. Where the computer is used for business applications or business-related personal applications, the two most commonly used **output devices** are the **printer** and the computer **screen** (Figure 1-6c).

Other frequently used names for the screen are the **monitor** or the **CRT**, which stands for **cathode ray tube**.

Auxiliary Storage Units

Auxiliary storage units store instructions and data when they are not being used by the processor unit. A common auxiliary storage device on personal computers is a disk drive (Figure 1-6d), which stores data as magnetic spots on a small plastic disk called a **diskette**. Another auxiliary storage device is called a **hard disk drive**. Hard disk drives contain nonremovable metal disks and provide larger storage capacities than diskette drives.

Each computer component plays an important role. The processing unit is where the actual processing of data occurs. The input devices, output devices, and auxiliary storage units that surround the processing unit are sometimes referred to as **peripheral devices**.

Categories of Computers

Figure 1-7 shows the following four major categories of computers: microcomputers, minicomputers, mainframe computers, and supercomputers.

FIGURE 1-7

(a) Microcomputers (below) are small desktop-sized computers. These machines have become so widely used that they are sometimes called "desktop appliances."
▼

(b) Minicomputers (right) can perform many of the functions of a mainframe computer, but on a smaller scale. ▶

(c) Mainframe computers (below) are large, powerful machines that can handle many users concurrently and process large volumes of data.
▼

(d) Supercomputers (left) are the most powerful and expensive computers.
◀

Computers are generally classified according to their size, speed, processing capabilities, and price. However, because of rapid changes in technology, firm definitions of these categories do not exist. This year's speed, performance, and price classification of a mainframe might fit next year's classification of a minicomputer. Even though they are not firmly defined, the categories are frequently referred to and should be generally understood.

Microcomputers (Figure 1-7a), also called **personal computers** or **micros**, are the small desktop-size systems that have become so widely used in recent years. These machines are generally priced under $10,000. This category also includes laptop, portable, and supermicro computers.

Minicomputers (Figure 1-7b) are more powerful than microcomputers and can support a number of users performing different tasks. Originally developed to perform specific tasks such as engineering calculations, their use grew rapidly as their performance and capabilities increased. These systems can cost from approximately $25,000 up to several hundred thousand dollars. The most powerful "minis" are called supermini-computers.

Mainframe computers (Figure 1-7c) are large systems that can handle numerous users, store large amounts of data, and process transactions at a very high rate. Mainframes usually require a specialized environment including separate air conditioning and electrical power. Raised flooring is often built to accommodate the many cables connecting the system components underneath. The price range for mainframes is from several hundred thousand dollars to several million dollars.

Supercomputers (Figure 1-7d) are the most powerful category of computers and, accordingly, the most expensive. The ability of these systems to process hundreds of millions of instructions per second is used for such applications as weather forecasting, space exploration, and other jobs requiring long, complex calculations. These machines cost several million dollars.

Computer Software

As previously mentioned, a computer is directed by a series of instructions called a computer program (Figure 1-8), which specifies the sequence of operations to be performed. To do this, the program must be stored in the main memory of the computer. Computer programs are commonly referred to as **software**.

Many instructions can be used to direct a computer to perform a specific task. For example, some instructions allow data to be entered from a keyboard and stored in main memory; some instructions allow data in main memory to be used in calculations, such as adding a series of numbers to

FIGURE 1-8

A computer program contains instructions that specify the sequence of operations to be performed. This program is written in a language called BASIC. The program instructs the computer to generate a telephone directory of names, area codes, and telephone numbers.

```
100 REM TELLIST          SEPTEMBER 22          SHELLY/CASHMAN
110                                                       REM
120 REM THIS PROGRAM DISPLAYS THE NAME, TELEPHONE AREA CODE
130 REM AND PHONE NUMBER OF INDIVIDUALS.
140                                                       REM
150 REM VARIABLE NAMES:
160 REM    A.....AREA CODE
170 REM    T$....TELEPHONE NUMBER
180 REM    N$....NAME
190                                                       REM
200 REM ***** DATA TO BE PROCESSED *****
210                                                       REM
220 DATA 714, "749-2138", "SAM HORN"
230 DATA 213, "663-1271", "SUE NUNN"
240 DATA 212, "999-1193", "BOB PELE"
250 DATA 312, "979-4418", "ANN SITZ"
260 DATA 999, "999-9999", "END OF FILE"
270                                                       REM
280 REM ***** PROCESSING *****
290                                                       REM
300 READ A, T$, N$
310                                                       REM
320 WHILE N$<> "END OF FILE"
330    PRINT N$, A, T$
340    READ A, T$, N$
350 WEND
360                                                       REM
370 PRINT " "
380 PRINT "END OF TELEPHONE LISTING"
390 END
```

obtain a total; some instructions compare two values stored in main memory and direct the computer to perform alternative operations based on the results of the comparison; and some instructions direct the computer to print a report, display information on the screen, draw a color graph on a screen, or store data on a disk.

Computer programs are written by people with specialized training. They determine the instructions necessary to process the data and place the instructions in the correct sequence so that the desired results will occur. Complex programs may require hundreds or even thousands of instructions.

Most end users do not write their own programs. In large corporations, the information processing department develops programs for unique company applications. In addition, programs required for common business and personal applications can be purchased from software vendors or stores that sell computer products. Purchased programs are often referred to as **applications software packages** or simply **software packages**.

Software is the key to productive use of computers. Without the proper software, a computer cannot perform the desired tasks. With the correct software, a computer can become a valuable tool.

Microcomputer Applications Software Packages

Personal computer users often use applications software packages. The four most commonly used packages, shown in Figure 1-9, are: word processing software, electronic spreadsheet software, computer graphics software, and database software.

Word processing software (Figure 1-9a) is used to create and print documents that would otherwise be prepared on a typewriter. A key advantage of word processing software is its ability to make changes easily in documents, such as correcting spelling, changing margins, and adding, deleting, or relocating entire paragraphs. These changes would be difficult and time consuming to make on a typewriter. Once created, the documents can be printed quickly and accurately.

Electronic spreadsheet software (Figure 1-9b) allows the user to add, subtract, and perform user-defined calculations on rows and columns of numbers. These numbers can be changed and the **spreadsheet** quickly recalculates the new results. Electronic spreadsheet software eliminates the tedious recalculations required with manual methods.

FIGURE 1-9

Commonly used microcomputer applications software packages. (*continued on next page*)

```
LETTER                              01/14
Space 01   Line 07  Page 01   Letter to Johnson
.........1.........2.........3.........4.........5
January 14

Harold A. Johnson
Yonnet Mfg. Co.
3342 Halliard Ave.
Hillsboro, UT 77531

Dear Mr. Johnson:

     I have received your letter concerning the
YT-9975 metal fasteners. We are interested in
testing the part. Would you please send one dozen
of the YT-9975 fasteners. Upon receipt, we shall
begin testing and let you know our decision in
two weeks.

          Sincerely,

          James L. Honnecut
          Vice President, Manufacturing
```

(a) **Word processing** is used to write letters, memos, and other documents.

JOHNSON MANUFACTURING CORPORATION
BUDGET FORECAST

FOR THE PERIOD 01/01 THRU 03/31

ITEM	JAN	FEB	MAR	TOTAL
SALES	112560	213450	211347	537357
RETURNS	1778	331	2381	4490
NET SALES	110782	213119	208966	532867
PROD COST	42773	85380	71858	200011
MARKETING	13507	36287	38042	87836
PLANT	21889	22229	23492	67610
G.A.	31227	41783	42139	115149
TOTAL COSTS	109396	185679	175531	470606
GROSS PROFIT	1386	27440	33435	62261
PROFIT %	.013	.129	.160	.117

(b) **Electronic spreadsheet** software is frequently used by people who work with numbers.

FIGURE 1-9

(continued)

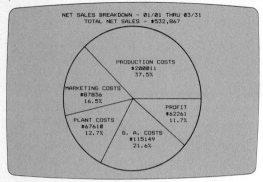

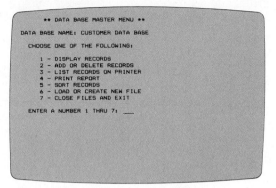

(c) Computer graphics software provides the ability to transform a series of numeric values into graphic form for easier analysis and interpretation.

(d) Database software allows the user to enter, retrieve, and update data in an organized and efficient manner.

Computer graphics software (Figure 1-9c) converts numbers and text into graphic output that visually conveys the relationships of the data. Some graphics software allows the use of color to further enhance the visual presentation. Line, bar, and pie charts are the most frequent forms of graphics output. Spreadsheet information is frequently converted into a graphic form, such as these charts. In fact, graphics capabilities are included in many spreadsheet packages.

Database software (Figure 1-9d) allows the user to enter, retrieve, and update data in an organized and efficient manner. These software packages have flexible inquiry and reporting capabilities that allow users to access the data in different ways.

A Typical Application: Budget Spreadsheet

Electronic spreadsheets are one of the most widely used applications software packages. In the following example, a user develops a budget spreadsheet for the first quarter of a year. The user enters the revenues and the costs for the first three months of the year. Then the spreadsheet program calculates the total revenues and total costs, the profit for each month (calculated by subtracting costs from revenues), and the profit percentage (obtained by dividing the profit by the revenues). In addition, the spreadsheet program calculates the total profit and the total profit percentage.

The diagrams in Figures 1-10, 1-11, and 1-12 show the steps that occur in order to obtain the spreadsheet output. A more complete description of these steps follows.

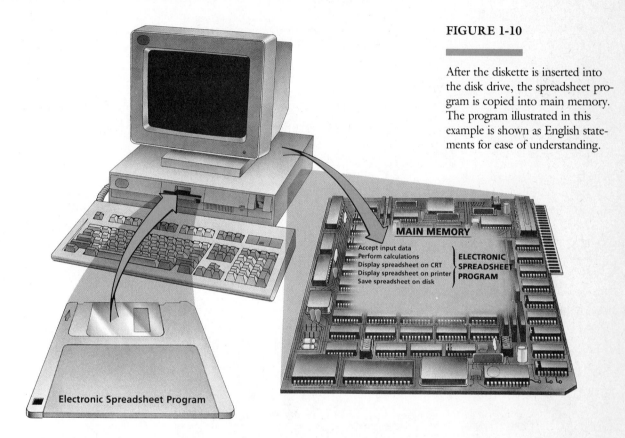

FIGURE 1-10

After the diskette is inserted into the disk drive, the spreadsheet program is copied into main memory. The program illustrated in this example is shown as English statements for ease of understanding.

MAIN MEMORY

Accept input data
Perform calculations
Display spreadsheet on CRT
Display spreadsheet on printer
Save spreadsheet on disk

ELECTRONIC
SPREADSHEET
PROGRAM

Electronic Spreadsheet Program

Loading the Program   For processing to occur, a computer program must first be stored in the main memory of the computer. The process of getting the program into memory is called loading the program. The spreadsheet program in this example is stored on a diskette. To load the program into the main memory of the computer, a copy of the spreadsheet program is transferred from the diskette into main memory.

In Figure 1-10, the diskette on which the program is stored is inserted into the disk drive. The user then issues the command to load the program from the diskette into main memory. After the program is loaded into main memory, the user directs the computer to begin executing the program.

Step 1—Input: Enter the Data With the electronic spreadsheet program in main memory, the first step is to input the data (Figure 1-11). This is accomplished by using a keyboard in the following way: (a) as the data is entered on the keyboard; (b) it is displayed on the screen; and (c) it is stored in main memory.

The data for this application consists of not only the numbers on which calculations are to be performed, but also some words indicating the contents of each of the columns and rows on the screen.

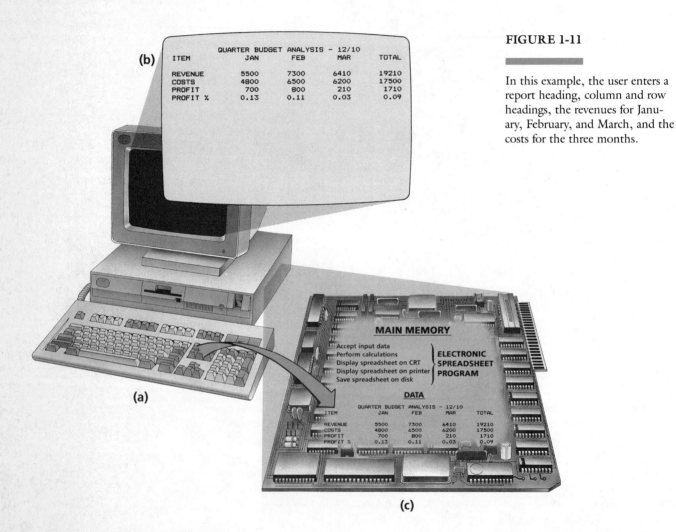

FIGURE 1-11

In this example, the user enters a report heading, column and row headings, the revenues for January, February, and March, and the costs for the three months.

Step 2—Process: Perform the Calculations As Figure 1-12 shows, after the user enters the data, the program calculates the profit for each month, the total revenue, costs and profit for the quarter, the profit percent for each month, and the total profit percent.

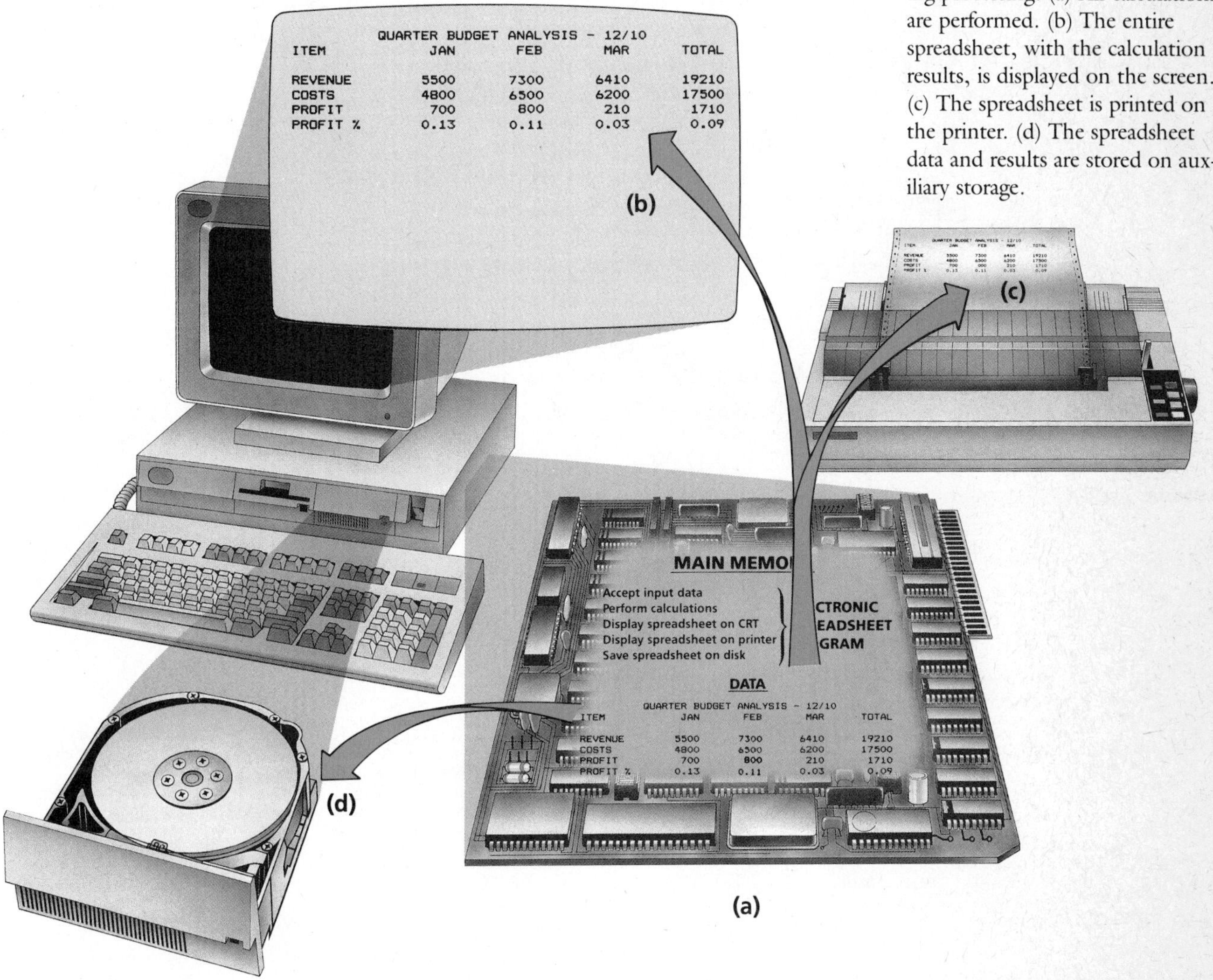

FIGURE 1-12

After the data has been entered, the program specifies the following processing: (a) All calculations are performed. (b) The entire spreadsheet, with the calculation results, is displayed on the screen. (c) The spreadsheet is printed on the printer. (d) The spreadsheet data and results are stored on auxiliary storage.

```
          QUARTER BUDGET ANALYSIS - 12/10
ITEM          JAN      FEB      MAR     TOTAL

REVENUE       5500     7300     6410    19210
COSTS         4800     6500     6200    17500
PROFIT         700      800      210     1710
PROFIT %      0.13     0.11     0.03     0.09
```

(b)

(c)

MAIN MEMO

Accept input data
Perform calculations
Display spreadsheet on CRT
Display spreadsheet on printer
Save spreadsheet on disk

CTRONIC
EADSHEET
GRAM

DATA

```
          QUARTER BUDGET ANALYSIS - 12/10
ITEM          JAN      FEB      MAR     TOTAL

REVENUE       5500     7300     6410    19210
COSTS         4800     6500     6200    17500
PROFIT         700      800      210     1710
PROFIT %      0.13     0.11     0.03     0.09
```

(d)

(a)

The preceding operations illustrate the calculating ability of computers. Whenever any calculations are performed on data, the data must be stored in main memory. The results of the calculations are also stored in main memory. If desired, the program can issue instructions to store the results on an auxiliary storage device, such as a hard disk or diskette.

Step 3—Output: Display the Results After the calculations have been completed, the program specifies that the spreadsheet, with the results of the calculations, is to be displayed on the screen. The program also specifies that the results are to be printed on the printer. When this instruction is executed, the spreadsheet is printed on paper so that the results of the processing can be used by someone other than the computer user.

Step 4—Storage: Save the Program and Data The spreadsheet is also stored on a disk, in this example a hard disk, so that at a later time it can be retrieved and utilized again.

What Are the Elements of an Information System?

Obtaining useful and timely information from computer processing requires more than just the equipment and software described so far. Other elements required for successful information processing include accurate data, trained information systems personnel, knowledgeable users, and documented procedures.

The equipment must be reliable and capable of handling the expected work load. The software must have been carefully developed and tested, and the data entered to be processed must be accurate. If the data is incorrect, the resulting information produced from it will be incorrect. Properly trained data processing personnel are required to run most medium and large computer systems. Users are sometimes overlooked as an important element of an information system, but with expanding computer use, users are taking increasing responsibility for the successful operation of information systems. This includes responsibility for the accuracy of both input and output information. In addition, users are taking a more active role in the development of computer applications. They work closely with information systems department personnel in the development of computer applications that relate to their areas of expertise. Finally, all information processing applications should have documented procedures covering not only the computer operations but any other related procedures as well.

To summarize, the six elements of an information system are: equipment, software, data, personnel, users, and procedures.

A Tour of an Information Systems Department

Many organizations use computers that concurrently process requests from more than one user. For example, one or more accounts receivable clerks could be entering cash receipts at the same time that one or more accounts payable clerks are entering invoices. Such systems are usually referred to as **multiuser computers**. Multiuser computers are generally under the control of a separate department of the company called the **information systems department**, the **data processing department**, or sometimes just the **computer department**.

The discussion that follows illustrates the elements of an information system by touring a typical information systems department with a multiuser computer.

Equipment

As indicated earlier, the hardware components of a computer system are input devices, processor, output devices, and auxiliary storage.

With multiuser computers, the primary input device is the **terminal**. A terminal is a device consisting of a keyboard and a screen, which is connected through a communication line or cable to the processor.

The processor unit of a multiuser computer, under the direction of the operating system, carries out the requests of the programs being processed. Modern computer processors are so fast that they can handle numerous users and provide quick response time.

The most commonly used output devices for a multiuser computer are a printer and a terminal. When large volumes of printed output must be produced, high-speed printers are used. The terminal can display both text material and graphics in either monochrome or color.

The two major types of auxiliary storage for a multiuser computer are **magnetic disk** and **magnetic tape**. Magnetic disk is the most widely used auxiliary storage for a multiuser computer.

When magnetic disk is used, data is recorded on an oxide-coated metal platter (the disk) as a series of magnetic spots. Magnetic tape units stores magnetic spots on a one-quarter to one-half inch tape on cassettes or reels. On systems with disk drives, tape is often used to store data that does not have to be accessed frequently. Another common use of tape is for backing up magnetic disks to protect against data loss such as in the case of disk drive failure.

Software

The information systems department keeps its software on either disks or tapes. Once the disk or tape containing the software is mounted on the disk or tape drive, the processor can run the software by reading it into main memory and executing the program instructions. Depending on the amount of disk storage available and how frequently a program is used, some software applications are always available for processing. An example would be order processing software that enters orders into the computer while the sales clerk is on the phone with the customer. Because a phone call can come in at any time, this software application must always be available for processing.

Data

Data exists throughout an organization and comes to the information systems department in many forms. Often data is in the form of **source documents**, which are original documents such as sales invoices. Sometimes there are no source documents. Then data can be entered directly into the system by users or it can be entered by machines that read special codes or labels. In all cases, the accuracy of the data is important because it will affect the usefulness of the resulting information.

Personnel

In order to implement applications on a computer, the information systems department usually employs people who have specialized training in computers and information processing. These employees may include data entry personnel to prepare and enter data into the computer; computer operators to run the computer; programmers to write specialized programs; systems analysts to design the software applications; a database administrator to control and manage data; and management to oversee the use of the computer.

FIGURE 1-13

Data entry personnel specialize in entering large amounts of data from source documents.

Data Entry Personnel **Data entry personnel** are responsible for entering large volumes of data into the computer system. Data is usually entered on terminals from source documents as shown in Figure 1-13.

Computer Operators The **computer operator** is responsible for a number of different tasks. When the computer is running, messages are displayed on the **operator's console** (Figure 1-14) indicating the status of the system. For example, a message may indicate that a special form, such as a check, must be placed in a printer. The operator responds to these messages in order to keep the computer running. In many instances, more than one operator is required to run a large computer.

FIGURE 1-14

The console allows the computer operator to monitor the multiuser computer system.

Computer Programmers **Computer programmers** design, write, test, and implement specialized programs that process data on a computer. The design specifications from the systems analyst tell the programmer what processing needs to be accomplished. It is the programmer's job to develop the specific programs of computer instructions that process the data and create the required information. The analyst specifies "what" is to be done; the programmer decides "how" to do it.

Systems Analysts **Systems analysts** are called on to review current or proposed applications within a company to determine if the applications should be implemented using a computer. Applications are considered for computer implementation if, among other things, productivity can be increased or more timely information can be generated to aid in the management of the company. If an application is to be "computerized," the analyst studies the application to identify the data used, how the data is processed, and other aspects of the application that are pertinent to the new system. The analyst then designs the new system by defining the data required for the computer application, developing the manner in which the data will be processed in the new system, and specifying the associated activities and procedures necessary to implement the application using the computer. Analysts work closely with both the people who will be using and benefiting from the new system and the programmers in the information systems department who will be writing the computer programs (Figure 1-15).

FIGURE 1-15

Programmers, analysts, and users all work closely in developing new computer applications.

Database Administrator An important function within the information systems department is the management of data. In many companies, this task is the responsibility of the **database administrator**. Among other things, the database administrator must develop procedures to ensure that correct data is entered into the system, that confidential company data is not lost or stolen, that access to company data is restricted to those who need the data, and that data is available when needed. This function is very important to most companies where billions of pieces of data are processed on the computer, and the loss or misappropriation of that data could be detrimental to business.

Information Systems Department Management Management within an information systems department is found at varying levels, depending on the size and complexity of the department. Most information systems departments have operations management, systems management, programming management, and a manager of the entire department. The **systems manager** oversees the activities in the systems analysis and design area of the department. The **programming manager** is in charge of all programmers within the department. Each of the previously mentioned managers may also have **project managers** within their area. The **operations manager** oversees the operational aspects of the department, including the scheduling, maintenance, and operation of the equipment. The information systems department manager is in charge of the entire department and may have the title **vice president of information systems** or **chief information officer**.

Users

Users interact with the information systems department in several ways. They are often the first to request that a specific application be computerized. When a systems analyst is assigned to study the application, the analyst will rely on the users' knowledge of the requirements to determine if computerization is feasible. Once an application is implemented, users usually maintain an ongoing relationship with the information systems department. They may request special reports or processing and make suggestions about improving the application.

Procedures

Written procedures are an important part of any information system. Procedures should be documented for all steps in the processing cycle, including those steps that are not computerized. Accurate, up-to-date procedures minimize processing errors, reduce training time for new employees, and serve as a guide for future changes to the application.

Summary of the Tour of an Information Systems Department

During the tour of the information systems department we have seen the six elements of an information system: equipment, software, data, personnel, users, and procedures. Each of these elements directly affects an organization's ability to successfully process data into useful information.

Qualities of Information

As we have discussed, the purpose of processing data is to create information. Just as data should have certain characteristics, so too should information. These characteristics are often called the "qualities of information." Terms used to describe these qualities include the following: accurate, verifiable, timely, organized, meaningful, useful, and cost effective.

Although it may seem obvious, the first quality of information is that it should be *accurate*. Inaccurate information is often worse than no information at all. As you may recall, accuracy was also a characteristic of data. And although accurate data does not guarantee accurate information, it is impossible to produce accurate information from erroneous data. The computer jargon term **GIGO** states this point very well; it stands for "Garbage In, Garbage Out."

Closely related to accuracy is the quality of information being *verifiable*. This means that if necessary, the user can confirm the information. For example, before relying on the amounts in a summary report, an accountant would want to know that the totals could be supported by details of transactions.

Another quality of information is that it must be *timely*. Although most information loses its value with time, some information, such as trends, becomes more valuable as time passes and more information is obtained. The important point here is that the timeliness must be appropriate for any decisions that will be made based on the information. Up-to-the-minute information may be required for some decisions while older information may be satisfactory or more appropriate for others.

To be of the most value, information should be *organized* to suit users' requirements. For example, a sales representative assigned to sell only to companies in a specific area would prefer to have a prospect list organized by zip code rather than a list that was only in alphabetical order.

Meaningful information means that the information is relevant to the person who receives it. Much information is only meaningful to specific individuals or groups within an organization. Extraneous and unnecessary information should be eliminated and the "audience" of the information should always be kept in mind.

To be *useful*, information should result in an action being taken or specifically not taken, as the case may be. Often, this quality can be improved through **exception reporting**, which focuses only on the information that exceeds certain limits. An example of exception reporting would be an inventory report showing items whose balance on hand is less than a predetermined minimum quantity. Rather than looking through an entire inventory report to find such items, the exception report would quickly bring these items to the attention of the persons responsible for inventory management.

Last, but not least, information must be *cost effective*. In other words, the cost to produce the information must be less than the "value" of the information. This can sometimes be hard to determine. If the value of the information cannot be determined, perhaps the information should only be produced as required instead of regularly. Many organizations periodically review the information they produce in reports to determine if the reports still have the qualities discussed above and their production cost can still be justified or possibly reduced.

Although the qualities of information have been discussed in conjunction with computer systems, these qualities apply to all information regardless of how it is produced. Knowing these qualities will help you evaluate the information you receive and provide every day.

Chapter Summary

This chapter presented a broad introduction to concepts and terminology that are related to computers. You now have an understanding of what a computer is, how it processes data into information, and which elements are necessary for a successful information system. The photo essay that follows the Review Questions in this chapter is a time line that shows the evolution of the computer industry. The following list summarizes the key topics discussed in this chapter.

1. A **computer** is an electronic device, operating under the control of instructions stored in its own memory unit, that can accept data (input), process data arithmetically and logically, produce output from the processing, and store the results for future use (p. 1.2).

2. A computer can perform **input**, **process**, **output**, and **storage** operations. These operations are called the **information processing cycle** (p. 1.2).

3. **Data** is defined as raw facts and consists of the numbers and words that a computer receives and processes to produce information (p. 1.2).

4. **Information** is data that has been processed into a form that has meaning and is useful (p. 1.2).

5. The production of information by processing data on a computer is called **information processing** (p. 1.3).

6. **Computer users** are the people who either directly use the computer or utilize the information it provides (p. 1.3).

7. A computer is a powerful tool because it is reliable and can process data quickly and accurately (p. 1.3).

8. A **computer program** is a detailed set of instructions that tells the computer exactly what to do (p. 1.3).

9. Using a computer, information processing can produce many different forms of information from a single set of data (p. 1.4).

10. Processing data on a computer is performed by computer equipment including input devices, the processor unit, output devices, and auxiliary storage units. Computer equipment is often referred to as **hardware** (p. 1.5).

11. **Input devices** are used to enter data into a computer (p. 1.6).

12. The **processor unit** includes the central processing unit (CPU) and main memory (p. 1.6).

13. The CPU controls and supervises the entire computer system and performs the actual arithmetic and logic operations on data, as specified by the program (p. 1.6).

14. **Arithmetic operations** are numeric calculations such as addition, subtraction, multiplication, and division that take place in the processor (p. 1.6).

15. **Logical operations** are comparisons of data in the processor to see if one value is greater than, equal to, or less than another value (p. 1.6).

16. **Main memory**, also called **primary storage**, consists of components that electronically store data and program instructions (p. 1.6).

17. **Output devices** are used to print or display data and information (p. 1.6).

18. **Auxiliary storage units** are used to store program instructions and data when they are not being used in the main memory of the computer (p. 1.7).

19. The four major categories of computers are microcomputers, minicomputers, mainframes, and supercomputers (p. 1.7).

20. Types of **microcomputers** include laptop, portable, desktop, and supermicro computers (p. 1.8).

21. **Minicomputers** address the needs of users who want more processing power than a microcomputer but do not need the power of a mainframe. Minicomputers can support a number of users performing different tasks (p. 1.8).

22. **Mainframe** computers are large systems that can handle numerous users, store large amounts of data, and process transactions at a very high rate (p. 1.8).

23. **Supercomputers**, the most powerful and expensive category of computers, can process hundreds of millions of instructions per second and perform long, complex calculations (p. 1.8).

24. **Software** is another name for computer programs (p. 1.8).

25. A computer program must first be loaded into main memory before it can be executed (p. 1.8, 1.11).

26. Programs purchased from computer stores or software vendors are called **applications software packages** (p. 1.9).

27. Four commonly used personal computer software packages are word processing, electronic spreadsheet, graphics, and database software (p. 1.9).

28. **Word processing software** is used to create and print documents (p. 1.9).

29. **Electronic spreadsheet software** performs calculations on rows and columns of numeric data based on formulas entered by the user (p. 1.9).

30. **Graphics software** provides the ability to transform numbers and text into a graphic format (p. 1.10).

31. **Database software** allows the user to enter, retrieve, and update data efficiently (p. 1.10).

32. The elements of an information system are equipment, software, data, personnel, users, and procedures (p. 1.14).

33. **Multiuser computers** can concurrently process requests from more than one user (p. 1.14).

34. A **terminal**, consisting of a keyboard and screen, is the most commonly used input device for a large computer (p. 1.15).

35. Modern computer processors are so fast that they can usually handle numerous users and still provide very quick response time (p. 1.15).

36. The most commonly used output devices for large computers are terminals and high-speed printers (p. 1.15).

37. Auxiliary storage devices used on a large computer include **magnetic disk** and **magnetic tape** (p. 1.15).

38. **Source documents** are original documents, such as sales invoices, from which data can be entered (p. 1.15).

39. Data can be entered directly into the computer by users or by machines (p. 1.16).

40. **Data entry personnel** prepare and enter data into the computer (p. 1.16).

41. **Computer operators** run the computer equipment and monitor processing operations (p. 1.16).

42. **Computer programmers** design, write, test, and implement programs that process data on a computer (p. 1.16).

43. **Systems analysts** review and design computer applications. Analysts work closely with users and programmers (p. 1.17).

44. A **database administrator** is responsible for managing a company's data (p. 1.17).

45. Management within an information systems department includes a **systems manager**, **programming manager**, **operations manager**, and a department manager, sometimes called the **vice president of information systems** or **chief information officer** (p. 1.18).

46. **Users** play an important role in the development of computer applications (p. 1.18).

47. Procedures should be documented for all steps in the processing cycle, including those steps that are not computerized (p. 1.18).

48. The terms used to describe the qualities of information include accurate, verifiable, timely, organized, meaningful, useful, and cost effective (p. 1.18).

49. **GIGO** is an acronym that stands for 'Garbage In, Garbage Out'' (p. 1.19).

Review Questions

1. What is the definition of a computer?
2. Identify and describe the four operations a computer can perform.
3. What is data? What is information? How is information derived from data?
4. What is the information processing cycle?
5. What are the four specific hardware units found on a computer? Describe each of them.
6. What is the difference between main memory and auxiliary storage? Why are both necessary?
7. What is computer software? Why is it critical to the operation of a computer?
8. Identify the four software packages most often used with personal computers.
9. Describe the processing of a typical application on a personal computer.
10. What are the six elements of an information system?
11. Identify some of the differences among microcomputers, minicomputers, mainframe computers, and supercomputers.
12. Who are some of the personnel who work in an information systems department?
13. What is the role of a systems analyst? How does that position differ from the job of a computer programmer?
14. What is the user's role in an information system?
15. Describe the qualities of information.
16. List the key developments in the evolution of the modern computer.

The Evolution of the Computer Industry

The electronic computer industry began about fifty years ago. This time line summarizes the major events in the evolution of the computer industry.

During the years 1943 to 1946, Dr. John W. Mauchly and J. Presper Eckert, Jr., completed the ENIAC (Electronic Numerical Integrator and Computer), the first large-scale electronic digital computer. The ENIAC weighed thirty tons, contained 18,000 vacuum tubes, and occupied a thirty by fifty foot space.

In 1952, the public awareness of computers increased when the UNIVAC I correctly predicted that Dwight D. Eisenhower would win the presidential election after analyzing only 5% of the tallied vote.

| 1937 | 1945 | 1950 | 1952 |

In 1951-52, after much discussion, IBM made the decision to add computers to their line of business equipment products. This led IBM to become a dominant force in the computer industry.

Dr. John von Neumann is credited with writing a report in 1945 describing a number of new hardware concepts and how to use stored programs. This brilliant breakthrough laid the foundation for the digital computers that have been built since then.

◄ Dr. John V. Atanasoff and his assistant, Clifford Berry, designed and began to build the first electronic digital computer during the winter of 1937-38. Their machine, the Atanasoff-Berry-Computer or ABC, provided the foundation for the next advances in electronic digital computers.

1.23

FORTRAN (FORmula TRANslator) was introduced in 1957. This programming language proved that efficient, easy-to-use computer languages could be developed. FORTRAN is still in use.

Dr. Hopper became instrumental in developing high-level languages such as COBOL, a business applications language that was introduced in 1960. COBOL uses English-like phrases and can be run on most brands of computers, making it one of the most widely used languages in the world.

In 1952, Dr. Grace Hopper, a mathematician and commodore in the U.S. Navy, wrote a paper describing how to program a computer with symbolic notation instead of the detailed machine language that had been used.

By 1959, over 200 programming languages had been created.

| 1952 | 1955 | 1957 | 1958 | 1959 | 1960 |

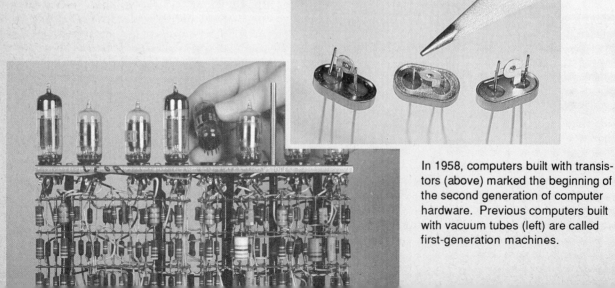

In 1958, computers built with transistors (above) marked the beginning of the second generation of computer hardware. Previous computers built with vacuum tubes (left) are called first-generation machines.

Dr. Ted Hoff of Intel Corporation is credited with developing the first microprocessor or microprogrammable computer chip, the Intel 4004, in 1969.

Third-generation computers were introduced in 1964. Their controlling circuitry is stored on chips. The family of IBM System/360 computers were the first third-generation machines.

| 1964 | 1965 | | 1968 | 1969 |

From 1958 to 1964, it is estimated, the number of computers in the U.S. grew from 2,500 to 18,000.

The 1960s saw the birth of the software industry. In 1968, Computer Science Corporation became the first software company to be listed on the New York Stock Exchange.

In 1965, Dr. John Kemeny of Dartmouth led the development of the BASIC programming language. BASIC is the most commonly used language on microcomputers. More people know how to program in BASIC than any other language.

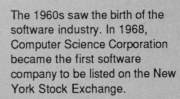

In 1969, under pressure from the industry, IBM announced that some of its software would be priced separately from the computer hardware. This "unbundling" opened up the industry to emerging software firms.

Digital Equipment Corporation (DEC) ▶ introduced the first minicomputer in 1965.

Fourth-generation computers emerged in 1970. These machines were built with chips that utilized LSI (large-scale integration). The chips used in 1965 could contain as many as 1,000 circuits. By 1970, the LSI chip could contain as many as 15,000.

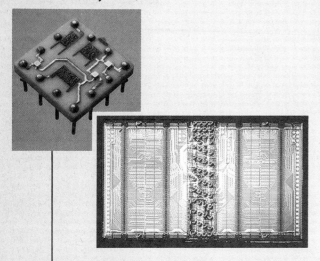

The VisiCalc spreadsheet program written by Dan Bricklin and Bob Frankston was introduced in 1979. This product was originally written to run on Apple II computers. Together, VisiCalc and Apple II computers became rapidly successful in the business community. Most people consider VisiCalc to be the single most important reason why microcomputers gained acceptance in the business world.

1970   **1975**   **1980**

The MITS, Inc., Altair computer was the first commercially successful microcomputer. It sold in kit form for less than $500.

In 1976, Steve Jobs and Steve Wozniak built the first Apple computer.

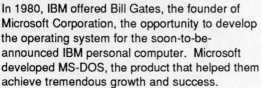

In 1980, IBM offered Bill Gates, the founder of Microsoft Corporation, the opportunity to develop the operating system for the soon-to-be-announced IBM personal computer. Microsoft developed MS-DOS, the product that helped them achieve tremendous growth and success.

The Lotus 1-2-3 integrated software package, developed by Mitch Kapor, was introduced in 1983. It combined spreadsheet, graphics, and database programs in one package.

1981   1982   1983

It is estimated that 313,000 microcomputers were sold in 1981. In 1982, the number jumped to 3,275,000.

The IBM PC was introduced in 1981, signaling IBM's entrance in the microcomputer marketplace. The IBM PC quickly garnered the largest share of the personal computer market and became the personal computer most often used in business.

The IBM Application System 400, introduced in 1988, made a significant impact on the minicomputer and mainframe market, allowing users to expand their computing capabilities more easily.

The Intel 80486 is the world's first 1,000,000 transistor microprocessor. It crams 1.2 million transistors on a sliver of silicon that measures .4" x .6" and can execute at 15 MIPS (million instructions per second). That's four times as fast as its predecessor, the 80386.

1987   1988   1989

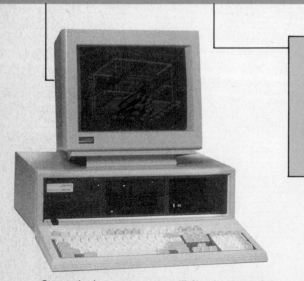

OS/2, an IBM microcomputer operating system, will enable microcomputers to be as powerful as many of today's minicomputers. Further, it will allow microcomputers to become multiuser systems, that is, multiple keyboards and screens can be attached to the same computer.

Several microcomputers utilizing the powerful Intel 80386 microprocessor were introduced in 1987. These machines can handle processing that previously only large systems could perform.

The computer industry will continue to evolve as improved technology and innovation lead to a variety of new computer applications.

Microcomputer Applications Software: User Tools

2

Objectives

- Identify the most widely used microcomputer applications software.
- Describe how microcomputer applications software can help users.
- Explain the key features of word processing, electronic spreadsheet, database, and graphics software.
- Define data and explain the terms used to organize data in an information processing system: field, record, file, database.
- Describe the key features of data communications, desktop publishing, electronic mail, and project management software.
- Explain integrated software and its advantages.
- List and describe five guidelines for purchasing microcomputer applications software packages.
- Identify microcomputer applications software learning aids and support tools.

Computer literate is a term you might have heard used to describe people who have an understanding of computers and how they are used in our modern world. Today, understanding the common applications used on microcomputers is often considered a part of being computer literate. In fact, a knowledge of these applications is now considered by many educators and employers to be more important than a knowledge of programming. Because of this, we place an introduction to microcomputer applications focusing on the four most widely used applications early in this book. Learning the features of each application will help you understand how microcomputers are used by people in our modern world and provide a foundation to help you learn.

Microcomputer Applications Software

The applications discussed in this chapter are referred to as **microcomputer applications software**. Word processing is a good example of applications software. Regardless of the type of business a company does, word processing can be used as a tool to help employees generate documents.

An important advantage of applications software is that you don't need any special technical skills or ability to use them. These programs are designed to be **user friendly**, in other words, easy to use. You do not need detailed computer instructions as you would if you were programming. Instead, you operate the software through simple commands. **Commands** are the instructions that you use to operate the software. For example, when you are finished using an application and you want to save your work, you issue an instruction called a "save" command. To use this command you might type SAVE WORKFILE. The word SAVE is the command and WORKFILE is the name under which your work will be stored.

User interfaces (Figure 2-1) are methods and techniques that make using an application simpler. They include function keys, screen prompts, menus, and icons. The **function keys** (Figure 2-1a) that are included on computer keyboards are a type of user interface. Pressing a function key in an applications program is a shortcut that takes the place of entering a command. The software defines exactly what the function key causes to happen. If you used a function key to perform the SAVE command described above, pressing one key instead of several could generate the entire command SAVE WORKFILE.

FIGURE 2-1

User interfaces.

(a) Function keys are programmed to execute commonly used instructions.

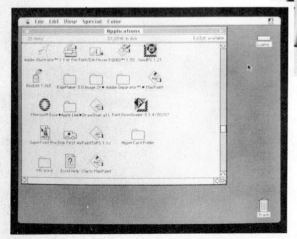

(b) Icons are symbols that represent activities that the computer can do. Selecting an icon instructs the computer to carry out the corresponding activity.

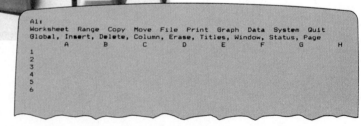

(c) Menus, like the one on the second line, offer a list of possible processing selections.

Screen **prompts** are the messages that the program displays to help you while you are using an application. **Icons** (Figure 2-1b) refer to pictures instead of words that are displayed on the screen to show you various program options. **Menus** (Figure 2-1c), a special kind of screen prompt, are used in applications to provide a list of processing options. You make a selection from the menu by pressing the number or letter key that corresponds with the desired option.

These are some of the features included in applications software packages that help to make them user friendly. These aids minimize the need for technical computer knowledge when you are using applications software packages.

The Four Most Common
Applications Software Packages

The four most widely used software packages are:

1. word processing software
2. electronic spreadsheet software
3. database software
4. graphics software

Although we will discuss these four applications on microcomputers, they are actually available on computers of all sizes. The concepts you will learn about each application package on microcomputers will also apply if you are working on a larger system.

Word Processing Software:
A Document Productivity Tool

Probably the most widely used applications software is word processing. If you need to create **documents**, such as letters or memos, you can increase your productivity by learning to use this software tool. Some of the popular packages used today include WordPerfect, WordStar, and Microsoft Word. This section discusses using a word processor to create a document.

Word processing software is used to prepare documents electronically (Figure 2-2). It allows you to enter text on the computer keyboard in the same manner as documents are created on a typewriter. As you enter the characters, they are displayed on the screen and stored in the computer's main memory. Because this is an

FIGURE 2-2

Last month's memo that will be changed for this month's meeting.

```
DATE:      June 21

FROM:      Julia Broderick, Vice President of Sales

TO:        All Sales Managers

SUBJECT:   Sales Meeting


A sales  meeting will  be held at  the Corporate  Training Center
from 8:00 AM to 12:00 noon, on Thursday, June 30.

This month's presentation will be on our new product line.

Please let  me know as  soon as possible  if you have  a schedule
conflict.
```

electronic format, it is easy to **edit** the document by making changes and corrections to the text. Errors may be corrected and words, sentences, paragraphs, or pages may be added or deleted. When the document is complete, you enter a command and have the computer send the document to the printer. The document's format is also under your control. You can specify the margins, define the page length, and select the print style. The document can be printed as many times as you like. Each copy is an original and looks the same as the other copies. The computer's storage capability allows you to store your documents so that they can be used again. It is an efficient way to file documents because many documents can fit on one disk. If you wish, previously stored documents can be combined to make new documents, and you do not have to reenter the text as you would on a typewriter.

The value of word processing is that it reduces the time required to prepare and produce written documents. Any editing you wish to do in the document is easy because the software allows you to make changes quickly and efficiently. In addition, the tedious task of typing a final draft is eliminated.

Most word processing packages include additional support features such as spelling checkers, a thesaurus, and some limited grammar checking.

Spelling Checkers

Spelling checker software allows you to check individual words or the entire document for correct spelling. To check individual words, you position the cursor at the start of the word and press a key defined by the software to indicate that the spelling is to be checked. The word in the text will then be checked against an electronic dictionary stored on a disk that is part of the spelling checker software. Some spelling checker dictionaries contain over 100,000 words.

When the entire document is checked for spelling, each word is compared against entries in the dictionary. If an exact match is not found, the word is highlighted. A menu is then superimposed on the screen, giving you a list of similar words that may be the correct spelling. You may select one of the words displayed on the menu, edit the highlighted word, leave the word unchanged, or add the word to the dictionary. Many users customize their software dictionaries by adding company, street, city, and personal names to the dictionary so that the software can check the correct spelling of those words.

Thesaurus

Thesaurus software allows you to look up synonyms for words in a document while you are using your word processor. Using a thesaurus is similar to using a spelling checker. When you want to look up a synonym for a word, you place the cursor on the word that you want to check, enter a command through the keyboard, and the thesaurus software displays a menu of possible synonyms. If you find a word you want to use, you select the desired word from the list and the software automatically incorporates it in the document by replacing the previous word.

Grammar Checkers

Grammar checker software can be used to check for certain grammar, writing style, and sentence structure errors. These programs can check documents for excessive usage of a word or phrase and can identify sentences that are too long. They can also show you words that have been repeated such as "and and" or words used out of context such as "four example."

A Word Processing Example

Figures 2-3 through 2-9 illustrate the following word processing example. Let's say the vice president of sales of a company wants to send a memo announcing a meeting of all sales personnel. She remembers that last month she sent a similar memo to just the sales managers. Thus, the first thing she does is load last month's memo (Figure 2-3) into main memory so it will appear on the screen. This memo might be stored on a hard disk or on a diskette.

Word processing changes are usually of three types: to **insert** data, **delete** data, or **move** data. Often it makes sense to do your insertions and deletions at the same time; as you edit your document, you delete the existing word or phrase and insert the new one. **Replace** is a combination of the delete and insert commands. With replace, you can scan a document for a single or multiple occurrence of a word or phrase and replace it with another or delete it entirely. Figure 2-3 shows the document with the text to be deleted. Figure 2-4 shows the document after the new text has been inserted.

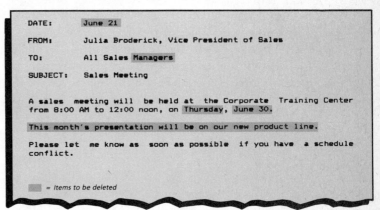

FIGURE 2-3

The shaded areas indicate text to be deleted.

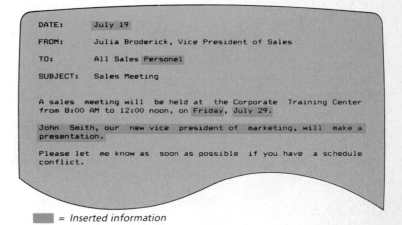

FIGURE 2-4

The shading on the computer screen shows the new text inserted into last month's memo.

The **move** command allows you to either cut (remove) or copy a sentence, paragraph, page, or block of text. In our example, the VP of sales, Julia Broderick, decided she wanted to move the existing paragraph 3 in front of the existing paragraph 2 (Figure 2-5). First she would highlight the text to be moved. Next she would indicate that she wants to "cut" and not "copy" the marked text. With a **cut**, you are removing text from an area. With a **copy**, the word processor makes a copy of the marked text but leaves the marked text where it was. After you perform either the cut or the copy, the word processor needs to know where you want to place or **paste** the text. This is usually done by moving the cursor to the point where you want the moved text to begin. You then give a command to execute the move. Figure 2-6 shows the cut text "pasted" into a position that now makes it the second paragraph.

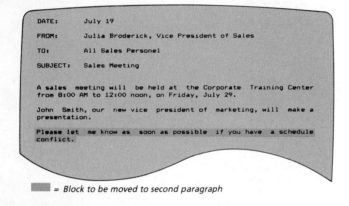

= Block to be moved to second paragraph

FIGURE 2-5

The shading shows the text to be moved from third to second paragraph.

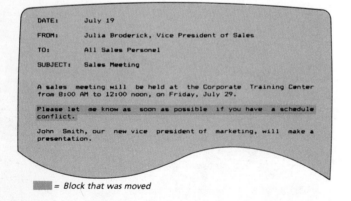

= Block that was moved

FIGURE 2-6

Memo after third paragraph was moved to second paragraph.

After the text changes are made, Julia runs a spelling checker. The spelling checker matches each word in the document against its spelling dictionary and discovers an unrecognized word: "personel." Figure 2-7 shows how a spelling checker might present two alternatives for the correct spelling of the word. Julia merely has to enter the letter B and the word processor will change "personel" to "personnel" (Figure 2-8).

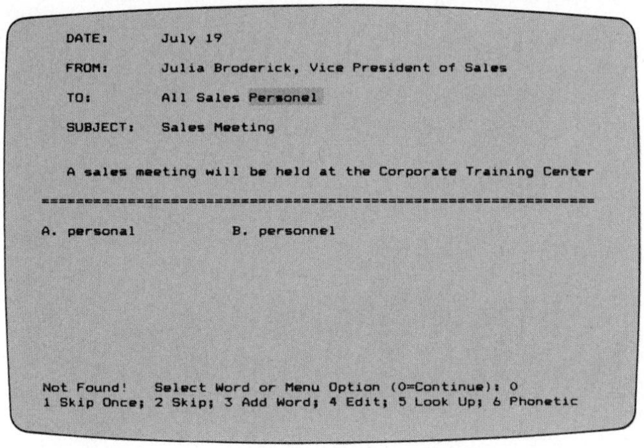

```
DATE:        July 19

FROM:        Julia Broderick, Vice President of Sales

TO:          All Sales Personel

SUBJECT:     Sales Meeting


A sales meeting will be held at the Corporate Training Center
==========================================================

A. personal          B. personnel




Not Found!   Select Word or Menu Option (0=Continue): 0
1 Skip Once; 2 Skip; 3 Add Word; 4 Edit; 5 Look Up; 6 Phonetic
```

= Incorrectly spelled word

FIGURE 2-7

Spelling checker highlighting unrecognized word and showing two possible spellings.

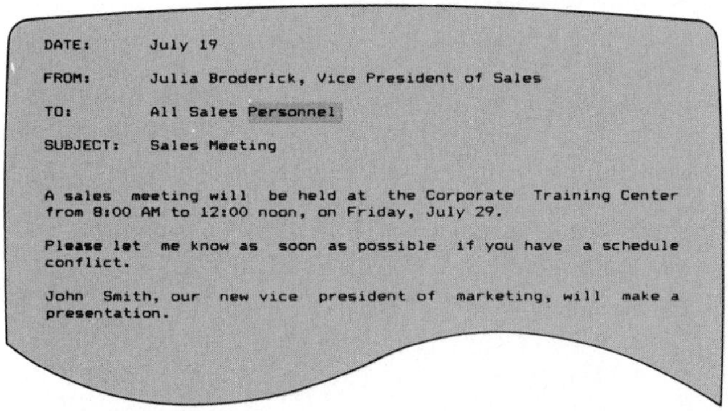

```
DATE:        July 19

FROM:        Julia Broderick, Vice President of Sales

TO:          All Sales Personnel

SUBJECT:     Sales Meeting


A sales  meeting will  be held at  the Corporate  Training Center
from 8:00 AM to 12:00 noon, on Friday, July 29.

Please let  me know as  soon as possible  if you have  a schedule
conflict.

John  Smith, our  new vice  president of  marketing, will  make a
presentation.
```

= Correctly spelled word

FIGURE 2-8

Correct spelling of "personnel" inserted into text by spelling checker.

Before printing the memo, Julia reviews its format. She decides that the document is too wide and increases the margins. Figure 2-9 shows the printed document with the wider, 1 1/2-inch, margins.

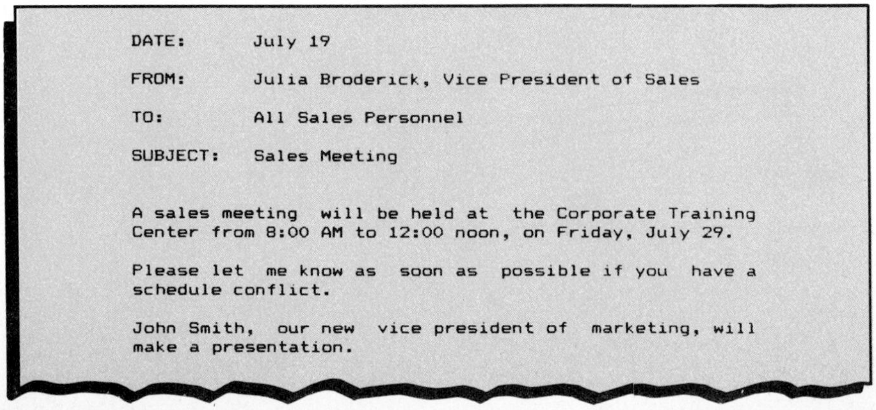

```
DATE:        July 19

FROM:        Julia Broderick, Vice President of Sales

TO:          All Sales Personnel

SUBJECT:     Sales Meeting


A sales meeting  will be held at  the Corporate Training
Center from 8:00 AM to 12:00 noon, on Friday, July 29.

Please let  me know as  soon as  possible if you  have a
schedule conflict.

John Smith,  our new  vice president of  marketing, will
make a presentation.
```

FIGURE 2-9

Memo after margins are changed

Now that the text and format are correct, Julia saves the document before printing it in case a system or power failure occurs during printing. Once saved, the document can be printed as often as necessary and is available for use or modification at a later date.

Word processing software is a productivity tool that allows you to create, edit, format, print, and store documents. Each of the many word processing packages available may have slightly different capabilities, but most have the features summarized in Figure 2-10.

WORD PROCESSING FEATURES	
INSERTION AND MOVING	**SEARCH AND REPLACE**
Insert character	Search and replace word
Insert word	Search and replace character strings
Insert line	**PRINTING**
Move sentences	Set top and bottom margins
Move paragraphs	Set left and right margins
Move blocks	Set tab stops
Merge text	Print columns
DELETE FEATURES	Single, double, triple space control
Delete character	Variable space control within text
Delete word	Right justify
Delete sentence	Center lines
Delete paragraph	Subscripts
Delete entire text	Superscripts
SCREEN CONTROL	Underline
Scroll up and down by line	Boldface
Scroll by page	Condensed print
Word wrap	Enlarged print
Uppercase and lowercase display	Special type fonts
Underline display	Proportional spacing
Screen display according to defined format	Headers
	Footers
Bold display	Page numbering
Superscript display	Print any page from document
Subscript display	

FIGURE 2-10

Common features of word processing software

Electronic Spreadsheet Software: A Number Productivity Tool

Electronic spreadsheet software allows you to organize numeric data into a table format called a **spreadsheet** or **worksheet**. Manual methods have long been used to organize numeric data in this manner (Figure 2-11). You will see that the data in an electronic spreadsheet is organized in the same manner as it is in a manual spreadsheet, one that is done by hand. Within a spreadsheet, data is organized horizontally in **rows** and vertically in **columns**. The intersection where a row and column meet is called a **cell** (Figure 2-12).

	PERSONAL EXPENSES	
	THIS YEAR	LAST YEAR
RENT	9600	8400
FOOD	2400	2150
UTILITIES	1200	800
AUTO	2200	1900
INSURANCE	900	860
ENTERTAINMENT	1250	1100
TOTAL EXPENSES	17550	15210

```
       A        B        C         D        E
 1                     PERSONAL EXPENSES
 2                     THIS YEAR        LAST YEAR
 3
 4     RENT            9600            8400
 5     FOOD            2400            2150
 6     UTILITIES       1200             800
 7     AUTO            2200            1900
 8     INSURANCE        900             860
 9     ENTERTAINMENT   1250            1100
10
11     TOTAL EXPENSES 17550           15210
12
13
14
15
16
17
18
```

FIGURE 2-11

The electronic spreadsheet on the right still uses the row and column format of the manual spreadsheet on the left.

Cells may contain two types of data: **labels** (text) and **values** (numbers and formulas). The labels are used to identify the data and to document the worksheet. Good spreadsheets are well documented and contain descriptive titles. The rest of the cells in a spreadsheet may appear to contain numbers. However, some of the cells actually contain formulas. The formulas perform calculations on the data in the spreadsheet and display the resulting value in the cell containing the formula.

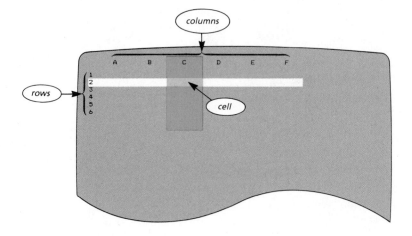

FIGURE 2-12

In a spreadsheet, rows refer to the horizontal lines of data. Columns refer to the vertical lines of data. Note that rows are identified by numbers and columns are identified by letters. The intersection of a row and column is called a cell. The highlighted cell is the cursor. You can move the cursor by pressing the arrow keys on the keyboard.

In a manual spreadsheet, each of the totals would have to be calculated by hand. In an electronic spreadsheet, the user enters a formula into a cell. Then the result for that cell is calculated and displayed automatically. Once a formula is entered into a cell, it can be copied to any other cell that requires a similar formula. As the formula is copied, the formula calculations are performed automatically.

One of the most powerful features of the electronic spreadsheet occurs when the data in a spreadsheet changes. To appreciate the capabilities of spreadsheet software, let's discuss how a change is handled in a manual system. When a value in a manual spreadsheet changes, it must be erased and a new value written into the cell. All cells that contain formulas referring to the value that changed must also be erased, recalculated, and the result reentered. For example, the row totals and column totals would be updated to reflect changes to any values within their areas. In large manual spreadsheets, accurately posting changes and updating the values affected can be time consuming. But posting changes on an electronic spreadsheet is easy. You change data in a cell by simply typing in the new value. All other values that are affected are updated *automatically*. While the updating happens very quickly, if you watch the screen closely you can sometimes see the values change. As row and column totals are updated, the changes are said to *ripple* through the spreadsheet.

An electronic spreadsheet's ability to recalculate when data is changed makes it a valuable tool for management personnel. This capability allows managers to perform "what if" testing by changing the numbers in a spreadsheet (Figure 2-13). The resulting values that are calculated by the spreadsheet software provide management with valuable decision support information based on the alternatives tested.

To illustrate this powerful tool, we will show you how to develop the spreadsheet that was used as an example in Chapter 1. You may remember that the completed spreadsheet contains revenues, costs, profit, and profit percentage for three months and the totals for the three months. By following Figures 2-14 through 2-18, you can see that the first step in creating the spreadsheet is to enter the labels or titles. These should be short but descriptive, to help you organize the layout of the data in your spreadsheet. The next step is to enter the data or numbers in the body of the spreadsheet, and finally the formulas. At this point you can give commands to print the spreadsheet and to store it on a disk.

FIGURE 2-13

The "what if" testing capability of electronic spreadsheets is a powerful tool used to aid managers in making decisions.

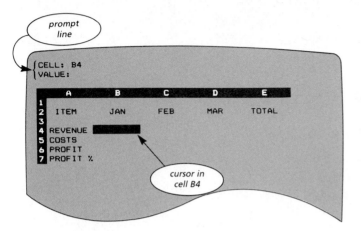

FIGURE 2-14

Labels identify rows and columns in a spreadsheet. The prompt line at the top left of the screen has two parts: CELL, which identifies the column and row being referenced; and VALUE, which identifies the value in the cell. The cursor is located in cell B4, the intersection of column B and row 4. No value has been entered into B4.

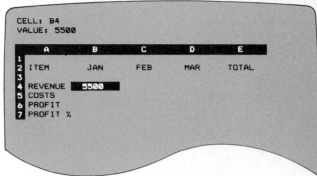

FIGURE 2-15

The value 5500 is entered and stored at cell B4. Note the entries in the display at the top left corner of the screen, identifying which value (in this case a number) has been entered into which cell.

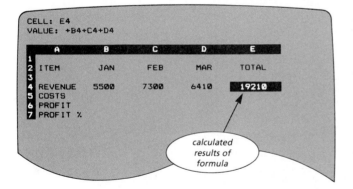

FIGURE 2-16

The arrow keys are used to move the cursor to cells in the spreadsheet. The values 7300 and 6410 are entered in cells C4 and D4. A formula is entered in cell E4. The formula specifies that the content of cell E4 is to be the sum of the values in cells B4, C4, and D4. The spreadsheet itself displays the numeric sum. The prompt line at the top of the screen, however, shows the formula used to calculate the value.

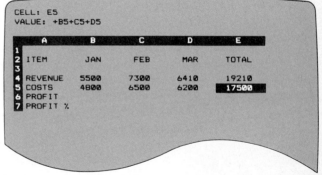

FIGURE 2-17

The formula required for cell E5 is similar to the one entered for cell E4; it totals the amounts in the three previous columns. When we copy the formula from E4 into E5, the software automatically changes the cell references from B4, C4, and D4 to B5, C5, and D5.

An electronic spreadsheet is a productivity tool that organizes and performs calculations on numeric data. Spreadsheets are one of the most popular applications software packages. They have been adapted to a wide range of business and nonbusiness applications. Some of the popular packages used today are Lotus 1-2-3, Excel, SuperCalc, Quattro, and VP-Planner. Most of the packages available will have the features shown in Figure 2-19.

FIGURE 2-18

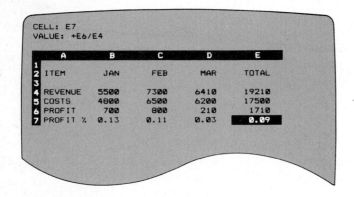

This screen shows the completed spreadsheet. The value in cell E7 is derived from the formula illustrated on the prompt line, which specifies that the value in cell E6 is to be divided by the value in cell E4. (The slash character indicates division.) Since the value in E6 is the total profit and the value in E4 is the total revenue, the result of the division operation is the profit percentage.

SPREADSHEET FEATURES

WORKSHEET
Global format
Insert column
Insert row
Delete column
Delete row
Set up titles
Set up windows

RANGE
Format range of data
Erase cells

COPY
Copy from cells
Copy to cells

MOVE
Move from cells
Move to cells

FILE
Save
Retrieve
Erase
List

PRINT
Set up margins
Define header
Define footer
Specify range to print
Define page length
Condensed print

FIGURE 2-19

Common features of spreadsheet software

Database Software: A Data Management Tool

Database software allows you to create electronic files on your computer and to retrieve, manipulate, and update the data you store in the files. Just as in a manual system, a file is a collection of related data. For example, to assist the sales clerk in a retail store, an item file is usually maintained to track inventory and prices. On the computer, the file is stored in an electronic format on an auxiliary storage device, such as a disk (Figure 2-20). Individual facts about an item, such as item number, quantity, and unit price, are referred to as **data items**, **data fields**, or **fields**.

A collection of related fields is called a **record**. In the item file in Figure 2-20, all the data that relates to item number A274 is collectively called record A274. A collection of related records is called a **file**.

Sometimes the word database is used interchangeably with the word file. However, the term **database** usually refers to a collection of data that is organized in multiple files. Understanding the difference between the terms file and database will help you to understand the difference between file management software and database software. In general, **file management software** allows you to work with one file at a time, while database software allows you to work with multiple files.

The screens in Figures 2-21 through 2-25 present the development of a personal checking account file and inquiry system using a file management system. The file management main menu (Figure 2-21) presents 5 choices: to create a file, enter data, update the file, display data, and terminate the processing of the file management system. To begin, you would select option 1, CREATE FILE.

When you select option 1, the FILE MANAGEMENT CREATE FILE information shown at the top of Figure 2-22 is displayed. A prompt asks you to enter a file name, the name under which the file being created will be stored on disk. In this example, you would enter the name CHECKING.

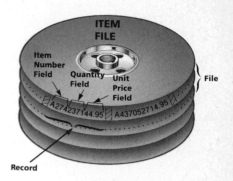

FIGURE 2-20

The item file consists of a record for each item the retail store sells. Each record includes an item number, quantity, and unit price.

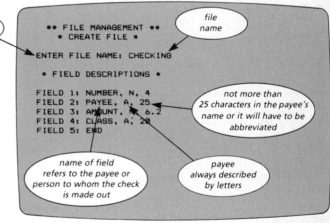

FIGURE 2-22

CREATE FILE screen showing definition of fields for records in the CHECKING file

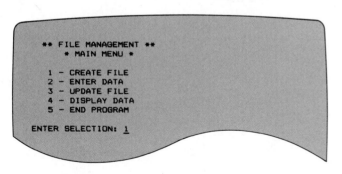

FIGURE 2-21

A typical main menu of file management software

You are then asked to enter descriptions for each field in the records to be stored in the file. A field description consists of a field name, the type of data to be stored in the field (A for alphanumeric, N for numeric data), and the number of characters in the field. In a numeric field, if digits are to appear to the right of the decimal point, you must specify the number of digits to the right. Thus, for the amount field, the designation 6.2 means there are six numeric digits in the field with two of those digits to the right of the decimal point.

Once you have defined the fields in the records, you enter data into the records. Therefore, you would choose main menu entry 2, ENTER DATA and Figure 2-23 would appear. The file management system prompts you to enter data for each record by typing the data to be stored in the field. Thus, after the field name NUMBER, you enter the check number. You complete each field in the same manner, and continue to enter data until all data is entered for the checking account file.

After the file has been defined and data has been stored in it, you can use the file to produce information. Therefore you would choose option 4, DISPLAY DATA, from the main menu. You are then asked to enter the commands that specify what should be displayed and how the data should be processed prior to being displayed. As Figure 2-24 shows, you stated that the data should be sorted on the field called NUMBER, and that all fields in the record should be displayed.

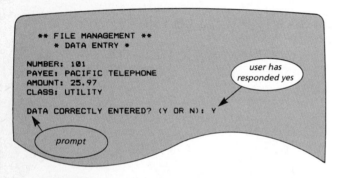

FIGURE 2-23

Data entry screen

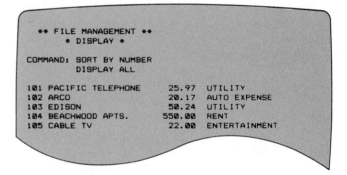

FIGURE 2-24

Display of all records sorted by record number

In Figure 2-25, you direct the system to display only those records where the class is equal to UTILITY and to print a total for the field AMOUNT. As a result, the report shows only those records for which the classification is UTILITY. The values in the amount field are totaled and printed after all records have been processed.

In addition to creating, retrieving, and storing data, most database and file management software provide for the manipulation of the data. This includes sorting the data in ascending or descending sequence by specifying a few simple English-like commands. Figure 2-26 lists some features of popular database software, such as dBASE III PLUS.

Note again that when using this microcomputer application, you do not need to have any special technical knowledge. Database software and file managers are software tools that are designed to help you easily and efficiently manage data electronically.

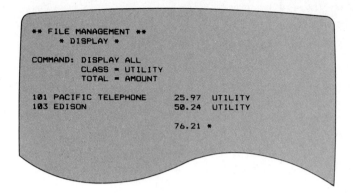

```
** FILE MANAGEMENT **
     * DISPLAY *

COMMAND: DISPLAY ALL
        CLASS = UTILITY
        TOTAL = AMOUNT

101 PACIFIC TELEPHONE    25.97  UTILITY
103 EDISON               50.24  UTILITY

                         76.21 *
```

FIGURE 2-25

Display of only the UTILITY class records with a total calculated on the amount

DATABASE FEATURES	
OPERATIONS Create database Copy data Delete data Sort data **EDITING** Display data Update data	**ARITHMETIC** Compute the average Count the records Sum data fields **OUTPUT** Retrieve data Produce a report

FIGURE 2-26

Common features of database software

Graphics Software: A Data Presentation Tool

Information presented in the form of a graph or a chart is commonly referred to as **graphics**. Studies have shown that information presented in graphic form can be understood much faster than information presented in writing. Three common forms of graphics are **pie charts**, **bar charts**, and **line diagrams** (Figure 2-27).

FIGURE 2-27

(a) Pie charts, so called because they look like pies cut into pieces, are particularly effective for showing the relationship of parts to a whole.

(b) Bar charts display blocks or bars to show relationships among data clearly and precisely.

(c) Line diagrams are particularly effective for showing movement or a change in the condition of the data.

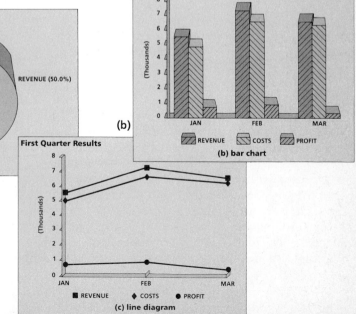

Today, there are many software packages of different capabilities that can create graphics, including most spreadsheet packages. The graphics capabilities of these packages can be grouped into two categories: analytical graphics and presentation graphics. Both kinds can transform numeric data into graphic form.

Analytical graphics is widely used by management personnel when reviewing information and when communicating information to others within their organization. For example, a production manager who is planning a meeting with the president of the company may use color graphics to depict the expenditures of the production department. This graphic display would have more impact and lead to better understanding than would a printed column of production figures.

As its name implies, **presentation graphics** goes beyond analytical graphics by offering the user a wide choice of presentation effects. These include three-dimensional displays, background patterns, multiple text fonts, and image libraries that contain illustrations of factories, people, coins, dollar signs, and other symbols that can be incorporated into the graphic.

To create graphics on your computer, you must follow the directions that apply to your graphics software package. Most packages will prompt you to enter the data the graph will represent, and then ask you to select the type of graph you would like. After entering the data, you can select several different graphic forms to see which one will best convey your message. When you decide on a graph, you can print it and also store it for future reference.

Using graphics software as a presentation tool allows you to efficiently create professional-quality graphics that can help you communicate information more effectively.

Other Popular Applications Software Packages

The four applications discussed so far, word processing, spreadsheet, database, and graphics, are the most widely used microcomputer applications. Four other packages that are finding increasing use are data communications, desktop publishing, electronic mail, and project management.

Data Communications

Data communications software is used to transmit data from one computer to another. It gives users access to online databases such as stock prices and airline schedules, and services such as home banking and shopping.

Microcomputer data communications software often involves using a telephone line connected to special communication equipment either inside or attached to the computer. Similar equipment must be present at the other computer that will be accessed. The data communications software is used to dial the other system and establish the communication connection. Once the connection is established, the user enters commands and responses that control the transmission of data from one computer to the other.

Desktop Publishing

Desktop publishing software allows the user to combine text and graphics to produce high-quality printed documents. Desktop publishing systems go far beyond the capabilities of typical word processing systems by providing many different type sizes and styles and the ability to merge charts, pictures, and illustrations with the text. Numerous special effects such as borders and backgrounds can also be used to enhance the appearance of a document. Businesses of all sizes are increasingly using desktop publishing systems to produce better-looking brochures and communications and to control the production of work that previously could only be done by graphic artists. Figure 2-28 shows examples of documents produced on a desktop publishing system.

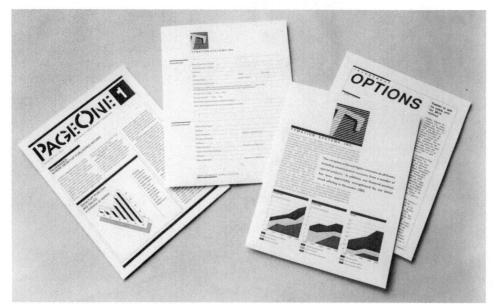

FIGURE 2-28

High-quality printed documents can be produced with desktop publishing software.

An important feature of desktop publishing is page composition. This means that a user is able to design on the screen an exact image of what a printed page will look like. This capability is called **WYSIWYG**—an acronym for "What You See Is What You Get." Some of the page composition or layout features that are available include the use of columns for text, the choice of different font (type) styles, and the placement and size of art on the page.

The art used in the documents created with desktop publishing usually comes from one of three sources:

1. It can be created on the computer with software that has graphics capabilities, such as software packages that are specifically designed to create graphics, or software such as spreadsheet packages that can create pie, line, and bar charts.
2. A scanner can be used to digitize pictures, photographs, and drawings and store them as files on auxiliary storage for use with desktop publishing software.

3. Art can be selected from "clip art" collections. These are collections of art that are stored on disks and are designed to integrate with popular desktop publishing packages (Figure 2-29).

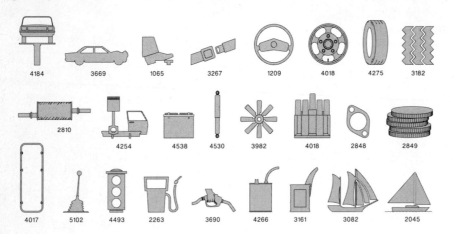

4184 3669 1065 3267 1209 4018 4275 3182

2810 4254 4538 4530 3982 4018 2848 2849

4017 5102 4493 2263 3690 4266 3161 3082 2045

FIGURE 2-29

Clip art consists of previously created figures, shapes, and symbols that can be added to documents. Users specify the numbers of the piece they want to use.

While the text for a document can be created with desktop publishing software, the word processing features of many desktop publishing packages are not as complete as those offered by word processing packages. Therefore, text is usually created with a word processor and then transferred into the desktop publishing package. As new versions of word processing and desktop publishing software are introduced, the capabilities of both applications will increase and the differences between the two applications will decrease. A number of word processing packages now offer desktop publishing features and the word processing features of desktop publishing packages continue to improve.

Electronic Mail

Electronic mail software provides the ability for users to communicate directly with other users by sending text messages electronically over communication channels. For example, if the sales manager, Florence Bolduc, wants to send a message congratulating Terry Willis and Sue Rodriguez for closing a recent sale, she would use the electronic mail software to (1) enter the message on her computer, (2) specify that Terry and Sue are to receive the message, and (3) enter a command to send the message. The software places the message in a file referred to as an electronic mailbox. When Terry and Sue use their computers to check for electronic mail, the message from Florence is displayed on their screens. This method of communication is much more efficient than the traditional method of creating and physically delivering a printed document. Correspondence that once took days to reach an individual can now be electronically transmitted from one user to another in seconds.

Project Management

Project management software allows users to plan, schedule, track, and analyze the events, resources, and costs of a project (Figure 2-30). For example, a construction company might use this type of software to manage the building of an apartment complex or a campaign manager might use it to coordinate the many activities of a politician running for office. The value of project management software is that it provides a method for managers to control and manage the variables of a project to help ensure that the project will be completed on time and within budget.

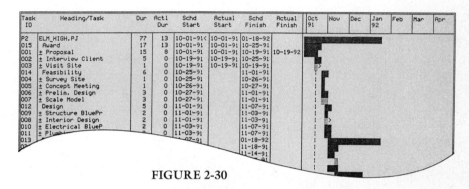

FIGURE 2-30

This output was prepared using project management software. It shows the individual tasks that make up the project and the elapsed time that each task is scheduled to take.

A Summary of Microcomputer Applications Software

Microcomputer applications software provides a way for tasks that are commonly performed in all types of businesses to be done on a computer. These applications are sometimes referred to as **productivity tools** because when they are used, they provide users with a more efficient way to do their work so that they become more productive. There are many popular types of microcomputer applications software (Figure 2-31).

FIGURE 2-31

A list of microcomputer applications software packages. These packages can be used by most organizations and are not limited to a specific type of business.

TYPE	PURPOSE	POPULAR PACKAGES
Word processing	Creates documents	WordPerfect, Microsoft Word
Spreadsheet	Manipulates rows and columns of numbers	Lotus 1-2-3, Excel
Database	Stores, organizes, and retrieves data	dBASE III, dBASE IV, RBASE
Graphics	Pictorial representation of data	Chart-Master, Harvard Graphics
Electronic mail	Transmits electronic messages	Microsoft Mail, In Box
Data communications software	Transmits data from one computer to another	PC Intercom
Desktop publishing	Lay out and create documents containing text and graphics	Ventura, PageMaker
Project management	Schedule and track a project's events and resources	Timeline, Super Project Expert

The most common include word processing, spreadsheets, database, and graphics applications. In addition, four others that are commonly used include data communications software, desktop publishing, electronic mail, and project management.

Integrated Software

Software packages such as electronic spreadsheet and word processing are generally used independently of each other. But what if you wanted to place information from a spreadsheet into a word processing document? The spreadsheet data would have to be reentered in the word processing document. This would be time consuming and errors could be introduced as you reentered the data. The inability of separate programs to communicate with one another and use a common set of data has been overcome through the use of integrated software.

Integrated software refers to packages that combine applications such as word processing, electronic spreadsheet, database, graphics, and data communications into a single, easy-to-use set of programs. Application packages that are included in integrated packages are designed to have a consistent command structure; that is, common commands such as those used to SAVE or LOAD files are the same for all the applications in the package. Besides the consistent presentation, a key feature of integrated packages is their ability to pass data quickly and easily from one application to another. For example, revenue and cost information from a database on daily sales could be quickly loaded into a spreadsheet. The spreadsheet could be used to calculate gross profits. Once the calculations are completed, all or a portion of the spreadsheet data can be passed to the graphics program to create pie, bar, line, or other graphs. Finally, the graphic (or the spreadsheet) can be transferred to a word processing document. A possible disadvantage of an integrated package is that individual integrated programs may not have all the features that are available in nonintegrated packages.

Integrated programs frequently use windows. A **window** is a rectangular portion of the screen that is used to display information. Windows can display help information about the commands of the program you are using or, with integrated packages, they can actually display data from another application. Many programs today can display multiple windows on the screen (Figure 2-32) and allow the user to move from one application window to another. Although they are called "windows" because of their ability to "see" into another part of the program, many people consider windows to be more like multiple sheets of paper on top of a desk. The papers can be shuffled, placed side by side, or moved entirely off the desk until needed again.

FIGURE 2-32

Windows on your screen let you see several applications at one time. In this example the user can plan projects using project management software (top left), pictorially present the plan using graphics software (bottom left), and write about the plan using word processing software (right).

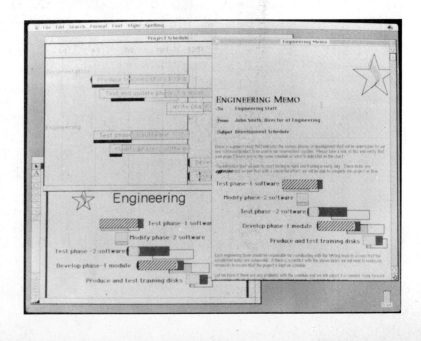

Guidelines for Purchasing Microcomputer Applications Software

Whenever you purchase applications software, you should make sure that the software will meet your needs. Do this by following these five steps:

1. Verify that the software performs the task you desire.
2. Verify that the software will run on your computer.
3. Make sure that the software is adequately documented. The written material that accompanies the software is known as **documentation**.
4. Purchase the software from a reputable store, distributor, or vendor.
5. Obtain the best value, but keep in mind that that might not mean the lowest price.

If you keep these factors in mind when buying applications software packages, you are likely to be pleased with the software you buy.

A good place to look when shopping for software is in computer magazines such as *InfoWorld* and *PC World*. These magazines regularly review software packages and publish articles and charts to help you choose the package best suited to your needs.

Learning Aids and Support Tools for Application Users

Learning to use an applications software package involves time and practice. Fortunately, several support tools are available to help you: tutorials, online help, trade books, and keyboard templates.

Tutorials are step-by-step instructions using real examples that show you how to use an application. Some tutorials are written manuals, but more and more, tutorials are in the software form, allowing you to use your computer to learn about a package.

Online help refers to additional instructions that are available within the application. In most packages, a function key or special combination of keys are reserved for the help feature. When you are using an application and have a question, pressing the designated ''help'' key will temporarily overlay your work on the screen with information on how to use the package. When you are finished using the help feature, pressing another key allows you to return to your work.

The documentation that accompanies software packages is frequently organized as reference material. This makes it very useful once you know how to use a package but difficult to use when you are first learning it. For this reason, many **trade books** are available to help users learn to use the features of microcomputer software packages. These books can usually be found where software is sold and are frequently carried in regular bookstores.

Keyboard templates are plastic sheets that fit around a portion of your keyboard. The keyboard commands to select the various features of the application programs are printed on the template. Having these prompts readily available is helpful for both beginners and experienced users.

Chapter Summary

The following list summarizes the key topics discussed in this chapter.

1. **Computer literate** is a term used to describe people who have an understanding of computers and how they are used in our modern world (p. 2.1).

2. Software that is useful to a broad range of users is sometimes referred to as **microcomputer applications software packages** (p. 2.2).

3. The four most widely used microcomputers applications software packages are word processing, electronic spreadsheet, database, and graphics (p. 2.3).

4. **Word processing software** is used to prepare documents electronically (p. 2.3).

5. Additional support features for a word processing application can include a spelling checker, thesaurus, and grammar checker (p. 2.4).

6. **Spelling checker software** allows you to check individual words or an entire document for correct spelling (p. 2.4).

7. **Thesaurus software** allows you to look up synonyms for words in a document while you are using your word processor (p. 2.4).

8. **Grammar checker software** identifies possible grammar, writing style, and sentence structure errors (p. 2.5).

9. Word processing software is a document productivity tool that allows you to create, edit, format, print, and store documents (p. 2.8).

10. **Electronic spreadsheet software** allows you to organize numeric data into a table format called a **spreadsheet** or **worksheet**. (p. 2.8).

11. A spreadsheet is composed of **rows** and **columns**. Each intersection of a row and column is a **cell** (p. 2.9).

12. A spreadsheet cell can contain a label (text) or a value (number or formula) (p. 2.9).

13. The "what if" capability of electronic spreadsheet software is a powerful tool that is widely used by management personnel for decision support information (p. 2.10).

14. **Database software** and **file management software** are used to organize, retrieve, manipulate, and update data that is stored in files (p. 2.12).

15. Individual facts are referred to as **data items, data fields**, or **fields** (p. 2.13).

16. A **record** is a collection of related fields (p. 2.13).

17. A collection of related records is called a **file** (p. 2.13).

18. In general, database software works with data that is stored in multiple files. File management software is designed to work with one data file at a time (p. 2.13).

19. Information presented in the form of a graph or a chart is commonly referred to as **graphics**. Three popular graphics used to present information include **pie charts, bar charts**, and **line diagrams** (p. 2.15).

20. **Data communications software** allows you to transmit data from one computer to another (p. 2.16).

21. **Desktop publishing software** can combine text and graphics to produce high-quality printed documents (p. 2.17).

22. Page composition, or the ability to design on the screen an exact image of what a printed page will look like, is an important feature of desktop publishing. This capability is called **WYSIWYG**, an acronym for "What You See Is What You Get" (p. 2.17).

23. **Electronic mail** software provides the ability for users to directly communicate with other users by sending text messages electronically over communication channels (p. 2.18).
24. **Project management software** allows users to plan, schedule, track, and analyze the events, resources, and costs of a project (p. 2.19).
25. **Integrated software** packages combine several applications in one package and allow data to be shared between the applications (p. 2.20).
26. When you purchase software, you should perform the following steps: (1) Verify that the software performs the task desired. (2) Verify that the software runs on your computer. (3) Make sure the software documentation is adequate. (4) Purchase the software from a reputable store, distributor, or vendor. (5) Obtain the best value (p. 2.21).
27. Aids such as tutorials, online help, trade books, and keyboard templates are useful in learning and using microcomputer applications (p. 2.21).

Review Questions

1. Define the term computer literate.
2. What is microcomputer applications software?
3. List the four most widely used microcomputer applications software packages and describe how each application helps users.
4. What is a spelling checker? Describe a typical procedure when a misspelled word is found.
5. Explain how management personnel use the "what if" capability of electronic spreadsheets. Why is this capability useful for decision support?
6. Define the terms field, record, file, and database.
7. What is the difference between database software and file management software?
8. List the three most commonly used charts. Draw an example of each.
9. What does the page composition feature of desktop publishing allow a user to do? What is WYSIWYG?
10. What is electronic mail? What is project management?
11. Describe the advantage of using integrated software. What is a possible disadvantage? What are windows and how are they used in integrated software packages?
12. List the five steps that should be performed when purchasing software.
13. List and describe four learning aids that can help you use microcomputer applications software packages.

Input to the Computer

3

Objectives

- Define the four types of input and how the computer uses each type.
- Describe the standard features of keyboards and explain how to use the cursor control and function keys.
- Identify the two types of terminals and how to use each type.
- Describe several input devices other than the keyboard and terminal.
- Define user interface.
- Define the term menu and describe various forms of menus.
- Discuss the differences between interactive and batch processing data entry.
- Describe online and offline data entry and the uses for each.
- Explain the term ergonomics and describe some of the changes that have occurred in equipment design.

In the information processing cycle, the input operation must take place before any data can be processed and any information produced. Without valid input data, a computer is not capable of producing any useful information.

When they were first utilized for business applications, nearly all computers used punched card equipment for input. The data was recorded on cards using a device called a keypunch. A keypunch is a machine that contains a keyboard and a punching mechanism. As the operator presses the keys, holes representing numbers, letters of the alphabet, or special characters are punched into the card. The cards are then collected together and read into main memory by a card reader.

Although punched cards and the card reader are still used today, they have, for the most part, been replaced by easier-to-use and more efficient input devices. This chapter examines the devices used for input, the ways that both hardware and software are designed to make input operations easier for the user, and the various methods of entering data into the computer.

What Is Input?

Input refers to the process of entering programs, commands, user responses, and data into main memory. These four types of input are used by a computer in the following ways:

- **Programs** are the sets of instructions that direct the computer to perform the necessary operations to process data into information. The program that is loaded and stored in main memory determines the processing that the computer will perform. When a program is first entered into a computer it is input by way of a keyboard. Once the program has been entered and stored on auxiliary storage, it can be transferred to main memory by a command.
- **Commands** are key words and phrases that the user inputs to direct the computer to perform certain activities. For example, if you want to use a payroll program, you might issue a command such as LOAD ''PAYROLL'' to load the program named PAYROLL into main memory from auxiliary storage. To begin the execution of the program you would enter another command such as RUN (Figure 3-1).
- **User responses** refer to the data that a user inputs in response to a question or message from the software. Usually these messages display on a screen and the user responds through a keyboard. One of the most common responses is to answer ''Yes'' or ''No'' to a question. Based on the answer, the computer program will perform specific actions. For example, in a spreadsheet program, typing the letter Y in response to the message ''Do you want to save this file?'' will result in the spreadsheet file being saved (written) to the auxiliary storage device.
- **Data** is raw facts; it is the source from which information is produced. It must be entered and stored in main computer memory for processing to occur. For example, data entered from sales orders can be processed by a computer program to produce sales reports useful to management. Data is the most common type of input.

FIGURE 3-1

In this example, the computer user first enters a command to load the program called ''PAYROLL'' and then issues the command RUN, which causes the program to be executed.

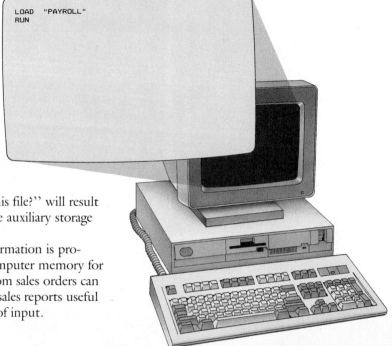

```
LOAD   "PAYROLL"
RUN
```

Regardless of the type, input is entered through some kind of input device. The next section of this chapter discusses the various types of available input devices.

The Keyboard

Keyboards are the most commonly used input devices. Users input data to a computer by pressing the keys on the keyboard. Keyboards are connected to other devices, such as a personal computer or a terminal, that have screens. As the user enters data on the keyboard, it displays on the screen.

The keyboards (Figure 3-2) used for computer input are very similar to the keyboards used on the familiar office machine, the typewriter. They contain numbers, letters of the alphabet, and some special characters. In addition, many computer keyboards are equipped with a special **numeric keypad** on the right-hand side of the keyboard. These numeric keys are arranged in an adding machine or calculator format and aid the user with data entry.

FIGURE 3-2

The enhanced IBM PS/2 keyboard contains a numeric keypad, cursor control keys, and function keys.

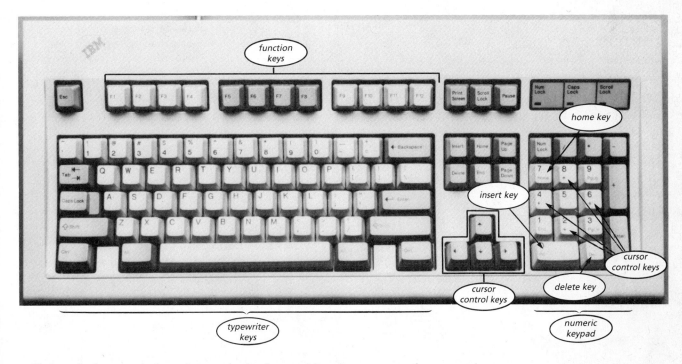

Keyboards also contain keys that can be used to position the cursor on the screen. A **cursor** is a symbol, such as a highlighted rectangle or an underline character, that indicates where on the screen the next character entered will be displayed. The keys that move the cursor are called **arrow keys** or **cursor control keys**. These keys include an up arrow, a down arrow, a left arrow, and a right arrow. When you press any of these keys, the cursor moves one space in the direction specified by the arrow. In addition, many keyboards contain other cursor control keys such as the Home key, which when pressed sends the cursor to the upper left position of the screen or document.

Some computer keyboards also contain keys that are used to alter or edit the text displayed on the screen. For example, the Ins (insert) and Del (delete) keys allow characters to be inserted or deleted from the screen.

Function keys are keys that are assigned certain tasks that assist the user. For example, a function key might be assigned as a help key when a computer is used for word processing. Whenever the key is pressed, messages will appear that give instructions pertaining to the word processor. Another use of function keys is to save keystrokes. Sometimes several keystrokes are required to accomplish a certain task, for example, printing a document. Some applications software packages are written so that the user can either enter the individual keystrokes or press a function key and obtain the same result.

The disadvantage of using a keyboard as an input device is that training is required to use it efficiently. Users who do not know how to type are at a disadvantage because of the time they spend looking for the correct keys to press.

Terminals

Terminals, sometimes called **display terminals** or **video display terminals (VDTs)**, consist of a keyboard and a screen. They fall into two basic categories: dumb terminals and intelligent terminals (Figure 3-3).

FIGURE 3-3

Terminals can be classified into two broad categories: dumb terminals and intelligent terminals. From appearance alone, it is often difficult to tell which category a terminal belongs to. In these photos the dumb terminal on the left lacks a processor.

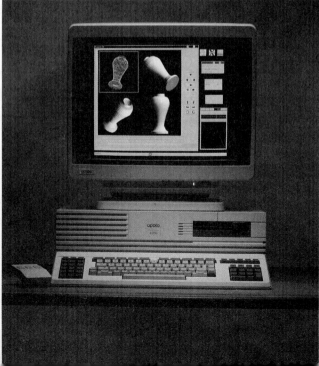

Dumb Terminals

A **dumb terminal** consists of a keyboard and a display screen that can be used to enter and transmit data to or receive and display data from a computer to which it is connected. A dumb terminal has no independent processing capability or auxiliary storage and cannot function as a stand-alone device.

Intelligent Terminals

Intelligent terminals are terminals whose processing capabilities are built in. These terminals are also known as **programmable terminals** because they can be programmed by the user to perform many basic tasks, including both arithmetic and logic operations. Personal computers are frequently used as intelligent terminals.

Intelligent terminals often contain not only the keyboard and screen associated with other terminals, but also are supported with disk drives and printers, so they can perform limited processing tasks when not communicating directly with the central computer. In some instances, when the user enters data, the data is checked for errors and some type of report is produced. In addition, the valid data that is entered is stored on the disk connected to the terminal. After the data has been entered and stored on disk, it is transmitted over communication lines to the central computer. This operation is called **uploading**, because the data is loaded from the smaller terminal "up" to the bigger main computer. Uploading is used most often when the data entered is to be processed in a batch processing mode.

The alternative to uploading is downloading. With **downloading**, data and/or programs are loaded "down" from the computer to the intelligent terminal. Downloading is often used to load the programs into the main memory unit of the terminal to accept and edit the data entered by the user.

As the amount of processing power that is incorporated into intelligent terminals increases, more processing can occur at the site of the terminal prior to sending the data to the central computer. This means that the large minicomputer or mainframe at the central site can perform the main processing and serve multiple users faster, rather than having to use its resources to perform tasks that can be performed by the intelligent terminal.

FIGURE 3-4

This point of sale terminal is specially designed for grocery store item entry. The checker can press separate keys to process the prices of produce, meat, and other items.

Special-Purpose Terminals

Terminals are found in virtually every environment that generates data for processing on a computer. While many are standard terminals like those previously described, others are designed to perform specific jobs and contain features uniquely designed for use in a particular industry.

The terminal shown in Figure 3-4 is called a point of sale terminal. **Point of sale terminals** allow data to be entered at the time and place where the transaction with a customer occurs, such as in fast-food restaurants or hotels. Point of sale terminals serve as input to either minicomputers located at the place of business or larger computers located elsewhere. The data entered is used to maintain sales records, update inventory, make automatic calculations such as sales tax, verify credit, and perform other activities associated with the sales transactions and critical to running the business. Point of sale terminals are designed to be easy to operate, requiring little technical knowledge.

Other Input Devices

Besides keyboards and terminals, there is an increasing variety of other input devices. This section describes some of the devices used for general-purpose applications.

The Mouse

The mouse, initially designed by Xerox, is a unique device used with personal computers and some computer terminals. A **mouse** is a small, lightweight device that easily fits in the palm of your hand. You move it across a flat surface such as a desktop (Figure 3-5) to control the movement of the cursor on a screen. The mouse is attached to the computer by a cable. On the bottom of the mouse is a ball. As the mouse moves across the flat surface, the computer electronically senses the movement of the ball. The movement of the cursor on the screen corresponds to the movement of the mouse. When you move the mouse left on the surface of a table or desk, the cursor moves left on the screen. When you move the mouse to the right, the cursor moves to the right, and so on.

On top of the mouse are one or more buttons. By moving the cursor on the screen and pressing the buttons, you can make menu choices, choose letters or words in a word processing application for addition or deletion, move data from one point on the screen to another, and perform many other actions that move and rearrange information displayed on the screen.

The primary advantage of a mouse is that it is easy to use. Proponents of the mouse say that with a little practice, a person can use a mouse to point to locations on the screen just as easily as using a finger. For some applications such as desktop publishing, a mouse is indispensable.

There are two major disadvantages of the mouse. The first is that it requires empty desk space where it can be moved about. The second disadvantage is that the user must remove a hand from the keyboard and place it on the mouse whenever the cursor is to be moved or a command is to be given. Some keyboard experts have noted that taking hands from the keyboard slows the effective data entry speed considerably. Thus, some people have said the mouse is not an effective tool in those environments where keying must be performed rapidly, such as in word processing applications. Others, however, say that using a mouse is far superior to using the cursor control keys on a keyboard.

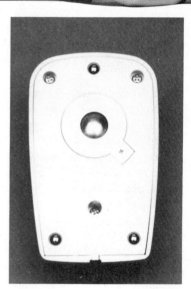

FIGURE 3-5

The mouse can be moved to control the cursor on the screen. Press the button at the top of the mouse to make selections or perform functions, depending on the software being used. The ball on the underside of the mouse moves as the user pushes the mouse around on a hard, flat surface. The movement of the ball causes the cursor to move correspondingly on the screen.

Touch Screens

Touch screens allow users to merely touch areas of the screen to enter data. They let the user interact with a computer by the touch of a finger, rather than typing on a keyboard or moving a mouse. The user enters data by touching words or numbers, or locations identified on the screen (Figure 3-6).

Several electronic techniques change a touch on the screen into electronic impulses that can be interpreted by the computer software. One of the most common techniques utilizes beams of infrared light that are projected across the surface of the screen. A finger or other utensil touching the screen interrupts the beams, generating an electronic signal. This signal identifies the location on the screen where the touch occurred. The software interprets the signal and performs the required function.

Touch screens are not used to enter large amounts of data. They are used, however, for applications in which the user must issue a command to the software to perform a particular task or must choose from a list of options to be performed.

There are both advantages and disadvantages of touch screens. A significant advantage is that they are very "natural" to use; that is, people are used to pointing to things. With touch screens, they can point to indicate the processing they want performed by the computer. In addition, touch screens are usually easy for the user to learn. As quickly as pointing a finger, the user's request is processed. Finally, touch screens allow absolute cursor movement; that is, the user can point a finger at the location where the cursor is to appear and it will. This can be considerably faster than repeatedly pressing arrow keys to move the cursor from one location on the screen to another.

Two major complaints are lodged against touch screens. First, the resolution of the touching area is not precise. Thus, while a user can point to a box or a fairly large area on the screen and the electronics can determine the location of the touch, it is difficult to point to a single character in a word processing application, for example, and indicate that the character should be deleted. In cases such as these, a keyboard is easier to use. A second complaint is that after a period of reaching for the screen, the user's arm may become tired.

Graphic Input Devices

Graphic input devices are used to translate graphic input data, such as photos or drawings, into a form that can be processed on a computer. Three major devices that are used for graphic input are light pens, digitizers, and graphics tablets. A **light pen** is used by touching it on the screen to create or modify graphics (Figure 3-7). A **digitizer** converts points, lines, and curves from a sketch, drawing, or photograph to digital impulses and transmits them to a computer (Figure 3-8). A **graphics tablet** works in a manner similar to a digitizer, but it also contains unique characters and commands that can be automatically generated by the person using the tablet.

FIGURE 3-7

Placing the light pen at a point on the screen activates a sensing device within the pen. The activated pen transmits the location of the light to the computer, where the program can perform the desired tasks.

FIGURE 3-8

The device in this aerospace engineer's hand reads and translates the coordinates on the printed wiring board layout into coordinates that can be stored in the computer and later used to reproduce the drawing on a screen or a printer.

Voice Input

One of the more exciting developments is the use of voice input, sometimes referred to as voice or speech recognition. As the name implies, **voice input** allows the user to enter data and issue commands to the computer with spoken words (Figure 3-9).

Most voice input devices require the user to "train" it first by speaking the words that will be used. As the words are spoken, they are digitized by the system; that is, they are broken down into digital components that the computer can recognize. After each word has been spoken several times, the system has developed a digital pattern for the word that can be stored on auxiliary storage. When the user later speaks a word to the system to request a particular action, the system compares the word to words that were previously entered and that it can "understand." When it finds a match, the software performs the activity associated with the word. For example, in voice-controlled word processing systems, spoken words can be used to control such functions as single and double spacing, choosing type styles, and centering text.

The major advantage of voice input is that the user does not have to key, move, or touch anything in order to enter data into the computer. It is expected that voice input will be a significant factor in the years to come.

FIGURE 3-9

This manager has just used his voice input system to request that sales data be presented in a bar graph. Often such systems have to be "trained" to recognize a particular user's voice.

Input Devices Designed for Specific Purposes

Some input devices have been designed to perform specific tasks. Here we illustrate a few of these devices.

Magnetic Ink Character Recognition

Magnetic ink character recognition or **MICR** is a type of machine-readable data. This type of data is read into the computer by input devices called **MICR readers**. MICR is found almost exclusively in the banking industry. In the 1950s, the industry chose MICR as the method to be used to encode and read the billions of checks written each year.

When MICR is used, special characters encoded on checks identify such items as the bank number and the account number. When a check is processed, the amount is also encoded on it by a bank operator. The items are encoded in special MICR characters

(Figure 3-10) using a special ink that can be magnetized during processing. MICR readers interpret the electronic signals generated from the magnetized characters so checks can be sorted and processed to prepare bank statements for customers. MICR devices can process over 1,000 checks per minute (Figure 3-11). MICR also is used in utility companies, credit card companies, and other industries that must process large volumes of data.

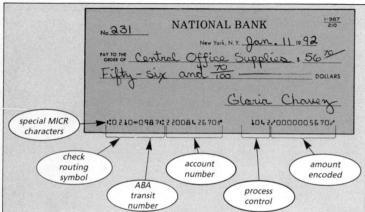

FIGURE 3-10

The characters at the bottom of a check can be read by MICR devices. All the banks in the United States and in many foreign countries use these codes for checks.

Scanners

Scanners include a variety of devices that "read" printed codes, characters, or images and convert them into a form that can be processed by the computer. This section describes several different types of scanning devices.

Optical Character Readers **Optical character recognition (OCR)** devices are scanners that read typewritten, computer-printed, and in some cases hand-printed characters from ordinary documents. OCR devices range

FIGURE 3-11

This MICR reader-sorter can process up to 1,200 documents per minute. After the documents are read, they are sorted into the vertical bins shown in the top center portion of the machine. This device can be connected directly to a computer to allow the documents to be processed as they are read.

from large machines that can automatically read thousands of documents per minute to hand-held wands (Figure 3-12).

An OCR device scans the shape of a character on a document, compares it with a predefined shape stored in its memory, and converts the character read into a corresponding bit pattern for storing in main memory. The standard OCR typeface, called OCR-A, is illustrated in Figure 3-13. The characters can be read easily by both humans and machines. OCR-B is a set of standard characters widely used in Europe and Japan.

Some optical character readers can read hand-printed characters. Building a machine able to read and interpret hand-printed characters is a challenging task even in this era of high technology. The characters must be carefully printed according to a strict set of rules regarding their shapes. The example in Figure 3-14 illustrates the shape of hand-printed characters that can be read with an OCR device.

FIGURE 3-12

This hand-held optical character recognition device is being used to read a typed document. Such wands can be used for both interactive and batch data entry.

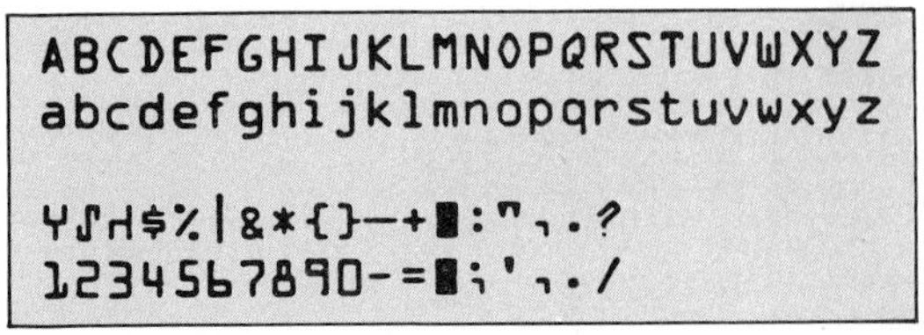

FIGURE 3-13

In the full OCR-A standard character set shown above, characters such as B and 8, S and 5, and zero and the letter O are designed so the reading device can easily distinguish between them.

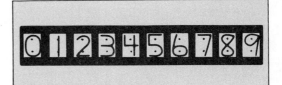

FIGURE 3-14

These hand-printed characters can be read by some types of OCR devices. The two small dots in each square identify where certain portions of each numeric digit must be placed.

The most widespread application for OCR devices is for reading turn-around documents prepared by computer printers. A **turn-around document** is designed to be returned to the organization that originally issued it. When the document is returned (''turned around''), the data on it is read by an OCR device. For example, many utility bills, department store bills, insurance premium statements, and so on request that the consumer return the statement with a payment (Figure 3-15). The statement is printed with characters that can be read by OCR devices. When the customer returns it, the machine reads it to give proper credit for the payment received. Some OCR devices, such as the one shown in Figure 3-16, are small enough to fit on top of a desk.

Optical Mark Readers An **optical mark reader (OMR)** is a scanning device that can read carefully placed pencil marks on specially designed documents. The pencil marks on the form usually indicate responses to questions and can be read and interpreted by a computer program. Optical mark readers are frequently used to score tests.

Laser Scanners A scanning device often used by modern grocery stores at checkout counters is a **laser scanner** (Figure 3-16). These devices use a laser beam to scan and read the special bar code printed on the products.

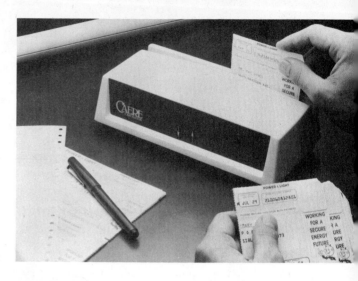

FIGURE 3-15

In this picture, utility company payment receipts are being read by an OCR device. These receipts are examples of turn-around documents because they were designed to be returned to the utility with the customer's payment.

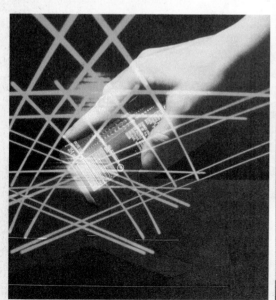

FIGURE 3-16

Most modern grocery stores use optical scanning devices such as the one shown here. A laser beam, emitted from the opening on the counter, reads the bar code on the product package. Most retail products have the Universal Product Code (UPC) imprinted somewhere on the label or package. The UPC code uniquely identifies both the manufacturer and the product. The scanning device is connected to a computer system that uses the UPC code to look up the price of the product and add the price into the total sale. A keyboard is used to code the numbers for items such as fruit, which do not have UPC labels.

Page Scanners A **page scanner** is a type of scanner that can convert an entire page of printed material into the individual characters and words that can be processed by a word processing program. Other types of scanners can convert images such as photos and art work for eventual use with desktop publishing systems (Figure 3-17).

FIGURE 3-17

The page scanner to the left of the PC can input text, graphics, or photographs for use in word processing or desktop publishing applications.

FIGURE 3-18

This portable data collection device is being used to take an inventory in a warehouse. The data is stored in memory and can later be transferred to a computer system for processing.

Image Processing As we've previously discussed, much of the information input to the computer is taken from source documents. Usually, only a portion of the information on the source document is input. But sometimes the entire source document is needed for data, such as a signature or a drawing. In these situations, organizations often implement image processing systems. **Image processing systems** use software and special equipment, including scanners, to input and store an actual image of the source document. These systems are like giant electronic filing cabinets that allow users to rapidly access and review exact reproductions of the original documents.

Data Collection Devices

Data entry is not confined to office environments or restricted to dedicated data entry personnel. **Data collection devices** are designed and used for obtaining data at the site where the transaction or event being reported takes place. For example, in Figure 3-18 a man is taking inventory in a warehouse. Rather than write down the number and type of items and then enter this data, he uses a portable data collection

device to record the inventory count in the device's memory. After he takes the inventory, the data can be transmitted to a computer for processing.

Unlike most input devices, data collection equipment is designed to be used in environments where heat, humidity, and cleanliness are difficult or impossible to control (Figure 3-19). In addition, data collection devices are often used by people whose primary task is not to enter the data. Entering the data is only a small portion of their job duties. Therefore, these devices must be easy to operate in any environment.

FIGURE 3-19

This photograph illustrates a data collection device that has been designed to accommodate the user. A data collection device should be simple and quick to operate, so that entering the data does not interfere with the main job of the person using it.

Using data collection devices can provide important advantages over alternative methods of input preparation. Because the data is entered as it is collected, clerical costs and transcription errors are reduced or eliminated. If the data collection devices are directly connected to the computer, the data is immediately available for processing.

Data collection devices range from portable devices that can be carried throughout a store or factory (such as in Figure 3-18) to sophisticated terminal systems with multiple input stations that feed directly into a central computer. These devices will continue to improve and find increased use in data entry applications.

Figure 3-20 summarizes the most commonly used input devices. While each device has advantages and disadvantages, each is appropriate for specific applications. Several of these devices incorporate a user interface to be more efficient.

DEVICE	DESCRIPTION
Keyboard	Most commonly used input device. Special keys may include numeric keypad, cursor control keys, and function keys.
Terminal	Video display terminals are dumb or intelligent.
Mouse	Small input device used to move the cursor on a screen and select options.
Touch screens	User interacts with the computer by touching the screen.
Graphic input	Light pens, digitizers, and graphics tablets translate graphic data into a form that can be processed by a computer.
Voice input	User enters data and issues commands with spoken words.
MICR reader	Used primarily in banking to read the magnetic ink characters printed on checks.
Scanner	A variety of devices that read printed codes, characters, or images.
Data collection	Used to input data where it is generated.

FIGURE 3-20

This table summarizes some of the more common input devices.

User Interfaces

With the widespread use of terminals and personal computers, input operations are performed by many types of users whose computer knowledge and experience varies greatly. Some users have a limited knowledge of computers and others have many years of experience. In addition, some users interact with computers daily, while others use them only occasionally. Information systems need to provide all users with a means of interacting with the computer efficiently. This is done through user interfaces.

A **user interface** is the combination of hardware and software that allows a user to communicate with a computer system. Through a user interface, users are able to input values that will: (1) respond to messages presented by the computer; (2) control the computer; and (3) request information from the computer. Thus, a user interface provides the means for communication between an information system and the user.

Both the hardware and software working together form a user interface. A terminal is an example of hardware that is frequently part of a user interface. The screen on the terminal displays messages to the user. The devices used for responding to the messages and controlling the computer include the keyboard, the mouse, and other types of input devices. The software associated with an interface are the programs. These programs determine the messages that are given to the user, the manner in which the user can respond, and the actions that will take place based on the user's responses.

The following sections discuss some of the user interface techniques that have been developed, such as prompts and menus, and how they have improved communication between the user and the computer.

Prompts

A **prompt** is a message to the user that displays on the screen and provides helpful information or instructions regarding some entry to be made or action to be taken. The example in Figure 3-21 illustrates the use of prompts. On the first line, the prompt ENTER LAST NAME: appears on the screen. This message tells the user to enter his or her last name.

After the user enters his or her last name, a second prompt displays. This prompt, ENTER DATE (MM/DD/YY), indicates not only what is to be entered but also the exact format it should have. MM/DD/YY means to enter the date as a two-digit month number followed by a slash (/), a two-digit day number followed by a slash, and a two-digit year number. Thus, the entry 04/05/90 is valid, but 4/5/90 is not.

To help ensure that the user inputs valid data, the software should use **data editing**, the ability to check the data for proper format and acceptable values. When data is entered incorrectly, a message should be displayed so that the user becomes aware of the error and can reenter the data. The example in Figure 3-22 illustrates what might occur when the data is not entered in the correct format. Note that an error message displays and requests the user to reenter the date.

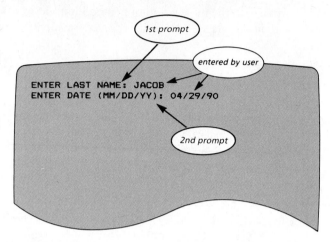

FIGURE 3-21

Prompts aid the user in entering data. They can tell the user what data to enter as well as the required format (as shown for the date entry). Prompts were one of the first types of interfaces designed to assist the user in utilizing the computer.

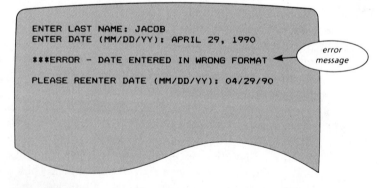

FIGURE 3-22

The software used for this screen checks the date entered and gives an error message if the date is entered in the wrong format.

Menus

A **menu** is a display on a screen that allows a user to make a selection from multiple alternatives. A menu generally consists of three parts (Figure 3-23): a title, the selections, and a prompt. The title identifies the menu and orients the user to the choices that can be made. The selections consist of both a means for identifying the choices and the words that describe them. The prompt asks the user to enter one of the selections.

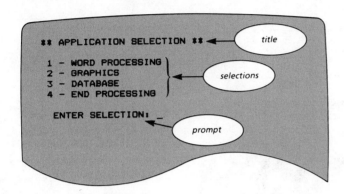

FIGURE 3-23

A menu consists of a title, the selections that can be made, and a prompt for the user to make an entry.

A program can request the user to select an activity from a menu in several ways. Figure 3-24 on the next page illustrates the most common techniques, each of which is described below.

1. **Sequential Number**   In Example 1, each of the selections is identified by a number. The user enters the number 1, 2, 3, or 4 to select the desired processing operation.
2. **Alphabetic Selection**   In Example 2 letters of the alphabet identify the various processing options.
3. **Cursor Positioning**   Example 3 illustrates a menu in which the choice is made by using the arrow or cursor control keys to position the cursor adjacent to the desired selection. Then the Enter key is pressed to make the choice.
4. **Reverse Video**   Example 4 illustrates using reverse video to highlight the selection. **Reverse video** means that the normal screen display pattern, such as amber on black, is reversed to highlight and draw attention to a certain character, word, or section of the screen. In the example, the directions instruct the user to move the reverse video from one selection to another by pressing the space bar. Pressing the space bar once moves the reverse video from the word processing option to graphics; pressing it again highlights the database option.
5. **Icon Selection**   In Example 5, the same reverse video method is used to highlight the choices, but the choices are also identified by graphic images or icons. An **icon** is a pictorial representation of a function to be performed on the computer. Pressing the space bar highlights each of the words under the graphic in reverse video. Pressing the Enter key executes the chosen function.

EXAMPLE 1 — Sequential Number

```
** APPLICATION SELECTION **

1 - WORD PROCESSING
2 - GRAPHICS
3 - DATABASE
4 - END PROCESSING

 ENTER SELECTION: _
```

type a number

EXAMPLE 2 — Alphabetic Selection

```
** APPLICATION SELECTION **

W - WORD PROCESSING
G - GRAPHICS
D - DATABASE
E - END PROCESSING

 ENTER SELECTION: _
```

type a letter

EXAMPLE 5 — Icon Selection

```
** APPLICATION SELECTION **
```

```
PRESS SPACE BAR TO IDENTIFY
SELECTION - THEN PRESS ENTER
```

select and press Enter

EXAMPLE 3 — Cursor Positioning

```
** APPLICATION SELECTION **

 WORD PROCESSING
 GRAPHICS
 DATABASE
 END PROCESSING

POSITION CURSOR TO MAKE
SELECTION - THEN PRESS ENTER
```

select and press Enter

EXAMPLE 4 — Reverse Video

```
** APPLICATION SELECTION **

 WORD PROCESSING
 GRAPHICS
 DATABASE
 END PROCESSING

 PRESS SPACE BAR TO HIGHLIGHT
 SELECTION - THEN PRESS ENTER
```

select and press Enter

FIGURE 3-24

This illustration shows five different types of menus and menu selection methods.

Submenus

Some applications require the use of several related menus. Menus that further define the operations that can be performed are called **submenus**.

The example in Figure 3-25 illustrates the main menu from Example 1 in Figure 3-24, which allows the user to select word processing, graphics, or database. When the word processing function is selected, a submenu appears. This submenu contains more detailed functions. Depending on the submenu selection, additional menus could be displayed. For example, if the user selected option 1, enter data, from the submenu shown in Figure 3-25, a third menu could appear that would display selections relative to margin settings, page length, and other word processing functions.

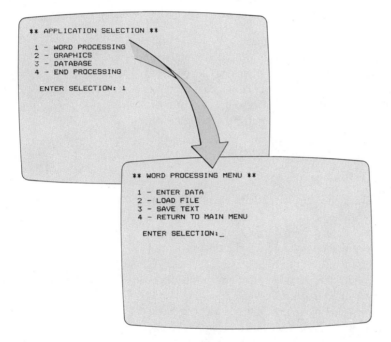

FIGURE 3-25

A submenu is used when additional selections can be made within an application. In this example, the submenu displays additional word processing selections.

Menus: Advantages and Disadvantages

Menus are a type of user interface that is used with all sizes and types of computers. There are both advantages and disadvantages to menus. Some of the advantages are:

1. The user does not have to remember special commands. He or she merely chooses a selection from a list of possible operations or functions.
2. The user can become productive with a minimum of training. Instead of having to learn a lot of technical computer information, he or she merely needs to understand the application and the results of choosing a particular option from the menu.
3. The user is guided through the application because only the options that are available are presented.

The disadvantage most often associated with menus, according to some experienced users, is that they can be slow and restrictive. For example, the menus illustrated in Figure 3-25 are good for the novice or infrequent computer user because they take him or her step-by-step through the possible operations that can be performed. The experienced user, however, knows what processing is required. Therefore, he or she may prefer to enter a few quick commands and immediately begin work instead of having to view and respond to two or more menus.

Data Entry for Interactive and Batch Processing

The information processing cycle (input, processing, output, storage) is usually implemented on a computer in one of two ways. These two methods are called interactive processing and batch processing. **Interactive processing** means that data is processed upon entry and output is produced immediately. In **batch processing**, data is collected and at some later time, all the data that has been gathered is processed as a group or "batch." The methods used to enter data for interactive and batch processing differs. We explain them in the following paragraphs.

Data Entry for Interactive Processing

Data entered in the interactive processing mode generates immediate output. In most interactive data entry, the person entering the data is communicating directly with the computer that will process the data. Therefore, data entry for interactive processing is said to be **online data entry**, meaning that the device from which the data is being entered is connected directly to the computer.

The output generated from interactive data entry processing is not always produced at the location where the data was entered. In Figure 3-26, for example, the data is entered from a terminal located in the order entry department. The data entered concerns a purchase by a customer. After the data is entered, a picking slip is printed in the warehouse. The worker in the warehouse would then retrieve the item purchased (in this case, a lawn mower) and package it for shipping. The terminal operator in the order entry department never sees the output generated, yet this is interactive processing because the data entered is processed immediately.

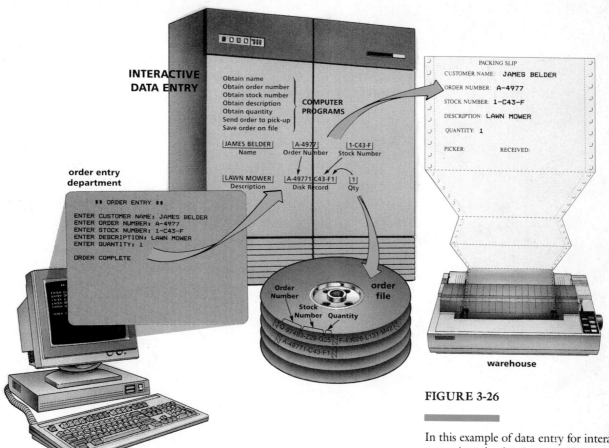

FIGURE 3-26

In this example of data entry for interactive processing, the data is entered by a terminal operator in the order entry department. The output generated, a picking slip, is printed in the warehouse. In addition, a record of the order is stored on disk.

Data Entry for Batch Processing

When data is entered for processing in the batch processing mode, it is stored on a storage medium (usually tape or disk) for processing at a later time. Data for batch processing can be entered in either an online or offline manner. As noted previously, online data entry means that the device from which the data is being entered is connected directly to the computer that will process it (Figure 3-27 on the next page).

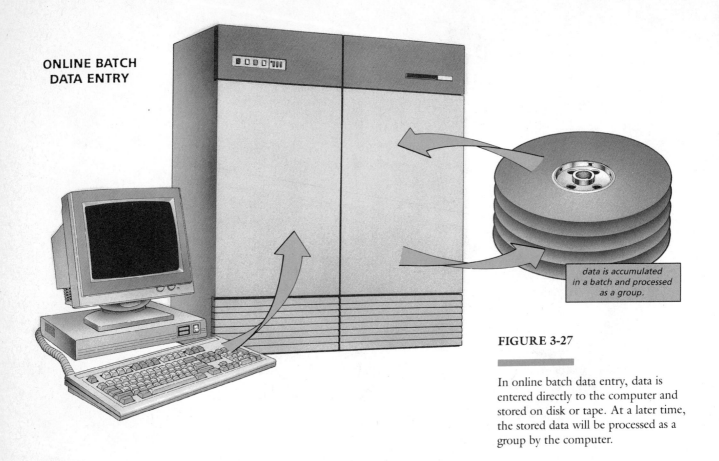

ONLINE BATCH
DATA ENTRY

data is accumulated
in a batch and processed
as a group.

FIGURE 3-27

In online batch data entry, data is
entered directly to the computer and
stored on disk or tape. At a later time,
the stored data will be processed as a
group by the computer.

Offline data entry means that the device from which the data is being entered is not
connected to the computer that will process it. Instead, the data is entered using a dedicated computer or other device devoted to the data entry function. This computer or
special device accepts the input data and stores it on disk or tape. At a later time, the
disk or tape can be transported to the site where the data will be entered for processing
in a batch mode to produce information.

Summary of Interactive and Batch Data Entry

Entering data to produce information can take place online or offline. Online data entry
is always used for interactive processing and often for batch processing as well. Offline
data entry is used for batch processing. With offline data entry, source documents from
which the data is obtained must be gathered prior to the data being entered. Regardless
of the processing method, producing information often requires a large amount of data
entry.

Ergonomics

To be efficient when you are using a computer, it is important that you be comfortable. Being comfortable results in less fatigue, better accuracy, and higher input rates, factors that are important to all users, but particularly to data entry personnel. **Ergonomics** is the study of the design and arrangement of equipment so that people will interact with the equipment in a healthy, comfortable, and efficient manner. As related to computer equipment, ergonomics is concerned with such factors as the physical design of the keyboard, screens, and related hardware, and the manner in which people interact with these hardware devices.

The first computer terminals contained the keyboard and screen as a single unit. The screen frequently displayed white characters on a black background. Early studies found significant user dissatisfaction with the terminals. One study reported that 90% of the personnel who used these terminals complained of health problems, including eye fatigue, blurred vision, itching and burning eyes, and back problems. As a result of these studies, a number of design recommendations for terminals were made. These recommendations included the following:

1. Computer keyboards should be detached from the screen so that they can be positioned on a desk for the convenience and comfort of the user.
2. The screen should be movable, and the angle at which the user views the contents of the screen should be adjustable.
3. Amber or green text on a black background is preferable to black characters on a white background or white characters on a black background.
4. The screen should be of high quality to eliminate any flickering of the image and characters on the screen. The characters displayed on the screen should appear as solid as possible.
5. The images on the screen should be in sharp focus over the entire screen area.
6. The screen should have an antiglare coating. Screen glare has been a common complaint of many terminal users, and it is known that glare can be harmful to eyes. A flat screen, now used on some terminals, can also reduce glare.
7. Screens that will display multiple elements of information should use color to distinguish the different elements, thus cutting down on the strain of looking for and identifying information displayed on the screen.

Figure 3-28 illustrates some of the above recommendations. The keyboard is detachable, the visual display unit is adjustable, and the screen has an antiglare coating.

FIGURE 3-28

This illustration shows some of the ergonomic factors that should be considered when using a terminal or personal computer for a long or repeated length of time.

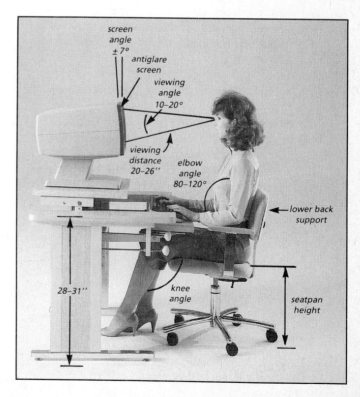

The illustration also shows the use of a lower back support. Note the position of the user's body in relation to the terminal.

As more and more workers use terminals and personal computers, the importance of ergonomically designed equipment increases. Manufacturers are now aware of the importance of ergonomic design and, as a result, are designing and building terminals and personal computers that incorporate ergonomic design for the health and comfort of users.

Chapter Summary

This chapter covered various aspects of input to the computer. We discussed the four types of input and how they are used, input devices, user interfaces, and data entry. After reading this chapter you should have a better overall understanding of computer input. The following list summarizes the key topics disussed in this chapter.

1. **Input** refers to the process of entering programs, commands, user responses, and data into the computer memory (p. 3.2).
2. The **keyboard** is the most commonly used input device. Special keys may include the **numeric keypad**, **cursor control keys**, and **function keys** (p. 3.3 and 3.4).
3. **Video display terminals** fall into two basic categories: **dumb terminals** and **intelligent terminals** (p. 3.5).
4. A **mouse** is a small input device used to control the movement of the cursor and to select options displayed on the screen (p. 3.6).
5. **Touch screens** allow the user to interact with a computer by merely touching the screen (p. 3.7).
6. **Light pens, digitizers**, and **graphics tablets** are graphic input devices used to translate graphic input data into a form that can be processed by the computer (p. 3.8).
7. **Voice input** allows the user to enter data and issue commands to a computer with spoken words (p. 3.9).
8. **Magnetic ink character recognition (MICR)** is a type of machine-readable data used almost exclusively in the banking industry (p. 3.9).

9. **Scanners** are devices that read printed codes, characters, or images and convert them into a form that can be processed by the computer (p. 3.10).
10. **Optical character recognition (OCR)** devices are scanners that read typewritten, computer-printed, and in some cases hand-printed characters from ordinary documents (p. 3.10).
11. An **optical mark reader (OMR)** is a scanning device that can read carefully placed pencil marks on a specially designed form (p. 3.12).
12. **Data collection devices** are designed and used for obtaining data at the site where the transaction or event being reported takes place (p. 3.13).
13. A **user interface** is the combination of hardware and software that allows a user to communicate with a computer system (p. 3.15).
14. A **prompt** is a message to the user that is displayed on the screen and provides information or instructions regarding some entry to be made or action to be taken (p. 3.16).
15. **Data editing** is used to check input data for proper format and acceptable values. It helps to ensure that valid data is entered by the user (p. 3.16).
16. A **menu** is a display on a screen that allows the user to select from multiple alternatives. There are several types of menu selection techniques including sequential and alphabetic selection, cursor positioning, reverse video, and icon selection (p. 3.17).
17. An **icon** is a pictorial representation of a function to be performed by the computer (p. 3.17).

18. The two methods used for processing data on a computer are interactive processing and batch processing (p. 3.20).
19. **Interactive processing** means that data is processed upon entry and output is produced immediately (p. 3.20).
20. In **batch processing**, data is collected and at some later time, all the data that has been gathered is processed as a group or batch (p. 3.20).
21. Data entry for interactive processing is said to be **online**, meaning that the device from which the data is being entered is connected directly to the computer (p. 3.20).
22. Data entry for batch processing can be online or **offline**. Offline means that the device from which the data is being entered is not connected to the computer that will process it (p. 3.22).
23. **Ergonomics** is the study of the design and arrangement of equipment so that people will interact with the equipment in a healthy, comfortable, and efficient manner (p. 3.23).
24. Manufacturers are now designing equipment that incorporates ergonomic design features (p. 3.24).

Review Questions

1. What are the four types of input and how are they used?
2. Describe the features available on a computer keyboard.
3. Name two types of display terminals. Describe each type.
4. Describe a mouse and list its advantages and disadvantages.
5. Describe three different types of graphic input devices.
6. What are data collection devices? How do they differ from other input devices?
7. What is a user interface? Why is it important?
8. Name five different menu selection methods.
9. What are the differences between data entry for interactive and for batch processing?
10. What is ergonomics? List and describe six ergonomic features that a terminal should have.

The Processor Unit

4

Objectives

- Identify the components of the processor unit and describe their use.
- Define a bit and describe how a series of bits in a byte is used to represent a character.
- Discuss how the ASCII and EBCDIC codes represent a character.
- Describe why the binary and hexadecimal numbering systems are used with computer systems.
- List and describe the four steps in a machine cycle.
- Discuss the three primary factors that affect the speed of the processor unit.
- Describe the characteristics of RAM and ROM memory. List several other types of memory.

The information processing cycle consists of input, processing, output, and storage operations. When an input operation is completed and both a program and data are stored in main memory, processing operations can begin. During these operations, the processor unit executes, or performs, the program instructions and processes the data into information.

This chapter examines the components of the processor unit, describes how main memory stores programs and data, and discusses the sequence of operations that occurs when instructions are executed on a computer.

What Is the Processor Unit?

While the term computer is used to describe the collection of devices that perform the information processing cycle, it is sometimes used more specifically to describe the processor unit. It is in the processor unit that the execution of computer programs and the manipulation of data takes place. The main components of the processor unit are the central processing unit or CPU and the main memory of the computer (Figure 4-1).

The Central Processing Unit

The central processing unit (CPU) contains the control unit and the arithmetic/logic unit. These two components work together using the program and data stored in main memory to perform the processing operations.

The CPU can be thought of as the "brain" of the computer. Just as the human brain controls the body, the control unit "controls" the computer. The **control unit** operates by repeating the following four operations: fetching, decoding, executing, and storing. **Fetching** means obtaining the next program instruction from main memory. **Decoding** is translating the program instruction into the commands that the computer can process. **Executing** refers to the actual processing of the computer commands, and **storing** takes place when the result of the instruction is written to main memory.

The second part of the CPU is the **arithmetic/logic unit**. This unit contains the electronic circuitry necessary to perform arithmetic and logical operations on data. Arithmetic operations include addition, subtraction, multiplication, and division. Logical operations consist of comparing one data item to another to determine if the first data item is greater than, equal to, or less than the other.

Main Memory

In addition to the CPU, **main memory** or **primary storage** is also contained in the processor unit of the computer. Main memory stores three items: (1) the *operating system* or software that directs and coordinates the computer equipment; (2) an *application program* containing the instructions that will direct the work to be done; and (3) the *data* currently being processed by the application program (Figure 4-2). Data is stored in areas of main memory referred to as input and output areas. These areas receive and send data to the input and output devices. Another area of main memory called working storage is used to store any other data that is needed for processing.

Within main memory, each storage location is called a **byte**. Just as a house on a street has a unique address that indicates its location on the street, each byte in the main memory of a computer has an address that indicates its location in memory (Figure 4-3). The number that indicates the location of a byte in memory is called a **memory address**. Whenever the computer references a byte, it does so by using the memory address of that location.

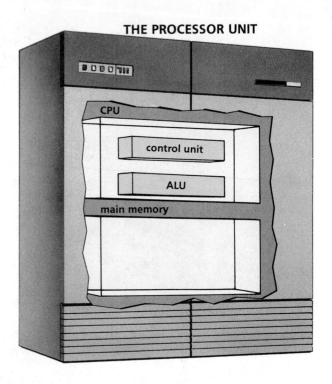

THE PROCESSOR UNIT

CPU
control unit
ALU
main memory

FIGURE 4-1

The processor unit of a computer contains two main components: the central processing unit (CPU) and main memory. The CPU includes the control unit and the arithmetic/logic unit.

FIGURE 4-2

Main memory is used to store several types of data and programs. As program instructions are executed and new data and programs are input and output, the allocation of memory space changes.

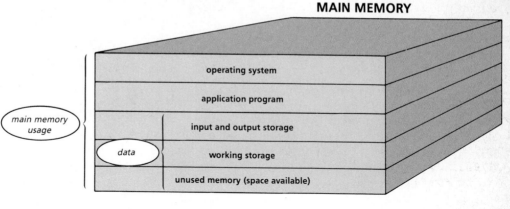

MAIN MEMORY

main memory usage

| operating system |
| application program |
| input and output storage |
| working storage |
| unused memory (space available) |

data

FIGURE 4-3

Just as each house on a street has its own address, each byte in main memory is identified by a unique address.

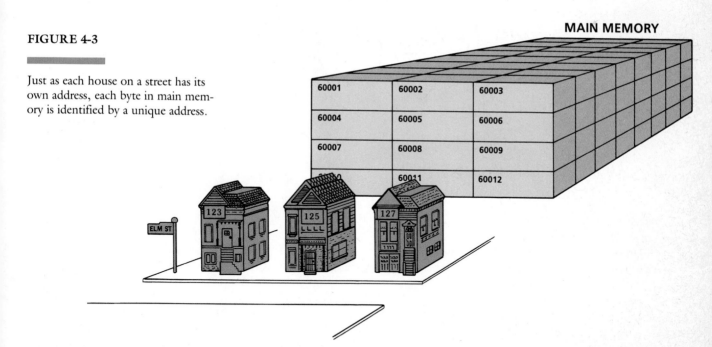

MAIN MEMORY

60001	60002	60003
60004	60005	60006
60007	60008	60009
	60011	60012

ELM ST 123 125 127

The size of main memory is normally measured in thousand-byte units called **kilobytes** (abbreviated as **K** or **KB**). Actually a kilobyte is a little larger than a thousand bytes—it is 1,024 bytes. For example, the memory size of a personal computer could be expressed as 640K, meaning that the computer contains approximately 640,000 bytes of main memory ($640 \times 1,000$). Most users round kilobyte to 1,000 and measure memory in this manner. If the exact size of memory is needed, it can be calculated by using the value 1,024. The exact size of 640K is 655,360 bytes ($640 \times 1,024$) of main memory.

Several other terms are used to describe memory size. When memory exceeds 1,000K or one million bytes, it is measured in **megabytes**, abbreviated **MB**. A billion bytes of memory, available on some large computers, is called a **gigabyte** or **GB**.

How Programs and Data Are Represented in Memory

Program instructions and data are made up of a combination of the three types of characters: alphabetic (A through Z), numeric (0 through 9), and special (all other characters). To understand how program instructions and data are stored in main memory, it is sometimes helpful to think of them as being stored character by character. Generally speaking, when we think of characters being stored in main memory, we think of one character being stored in one memory location or byte. Thus, the name TOM would take three memory locations or bytes because there are three letters in that name. The number $157.50 would take seven memory locations or bytes because there are seven characters (including the $ and .) in the number (Figure 4-4).

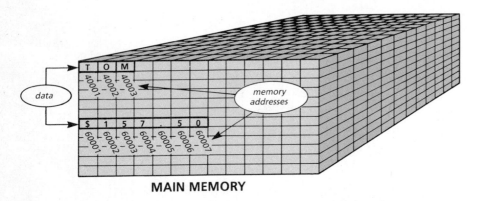

MAIN MEMORY

FIGURE 4-4

Each character (alphabetic, numeric, or special) usually requires one memory location (byte) for storage.

A byte contains eight bits. A **bit** is an element of a byte that can represent only two values. It can either be "off," represented in Figure 4-5 by an open circle, or "on," represented by a filled-in circle. Each alphabetic, numeric, and special character stored in the memory of the computer is represented by a combination of on and off bits. The computer can distinguish between characters because the combination of off and on bits assigned to each character is unique.

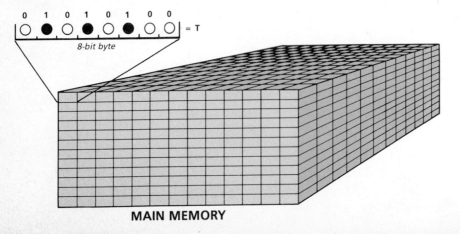

MAIN MEMORY

FIGURE 4-5

A graphic example of an eight-bit byte with two bits on and six bits off. The on bits (filled-in circles) represent the binary number 1 and each of the off bits (open circles) represent binary 0. (This combination of bits represents the letter T in ASCII code).

A mathematical way of representing the off and on conditions of a bit is to use 0 to represent off and 1 to represent on. The **binary** number system (base 2) represents quantities by using only the two symbols, 0 and 1. For this reason, binary is used to represent the electronic status of the bits inside the processing unit (Figure 4-5). The term bit was derived from the words *b*inary dig*it*.

Two popular codes that use combinations of zeros and ones for representing characters in memory are the ASCII and EBCDIC codes. A chart summarizing these codes is shown in Figure 4-6. Notice how the combination of bits, represented in binary, is unique for each character.

SYMBOL	ASCII	EBCDIC	SYMBOL	ASCII	EBCDIC	SYMBOL	ASCII	EBCDIC
(space)	00100000	01000000	?	00111111	00110111	^	01011110	
!	00100001	01011010	@	01000000	01111100	_	01011111	
''	00100010	01111111	A	01000001	11000001	a	01100001	10000001
#	00100011	01111011	B	01000010	11000010	b	01100010	10000010
$	00100100	01011011	C	01000011	11000011	c	01100011	10000011
%	00100101	01101100	D	01000100	11000100	d	01100100	10000100
&	00100110	01010000	E	01000101	11000101	e	01100101	10000101
'	00100111	01111101	F	01000110	11000110	f	01100110	10000110
(	00101000	01001101	G	01000111	11000111	g	01100111	10000111
)	00101001	01011101	H	01001000	11001000	h	01101000	10001000
*	00101010	01011100	I	01001001	11001001	i	01101001	10001001
+	00101011	01001110	J	01001010	11010001	j	01101010	10010001
,	00101100	01101011	K	01001011	11010010	k	01101011	10010010
–	00101101	01100000	L	01001100	11010011	l	01101100	10010011
.	00101110	01001011	M	01001101	11010100	m	01101101	10010100
/	00101111	01100001	N	01001110	11010101	n	01101110	10010101
0	00110000	11110000	O	01001111	11010110	o	01101111	10010110
1	00110001	11110001	P	01010000	11010111	p	01110000	10010111
2	00110010	11110010	Q	01010001	11011000	q	01110001	10011000
3	00110011	11110011	R	01010010	11011001	r	01110010	10011001
4	00110100	11110100	S	01010011	11100010	s	01110011	10100010
5	00110101	11110101	T	01010100	11100011	t	01110100	10100011
6	00110110	11110110	U	01010101	11100100	u	01110101	10100100
7	00110111	11110111	V	01010110	11100101	v	01110110	10100101
8	00111000	11111000	W	01010111	11100110	w	01110111	10100110
9	00111001	11111001	X	01011000	11100111	x	01111000	10100111
:	00111010	01111010	Y	01011001	11101000	y	01111001	10101000
;	00111011	01011110	Z	01011010	11101001	z	01111010	10101001
<	00111100	01001100	[	01011011	01001010	{	01111011	
=	00111101	01111110	\	01011100		}	01111101	
>	00111110	01101110	]	01011101	01011010			

FIGURE 4-6

This chart shows alphabetic, numeric, and special characters as they are represented in the ASCII and EBCDIC codes. Note how each character is represented in binary using zeros and ones.

Note: Blanks in EBCDIC columns mean that the symbol is not represented in EBCDIC code.

The ASCII Code

The **American Standard Code for Information Interchange**, called **ASCII** (pronounced "ASK-EE"), is the most widely used coding system to represent data. The

example in Figure 4-7 illustrates the
letter T stored in an eight-bit byte
in main memory using the ASCII
code.

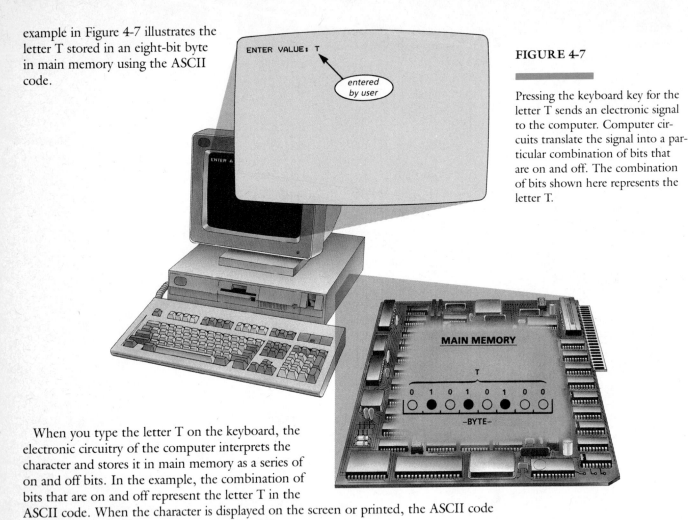

ENTER VALUE: T

entered
by user

MAIN MEMORY

T

0 1 0 1 0 1 0 0

–BYTE–

FIGURE 4-7

Pressing the keyboard key for the
letter T sends an electronic signal
to the computer. Computer circuits translate the signal into a particular combination of bits that
are on and off. The combination
of bits shown here represents the
letter T.

When you type the letter T on the keyboard, the
electronic circuitry of the computer interprets the
character and stores it in main memory as a series of
on and off bits. In the example, the combination of
bits that are on and off represent the letter T in the
ASCII code. When the character is displayed on the screen or printed, the ASCII code
is translated back into the alphabetic symbol T.

Only 128 ASCII codes are shown in Figure 4-6. There are 128 more for a total of 256
code combinations. Many of the 128 codes not shown in Figure 4-6 represent special
keys on the keyboard, like the Home key, End key, and arrow keys.

The EBCDIC Code

The ASCII code is widely used on personal computers and many minicomputers.
Another common coding scheme used primarily on mainframes is called the **Extended
Binary Coded Decimal Interchange Code** or **EBCDIC** (pronounced "EB-SEE-
DICK"). Some of the 256 EBCDIC codes are shown in Figure 4-6.

Binary Representation of Numbers

When the ASCII or EBCDIC codes are used, each character that is represented is stored in one byte of memory. Note, however, that there are other binary formats of data representation that allow multiple digits to be stored in one byte or memory location.

Parity

Regardless of whether ASCII, EBCDIC, or other binary methods are used to represent characters in main memory, it is important that the characters be stored accurately. For each byte of memory, most computers have at least one extra bit, called a **parity bit**, that is used by the computer for error checking. A parity bit can detect if one of the bits in a byte has been inadvertently changed. Such an error could occur because of voltage fluctuations, static electricity, or a memory chip failure.

Computers are either odd or even parity machines. In computers with **odd parity**, the total number of "on" bits in the byte (including the parity bit) must be an odd number (Figure 4-8). In computers with **even parity**, the total number of on bits must be an even number. Parity is checked each time a memory location is used. When data is moved from one location to another in main memory, the parity bits of both the sending and receiving locations are compared to see if they are the same. If the system detects a difference or if the wrong number of bits is on (for example, an even number in a system with odd parity), an error message displays. Some computers use multiple parity bits that enable them to detect and correct a single bit error and detect multiple bit errors.

FIGURE 4-8

In a computer with odd parity, the parity bit is turned on or off in order to make the total number of on bits (including the parity bit) an odd number. Here, the letters T and O have an odd number of bits and the parity bit is left off. However, the number of bits for the letter M is even, so in order to achieve odd parity, the parity bit is turned on. Turning on the parity bit makes the total number of bits in the byte an odd number (five).

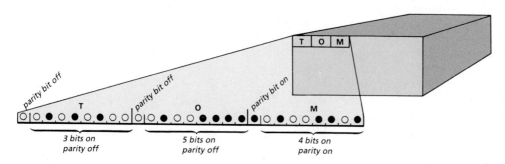

Number Systems

This section describes the number systems that are used with computers. While thorough knowledge of this subject is required for technical computer personnel, a general understanding of number systems and how they relate to computers is all most users need.

As you have seen, the binary (base 2) number system is used to represent the electronic status of the bits in main memory. It is also used for other purposes, such as addressing the memory locations. Another number system that is commonly used with computers is **hexadecimal** (base 16). Figure 4-9 shows how the decimal values 0 through 15 are represented in binary and hexadecimal.

The mathematical principles that apply to the binary and hexadecimal number systems are the same as those that apply to the decimal number system. To help you better understand these principles we will start with the familiar decimal system, then progress to the binary and hexadecimal number systems.

DECIMAL	BINARY	HEXADECIMAL
0	0000	0
1	0001	1
2	0010	2
3	0011	3
4	0100	4
5	0101	5
6	0110	6
7	0111	7
8	1000	8
9	1001	9
10	1010	A
11	1011	B
12	1100	C
13	1101	D
14	1110	E
15	1111	F

FIGURE 4-9

The chart shows the binary and hexadecimal representation of decimal numbers 0 through 15. Note how letters represent the numbers 10 through 15.

The Decimal Number System

The decimal number system is a base 10 number system (note that "deci" means 10). The *base* of a number system indicates how many symbols are used in it. Decimal uses the 10 symbols 0 through 9. Each of the symbols in the number system has a value associated with it. For example, you know that 3 represents a quantity of three and 5 represents a quantity of five. The decimal number system is also a positional number system. This means that in a number such as 143, each position in the number has a value associated with it. When you look at the decimal number 143, you know that the 3 is in the ones, or units, position and represents three ones or (3×1); the 4 is in the tens position and represents four tens or (4×10); and the 1 is in the hundreds position and represents one hundred or (1×100). The number 143 is the sum of the values in each position of the number $(100 + 40 + 3 = 143)$. Figure 4-10 is a power chart showing how the positional values (hundreds, tens, and units) for a number system can be calculated. Starting on the right and working to the left, we raise the base of the number system, in this case 10, to consecutive powers $(10^2\ 10^1\ 10^0)$. These calculations are a mathematical way of computing the place values in a number system.

power of 10	10^2	10^1	10^0
positional value	100	10	1
number	1	4	3

$$(1 \times 100) + (4 \times 10) + (3 \times 1) =$$
$$100 + 40 + 3 = 143$$

FIGURE 4-10

This chart shows the positional values in the decimal number 143.

When you use number systems other than decimal, the same principles apply. The base of the number system indicates the number of symbols that are used and each position in a number system has a value associated with it. The positional value can be calculated by raising the base of the number system to consecutive powers.

The Binary Number System

As we have discussed, binary is a base 2 number system ("bi" means two), and the symbols that are used are 0 and 1. Just as each position in a decimal number has a place value associated with it, so does each position in a binary number. In binary, the place values are successive powers of two (such as 2^3 2^2 2^1 2^0) or (8 4 2 1). To construct a binary number, ones are placed in the positions where the corresponding values add up to the quantity that is to be represented and zeros are placed in the other positions. For example, the binary place values are (8 4 2 1) and the binary number 1001 has ones in the positions for the values 8 and 1 and zeros in the positions for 4 and 2. Therefore, the quantity represented by 1001 is 9 (8 + 0 + 0 + 1) (Figure 4-11).

power of 2	2^3	2^2	2^1	2^0
positional value	8	4	2	1
binary	1	0	0	1

$$(1 \times 8) + (0 \times 4) + (0 \times 2) + (1 \times 1) =$$
$$8 + 0 + 0 + 1 = 9$$

FIGURE 4-11

This chart shows how to convert the binary number 1001 to the decimal number 9. Each place in the binary number represents a successive power of 2.

The Hexadecimal Number System

Many computers use a base 16 number system called hexadecimal. The hexadecimal number system uses 16 symbols to represent values. These include the symbols 0 through 9 and A through F (Figure 4-9). The mathematical principles previously discussed also apply to hexadecimal (Figure 4-12).

power of 16	16^1	16^0
positional value	16	1
hexadecimal	A	5

$$(10 \times 16) + (5 \times 1) =$$
$$160 + 5 = 165$$

FIGURE 4-12

This chart shows how the hexadecimal number A5 is converted into the decimal number 165. Note that the value 10 is substituted for the A during computations.

The primary reason why the hexadecimal number system is used with computers is because it can represent binary values in a more compact form and because the conversion between the binary and the hexadecimal number systems is very efficient. An eight-digit binary number can be represented by a two-digit hexadecimal number. For example, in the EBCDIC code (used by some computers to represent data), the decimal number 5 is represented as 11110101. This value can be represented in hexadecimal as F5.

One way to convert a binary number to a hexadecimal number is to divide the binary number (from right to left) into groups of four digits; calculate the value of each group; and then change any two-digit values (10 through 15) into the symbols A through F that are used in hexadecimal (Figure 4-13).

positional value	8421	8421
binary	1111	0101
decimal	15	5
hexadecimal	F	5

FIGURE 4-13

This chart shows how the EBCDIC code 11110101 for the value 5 is converted into the hexadecimal value F5.

Summary of Number Systems

As mentioned at the beginning of the section on number systems, binary and hexadecimal are used primarily by technical computer personnel. For the general user, a complete understanding of numbering systems is not required. The concepts that you should remember about number systems are that binary is used for purposes such as representing the electronic status of the bits in main memory and also for memory addresses. Hexadecimal is used to represent binary in a more compact form.

How the Processor Unit Executes Programs and Manipulates Data

The program instructions that users write are usually in a form similar to English. Before these instructions can be executed, they must be translated by the computer into a form called machine language instructions. A **machine language instruction** is one that the electronic circuits in the CPU can interpret and convert into one or more of the commands in the computer's instruction set. The **instruction set** contains the commands such as add or move that the computer's circuits can directly perform. To help you understand how the processor unit works, let's look at an example of a machine language instruction.

Machine Language Instructions

A machine language instruction is usually composed of three parts: an operation code, values indicating the number of characters to be processed by the instruction, and the addresses in main memory of the data to be used in the execution of the instruction (Figure 4-14).

The **operation code** is a unique value that is stored in the first byte in the instruction. This unique value indicates what operation is to be performed. For example, the letter A stored as the operation code might indicate that an *add*ition operation is to occur. The letter M might mean that a *move* operation is to take place.

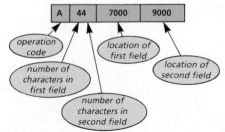

FIGURE 4-14

A machine language instruction consists of an operation code, the lengths of the fields to be processed, and the leftmost main memory addresses of the fields.

The number of characters to be processed is included in the machine language instruction so that the CPU will manipulate the proper number of bytes. For example, if a four-digit field were to be added to another four-digit field, the number of characters specified in the instruction for each field would be four.

The leftmost main memory addresses of the fields involved in the operation are also specified in the instruction. This specification of the main memory address enables the CPU to locate where in main memory the data to be processed is stored.

The illustration in Figure 4-15 shows the steps involved in executing a computer instruction. The instruction A44 7000 9000 indicates that the four-digit fields that begin in locations 7000 and 9000 are to be added together. When this instruction is executed, the following steps occur:

1. The instruction is fetched from main memory and placed in an instruction register. An **instruction register** is an area of memory within the control unit of the CPU that can store a single instruction at a time.
2. After the control unit decodes the instruction, it fetches the data specified at the two addresses in the instruction from main memory.
3. The arithmetic/logic unit executes the instruction by adding the two numbers.
4. The control unit then stores the result of the processing by moving the sum to main memory.

This basic sequence of fetch the instruction, decode the instruction, execute the instruction, and store the results is the way most computers process instructions.

The Machine Cycle

The four steps illustrated in Figure 4-16, fetch, decode, execute, and store, are called the **machine cycle**. As shown in Figure 4-16, the machine cycle is made up of the instruction cycle and the execution cycle. The **instruction cycle** refers to the fetching of the next program instruction and the decoding of that instruction. The **execution cycle** includes the execution of the instruction and the storage of the processing results.

FIGURE 4-15

Executing a program instruction

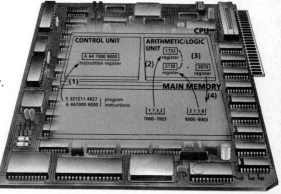

FIGURE 4-16

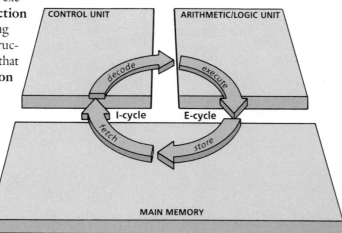

The machine cycle consists of four steps: fetching the next instruction, decoding the instruction, executing the instruction, and storing the result. Fetching and decoding are considered part of the instruction or I cycle. Executing and storing are considered part of the execution or E cycle.

When the computer is again ready to fetch the next program instruction, one machine cycle is completed.

Processor Speeds

Although the machine cycle may appear to be cumbersome and time consuming, computers can perform millions of machine cycles in one second. In fact, the processing speed of computers is often compared in **MIPS**—million instructions per second. A computer with a rating of 1 MIPS could process one million instructions per second. The most powerful personal computers today are rated at between 10 and 15 MIPS. Larger computers can process 75 to 100 MIPS and supercomputers are capable of over 200 MIPS.

The speed in which a computer can execute the machine cycle is influenced by three factors: the system clock, the buses, and the word size (Figure 4-17).

FACTOR	AFFECT ON SPEED
System clock	The clock generates electronic pulses used to synchronize processing. Faster clock speed results in more operations in a given amount of time.
Bus	The bus determines how much data can be transferred at any one time. A 32-bit bus can transfer twice as much data at one time as a 16-bit bus.
Word size	Word size is the number of bits that can be manipulated at any one time. A computer with a 32-bit word size can manipulate twice as much data at one time as a system with a 16-bit word size.

FIGURE 4-17

Factors affecting computer speed

System Clock

The control unit utilizes the **system clock** to synchronize, or control the timing, of all computer operations. The system clock generates electronic pulses at a fixed rate, measured in **megahertz**. One megahertz equals one million pulses per second. The speed of the system clock varies among computers. Some personal computers can operate at speeds in excess of 30 megahertz.

Buses

As we explained, computers store and process data as a series of electronic bits. These bits are transferred internally within the circuitry of the computer along paths capable of transmitting electrical impulses. The bits must be transferred from input devices to memory, from memory to the CPU, from the CPU to memory, and from memory to output devices. Any path along which bits are transmitted is called a **bus** or **data bus**.

Buses can transfer eight, 16, 32, or 64 bits at a time. An eight-bit bus has eight lines and can transmit eight bits at a time. On a 16-bit bus, bits can be moved from place to place 16 bits at a time and on a 32-bit bus, bits are moved 32 bits at a time.

The larger the number of bits that are handled by a bus, the faster the computer can transfer data. For example, assume a number in memory occupies four eight-bit bytes. With an eight-bit bus four steps would be required to transfer the data from memory to the CPU because on the eight-bit data bus, the data in each eight-bit byte would be transferred in an individual step. A 16-bit bus has 16 lines in the data bus, so only two transfers would be necessary to move the data in four bytes. And on a 32-bit bus, the entire four bytes could be transferred at one time. The fewer number of transfer steps required, the faster the transfer of the data occurs.

Word Size

Another factor that affects the speed of a computer is the word size. The **word size** is the number of bits that the CPU can process at one time, as opposed to the bus size, which is the number of bits the computer can transmit at one time. Like data buses, the word size of a machine is measured in bit sizes. Processors can have eight-, 16-, 32-, or 64-bit word sizes. A processor with an eight-bit word size can manipulate eight bits at a time. If two four-digit numbers are to be added in the ALU of an eight-bit processor, it will take four operations because a separate operation will be required to add each of the four digits. With a 16-bit processor, the addition will take two operations and with a 32-bit processor, only one operation would be required to add the numbers together. Sometimes the word size of a computer is given in bytes instead of bits. For example, a word size of 16 bits may be expressed as a word size of two bytes because there are eight bits in a byte. The larger the word size of the processor, the faster the computer is able to process data.

In summary, the speed of a computer is influenced by the system clock, the size of the buses, and the word size. When you purchase a computer, the speed requirements you want should be based on your intended use of the computer. Eight-bit computers may be useful and fast enough for personal and educational applications. Sixteen-bit computers are widely used today for applications such as word processing, electronic spreadsheets, or database. Thirty-two-bit computers are considered very powerful and are useful for multiuser systems and applications that require complex and time-consuming calculations, such as graphics. A few personal computers, many minicomputers, and most mainframes are 32-bit computers. Most supercomputers are 64-bit computers.

Architecture of Processor Units

The processor unit of a computer can be designed and built in many different ways. For example, the processor for a personal computer may be housed on a single printed circuit board while a larger machine may require a number of circuit boards for the CPU, main memory, and the related electronic circuitry.

Microprocessors

The smallest processor, called a **microprocessor** (Figure 4-18), is a single integrated circuit that contains the CPU and sometimes memory. An **integrated circuit**, also called an **IC**, **chip**, or **microchip**, is a complete electronic circuit that has been etched on a small chip of nonconducting material such as silicon. Microcomputers are built using microprocessors for their CPU. Figure 4-19 lists the microprocessors commonly used in personal computers today and those that are expected to be used in the next generation of personal computers.

FIGURE 4-18

A microprocessor contains the electronic circuits that perform the operations of a computer.

FIGURE 4-19

A comparison of some of the more widely used microprocessor chips.

MICROPROCESSOR	MANUFACTURER	WORD SIZE (BITS)	I/O BUS WIDTH (BITS)	CLOCK SPEED MHz)	MICROCOMPUTERS USING THIS CHIP
6502	MOS Technology	8	8	4	Apple IIe Atari 800
8088	Intel	16	8	8	IBM PC and XT HP 150 Compaq Portable
8086	Intel	16	16	8	Compaq Deskpro Many IBM compatibles
80286	Intel	16	16	8–12	IBM PC/AT Compaq Deskpro 286
68000	Motorola	32	16	12.5	Apple Macintosh SE Commodore Amiga
68020	Motorola	32	32	12.5–32	Apple Macintosh II
80386	Intel	32	32	16–32	Compaq Deskpro 386 IBM PS/2
68030	Motorola	32	32	16–32	Apple Macintosh SE/30
68040	Motorola	32	32	50	Engineering Workstations
80486	Intel	32	32	50	IBM PS/2

Coprocessors

One way computers can increase their productivity is through the use of a **coprocessor**, a special microprocessor chip or circuit board designed to perform a specific task. For example, math coprocessors are commonly added to computers to greatly speed up the processing of numeric calculations. Other types of coprocessors extend the capability of a computer by increasing the amount of software that will run on the computer.

Parallel Processing

Most computers contain one central processing unit (CPU) that processes a single instruction at a time. When one instruction is finished, the CPU begins execution of the next instruction, and so on until the program is completed. This method is known as **serial processing**. **Parallel processing** involves the use of multiple CPUs, each with their own memory. Parallel processors divide up a problem so that multiple CPUs can work on their assigned portion of the problem simultaneously. As you might expect, parallel processors require special software that can recognize how to divide up problems and bring the results back together again.

RISC Technology

As computers have evolved, more and more commands have been added to hardware instruction sets. In recent years, however, computer designers have reevaluated the need for so many instructions and have developed systems based on RISC technology. **RISC**, which stands for reduced instruction set computing (or computers), involves reducing the instructions to only those that are most frequently used. Without the burden of the occasionally used instructions, the most frequently used instructions operate faster and overall processing capability or *throughput* of the system is increased.

   In summary, you can see that there are many different types of processor architecture that are used on computers. Regardless of the architecture used, the important concept to remember is that the processor units on all computers perform essentially the same functions.

Types of Memory

As we noted, electronic components are used to store data in computer memory. The actual materials and devices used for memory have changed throughout the years. The first device used for storing data was the vacuum tube. After the vacuum tube, core memory was used. **Core memory** consisted of small, ring-shaped pieces of material that could be magnetized, or polarized, in one of two directions. The polarity indicated whether the core was on or off. Today, semiconductor memory is used in virtually all computers. **Semiconductor memory** is an integrated circuit containing millions of transistors. A **transistor** is an electronic component that can be either on or off and represents a bit in memory.

When core memory was used as main memory, the time required to access data stored in the memory was measured in **microseconds** (millionths of a second). Access to data stored in semiconductor memory is measured in **nanoseconds** (billionths of a second). In addition, the cost of semiconductor memory is just a fraction of the cost for core memory. Today you can buy 64K of semiconductor memory for about $30, whereas 64K of core memory once cost as much as $15,000. Figure 4-20 shows how the storage capacity of semiconductor memory has increased over recent years, while the cost of semiconductor memory has decreased. The trend is expected to continue. It has been predicted that by the end of the century it will be possible to store over a billion components on a chip.

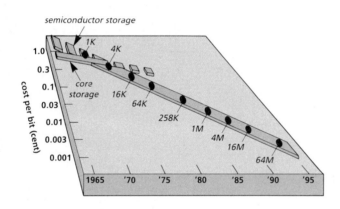

FIGURE 4-20

The chart shows the declining cost and increased storage capacity of semiconductor storage.

As you can see, semiconductor memory is compact, fast, and inexpensive. Several different types of semiconductor memory chips are used in computers. They are RAM, ROM, PROM, EPROM, and EEPROM chips.

RAM Memory

Random access memory, or **RAM**, is the name given to the integrated circuits or chips that are used for main memory. It is the type of memory that we have discussed so far in this chapter. Data and programs are transferred into and out of RAM and data stored in RAM is manipulated by computer program instructions.

There are two types of RAM memory chips: dynamic RAM and static RAM. **Dynamic RAM** chips are smaller and simpler in design than static RAM chips. With dynamic RAM the current or charge on the chip is periodically refreshed or regenerated by special regenerator circuits in order for the chip to retain the stored data. **Static RAM** chips are larger and more complicated than dynamic RAM and do not require the current to be periodically regenerated. The main memory of most computers uses dynamic RAM chips.

The example in Figure 4-21 illustrates the processing that could occur as a series of area codes are entered into RAM (computer memory) from a terminal. The first area code, 212, is entered from the keyboard and stored at memory locations 66000, 66001, and 66002. Once in memory, this field can be processed as required.

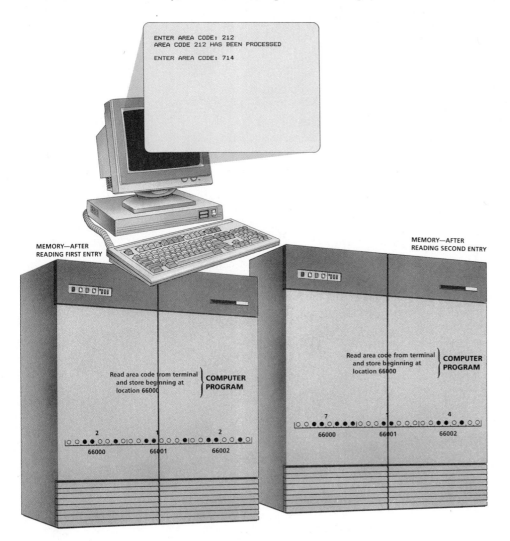

ENTER AREA CODE: 212
AREA CODE 212 HAS BEEN PROCESSED

ENTER AREA CODE: 714

MEMORY—AFTER
READING FIRST ENTRY

MEMORY—AFTER
READING SECOND ENTRY

Read area code from terminal
and store beginning at
location 66000 COMPUTER
PROGRAM

Read area code from terminal
and store beginning at
location 66000 COMPUTER
PROGRAM

FIGURE 4-21

The instruction in the program specifies that the area code is to be read into adjacent memory locations beginning with location 66000. After the data is placed in these locations, it can be processed by the program. When the same instruction is executed the second time, the value 714 entered by the terminal operator is stored in locations 66000, 66001, and 66002, where it can be processed by the same instructions that processed area code 212.

When the instruction to read (input) data into memory from the keyboard is executed again, the second area code entered from the keyboard, area code 714, replaces the previous value (212) at locations 66000, 66001, and 66002 in memory. Area code 714 is then processed by the same instructions that processed area code 212.

When data is moved from one location to another in main memory, the data at the receiving location is replaced by the new data. The data in the sending location remains intact. Data is not removed from one location and placed in another location. Instead, the data remains in the sending location and a copy of the data is transferred to and stored in the new location.

Another aspect of RAM memory is that it is said to be **volatile** because the programs and data stored in RAM are erased when the power to the computer is turned off. Auxiliary storage is used to store programs or data that may be needed for future use.

ROM Memory

ROM stands for **read only memory**. With ROM, data is permanently recorded in the memory when it is manufactured. ROM memory retains its contents even when the power is off. The data or programs that are stored in ROM can be read and used, but cannot be altered, hence the name "read only." ROM is used to store items such as the instruction set of the computer. In addition, many of the special-purpose computers used in automobiles, appliances, and so on use small amounts of ROM to store instructions that will be executed repeatedly. Instructions that are stored in ROM memory are called **firmware** or **microcode**.

Other Types of Memory

PROM means **programmable read only memory**. PROM acts the same as ROM when it is part of the computer; that is, it can only be read and its contents cannot be altered. With PROM, however, the data or programs are not stored in the memory when they are manufactured. Instead, PROM can be loaded with specially selected data or programs prior to installing it in a computer. A variation of PROM is **EPROM** (pronounced "EE-PROM"), which means **erasable programmable read only memory**. In addition to being used in the same way as PROM, EPROM allows the user to erase the data stored in the memory and to store new data or programs in the memory. EPROM is erased through the use of special ultraviolet light devices that destroy the bit settings within the memory.

EEPROM (pronounced "double-E-PROM"), or **electronically erasable programmable read only memory**, allows the stored data or programs to be erased electrically. The advantage of EEPROM is that it does not have to be removed from the computer to be changed.

Chapter Summary

In this chapter we examined various aspects of the processor unit including its components, how programs and data are stored, and how the processor executes program instructions to process data into information. While a detailed understanding of this material is not a prerequisite for computer literacy, understanding these principles will increase your overall comprehension of how processing occurs on a computer. The following list summarizes the key topics discussed in this chapter.

1. The central processing unit and the main memory are contained in the processor unit (p. 4.2).
2. The central processing unit or CPU contains the **control unit** and the **arithmetic/logic unit**. The control unit directs and coordinates all the activities on the computer. The arithmetic/logic unit performs arithmetic and logic operations (p. 4.2).
3. The **main memory**, also called **primary storage**, stores programs and data (p. 4.2).
4. Each storage location in main memory is called a **byte** and is identified by a **memory address** (p. 4.2).
5. The size of main memory is normally expressed in terms of **kilobytes** (approximately 1,000 bytes) of storage. A computer with 640K has approximately 640,000 memory locations (p. 4.3).
6. A byte consists of eight **bits**. A bit can represent only two values—off and on (p. 4.4).
7. When a letter is entered into main memory from a keyboard, the electronic circuitry interprets the character and stores the character in memory as a series of on and off bits. The computer can distinguish between characters because the combination of off and on bits assigned to each character is unique (p. 4.4).
8. One of the most widely used codes to represent characters is the **American Standard Code for Information Interchange**, called the **ASCII code** (p. 4.5).
9. A code used for mainframes is the **Extended Binary Coded Decimal Interchange Code (EBCDIC)** (p. 4.6).
10. Computers use **parity bits** for error checking (p. 4.7).
11. The **binary** (base 2) number system is used by the computer for purposes such as memory addresses and representing the electronic status of the bits in main memory. **Hexadecimal** (base 16) is used to represent binary in a more compact form (p. 4.8–4.9).
12. A **machine language instruction** can be decoded and executed by the CPU (p. 4.10).
13. A machine language instruction is usually composed of an **operation code**, values indicating the number of characters to be processed, and main memory addresses of the data to be processed (p. 4.10).
14. Steps in the **machine cycle** consist of: fetch the next instruction; decode the instruction; execute the instruction; store the results (p. 4.11).
15. The speed of a computer is influenced by the system clock, the bus size, and the word size (p. 4.12).
16. The **system clock** is used by the control unit to synchronize all computer operations (p. 4.12).
17. A **bus** is any line that transmits bits between memory and the input/output devices, and between memory and the CPU (p. 4.12).
18. The number of bits that the CPU can process at one time is called the **word size** (p. 4.13).
19. A computer's word size can be eight-bit, 16-bit, 32-bit, or 64-bit machines (p. 4.13).
20. **Microprocessors** are used for the CPU in microcomputers (p. 4.14).
21. **Coprocessors** can be used to enhance and expand the capabilities of a computer (p. 4.15).
22. Parallel processors divide up a problem so that multiple CPUs can work on their assigned portion of the problem simultaneously (p. 4.15).
23. **RISC** technology involves reducing a computer's instruction set to only those instructions that are most frequently used (p. 4.15).
24. **Core memory** consisted of small, ring-shaped pieces of material that could be magnetized, or polarized, in one of two directions (p. 4.15).
25. **Semiconductor memory** is now used in most computers. It consists of transistors etched into a semiconductor material such as silicon (p. 4.15).

26. **A microsecond** is a millionth of a second. A **nanosecond** is a billionth of a second. Access to data stored in semiconductor memory is measured in nanoseconds (p. 4.16).

27. **RAM**, which stands for **random access memory**, is used for main memory (p. 4.16).

28. Once a character is stored at a location in RAM memory, it will remain there until another character is placed into the same location. When the electrical power supply is turned off, all programs and data in RAM are erased (p. 4.17–4.18).

29. **ROM** stands for **read only memory**. Data or programs are stored in ROM when the memory is manufactured, and they cannot be altered (p. 4.18).

30. **PROM** means **programmable read only memory**. PROM acts the same as ROM except data can be stored into the PROM memory prior to being installed in the computer (p. 4.18).

31. **EPROM**, or **erasable programmable read only memory**, can be erased through the use of special ultraviolet devices (p. 4.18).

32. **EEPROM** or **electronically erasable programmable read only memory**, can be electronically erased without being removed from the computer (p. 4.18).

Review Questions

1. Identify the two components of the central processing unit and describe the functions of each.

2. Define the terms bit and byte. Illustrate how the number 14 is represented in binary, hexadecimal, ASCII, and EBCDIC.

3. What does the letter K stand for when referring to main memory?

4. Describe how a group of characters entered into the computer as a field are stored in main memory. Draw a diagram to illustrate how the letters in your first name would be stored using the ASCII code. Begin at main memory address 45663.

5. What is parity and how is it used?

6. What are the two number systems that are used with computers? Why are they used?

7. What are the components of a machine language instruction? Describe the steps that occur in main memory and the CPU when two numbers are added together.

8. What are the three factors that influence the speed of a processor?

9. What is a microprocessor and how is it used?

10. Define each of the following terms: RAM, ROM, PROM, EPROM, EEPROM.

Output from the Computer 5

Objectives

- Define the term output.
- List the common types of reports and graphs that are used for output.
- Describe the classifications of printers.
- List the types of printers used with personal computers and describe how they work.
- Discuss the quality of output obtainable from various types of printers.
- Describe printers used with large computers.
- Describe the types of screens available and list common screen features.
- List and describe other types of output devices used with computers.

Output is the way the computer communicates with the user; therefore it is important to know the many ways this communication can take place. This chapter discusses the types of output and the devices computers use to produce output.

What Is Output?

Output is data that has been processed into a useful form called information that can be used by a person or a machine. Output that is used by a machine, such as a disk or tape file, is usually an intermediate result that eventually will be processed into output that can be used by people. Computer output exists in a variety of forms.

Common Types of Output

The type of output generated from the computer depends on the needs of the user and the hardware and software that are used. The two most common types of output are reports and graphics. These types of output may be printed on a printer or displayed on a screen. Output that is printed is called **hard copy** and output that is displayed on a screen is called **soft copy**.

Reports

Most people think of reports as items printed on paper or displayed on a screen. But information printed on forms such as invoices or payroll checks can also be considered types of reports. One way to classify reports is by who uses them. An **internal report** is used by individuals in the performance of their jobs. For example, a daily sales report that is distributed to sales personnel is an internal report because it is used only by personnel *within* the organization. An **external report** is used outside the organization. Payroll checks that are printed and distributed to employees each week are external reports.

Reports may be classified by the way they present information. Three types of reports are common: detail reports, summary reports, and exception reports.

In a **detail report**, each line on the report usually corresponds to one record that has been read and processed. Detail reports contain a great deal of information and can be quite lengthy. They are usually required by individuals who need access to the day-to-day information that reflects the operating status of the organization. For example, people in the sales department of a retail store should have access to the number of units sold of each product. The units sold report in Figure 5-1 contains a line for each item, which corresponds to each record processed.

As the name implies, a **summary report** summarizes data. It contains totals for certain values found in the records processed. The report illustrated in Figure 5-2 contains a summary of the units sold for each department. The information on the summary report consists of totals from the information contained in the detail report in Figure 5-1. Summary reports are most useful for individuals who do not require a detailed knowledge of each transaction. For example, detail reports contain more information

FIGURE 5-1 ▆▆▆▆▆▆▆▆

The data for this detail report was obtained from each record that was read and processed. A line was printed for each record.

UNITS SOLD REPORT				
DEPT.	DEPT NAME	ITEM	DESCRIPTION	QTY SOLD
10	MENS FURNISHINGS	105	T-SHIRT	3
10	MENS FURNISHINGS	109	SOCKS	127
12	SLEEPWEAR	199	ROBE	6
14	MENS ACCESSORIES	266	HAT	4

FIGURE 5-2 ▆▆▆▆▆▆▆▆

This summary report contains the sales for each department. The report can be prepared from the same data that prepared the report in Figure 5-1.

SALES BY DEPARTMENT			
DEPT. NO.	DEPT. NAME	UNITS SOLD	SALES $
10	MENS FURNISHINGS	130	653.35
12	SLEEPWEAR	6	189.70
14	MENS ACCESSORIES	4	98.00

than most managers have time to review. With a summary report, however, a manager can quickly review information in summarized form.

An **exception report** contains information that is outside of "normal" user-specified values or conditions and thus is an "exception" to the majority of the data. For example, if an organization with an inventory wanted to have an on-hand quantity of more than 25 of every inventory item at all times, it would design an exception report to tell them if the amount of any inventory items fell below this level. An example of such a report is shown in Figure 5-3.

Exception reports help users to focus on situations that may require immediate decisions or specific actions. The advantage of exception reports is that they save time and money. In a large department store, for example, there may be over 100,000 inventory items. A detail report containing all inventory items could be longer than 2,000 pages. To search through the report to determine the items whose on-hand quantity was less than 25 would be a difficult and time-consuming task. The exception report, however, could extract these items, which might number 100–200, and place them on a two- to four-page report that could be prepared in just a few minutes.

```
INVENTORY EXCEPTION REPORT

ITEM        ITEM            QUANTITY
 NO.        DESCRIPTION     ON HAND

 105        T-SHIRT            24
 125        SCARF               3
 126        BELT               17
```

FIGURE 5-3

This exception report lists inventory items with a quantity of less than 25. They could have been selected from thousands of inventory records. Only these items met the user's "exception criteria."

Graphics

Another common type of output is computer graphics. In business, **computer graphics** are often used to assist in analyzing data. Computer graphics display information in the form of charts, graphs, or pictures so that the information can be understood easily and quickly (Figure 5-4). Facts contained in a lengthy report and data relationships that are difficult to understand in words can often be summarized in a single chart or graph.

In the past, graphics were not widely used in business because each time data was revised, a graphic artist would have to redraw the chart or graph. Today, relatively inexpensive graphics software makes it possible to redraw a chart, graph, or picture within seconds rather than the hours or days that were previously required. Many applications software packages, such as spreadsheets, include graphics capabilities. As we discussed in Chapter 2, the three most popular types of charts and graphs are pie charts, bar charts, and line diagrams.

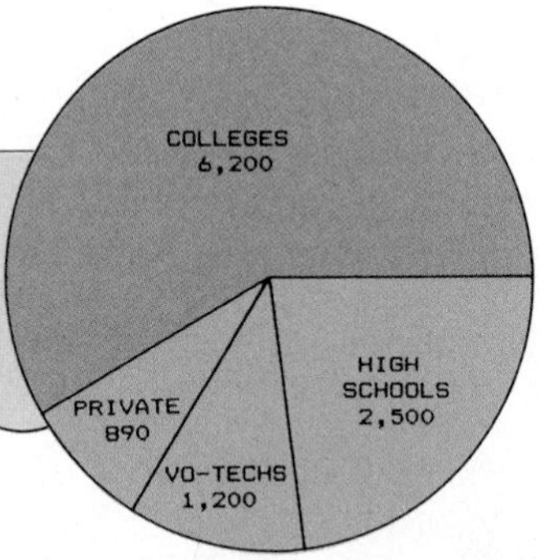

FIGURE 5-4

This small report lists sales of magazines by school category. With the addition of the pie chart graphic, however, the manager can easily see that colleges account for more than half the sales and that private schools represent a small percentage of the sales. Both the report and the graphic use the same information, but the graphic helps the manager to understand the information more quickly.

```
SALES BY CATEGORY

HIGH SCHOOLS      2,500
COLLEGES          6,200
VO-TECHS          1,200
PRIVATE SCHOOLS     890
```

COLLEGES 6,200
PRIVATE 890
HIGH SCHOOLS 2,500
VO-TECHS 1,200

Computer graphics offers a powerful tool for the business user who must present data in a meaningful manner or for the manager who must review, analyze, and make decisions based on data relationships.

A variety of devices are used to produce the output created in the information processing cycle. The following paragraphs describe the most commonly used output devices.

Printers

Printing requirements vary greatly among computer users. For example, the user of a personal computer generally uses a printer capable of printing 100 to 200 lines per minute. Users of mainframe computers, such as utility companies that send printed bills to hundreds of thousands of customers each month, need printers that are capable of printing thousands of lines per minute. These different needs have resulted in the development of printers with varying capabilities. Due to the many choices available and because printed output is so widely used, users must be familiar with the factors to consider when choosing a printer (Figure 5-5).

QUESTION	EXPLANATION
How much output will be produced?	Desktop printers are not designed for continuous use. High volume (more than several hundred pages a day) requires a heavy-duty printer.
Who will use the output?	Most organizations want external reports to be prepared on a high-quality printer.
Where will the output be produced?	If the output will be produced at the user's desk, a sound enclosure may be required to reduce the noise of some printers to an acceptable level.
Are multiple copies required?	Some printers cannot use multipart paper.

FIGURE 5-5

Factors that affect the choice of a printer

How Are Printers Classified?

Printers can be classified by how they transfer characters from the printer to the paper, either by impact or nonimpact, and by printer speed.

Impact and Nonimpact   **Impact printers** transfer the image onto paper by some type of printing mechanism striking the paper, ribbon, and character together. One technique is **front striking**, in which the printing mechanism that forms the character strikes a ribbon against the paper from the front to form an image. This is similar to the method used on typewriters. The second technique utilizes a **hammer striking** device. The ribbon and paper are struck against the character from the back by a hammer to form the image on the paper (Figure 5-6).

A number of technologies are used to accomplish nonimpact printing. **Nonimpact printing** means that printing occurs without having a mechanism striking against a sheet of paper. For example, ink is sprayed against the paper or heat is used to transfer the character.

Each of these two methods of printing has its advantages and disadvantages. Impact printing can be noisy because the paper is struck when printing occurs. But because the paper is struck, carbon paper can be used to create multiple copies of a report, such as an invoice, that go to different people. Although nonimpact printers cannot create carbon copies, they are very quiet and are ideal for desktop applications where the normal requirements only call for a single printed copy.

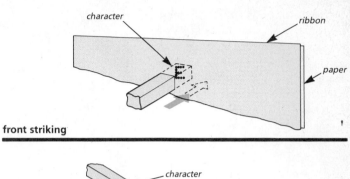

front striking

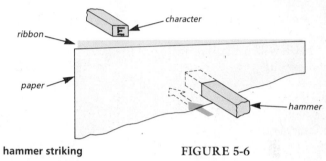

hammer striking   **FIGURE 5-6**

Impact printers operate in one of two ways: front striking or hammer striking.

Speed   Another way to classify printers is by the speed at which they print. Printers can be classified as low speed, medium speed, high speed, and very high speed.

Low-speed printers print one character at a time. The rate of printing for low-speed printers is expressed in the number of characters that can be printed in one second. Low-speed printers can print from 15 to 600 characters per second.

Medium-speed and **high-speed printers** print multiple characters on a line at the same time. For this reason they are called **line printers**. The rate of printing for these machines is stated in terms of the number of lines per minute that can be printed. **Medium-speed printers** can print from 300 to 600 lines per minute. Printers that can print from 600 to 3,000 lines per minute are classified as **high-speed printers**.

Very high-speed printers can print in excess of 3,000 lines per minute; some, more than 20,000 lines per minute. Very high-speed printers are often called **page printers** because they print an entire page at one time.

Printer Features

To decide which printer to choose for a particular job, it is important to know the different features that a printer might have. Common feature choices include carriage size, type of paper feed mechanism, and bidirectional printing capability.

Carriage Size Most printers are built with either a standard or wide carriage. A **standard carriage** printer can accommodate paper up to 8 1/2 inches wide. A **wide carriage** printer can accommodate paper up to 14 inches wide. Using a normal character size, most printers can print 80 characters per line on a standard carriage and 132 characters per line on a wide carriage.

Feed Mechanism The feed mechanism determines how the paper is moved through the printer. Two types of feed mechanisms are found on printers, tractor feed and friction feed. **Tractor feed mechanisms** transport continuous form paper through the printer by using sprockets, small protruding prongs of plastic or metal, which fit into holes on each side of the paper. The pages of **continuous form paper** are connected for continuous flow through the printer (Figure 5-7). Where it is necessary to feed single sheets of paper into the printer, **friction feed mechanisms** are used. As the name implies, paper is moved through friction feed printers by pressure on the paper and the carriage, as it is on a typewriter. As the carriage rotates, the paper is transported through the printer.

Bidirectional Printing Some printers are designed to print in a **bidirectional** manner. That is, the print head, the device that contains the mechanism for transferring the character to the paper, can print as it moves from left to right, and from right to left. The printer does this by storing the next line to be printed in its memory and then printing the line forward or backward as needed. Bidirectional printing can almost double the number of characters that can be printed in a given period of time.

FIGURE 5-7

Each sheet of continuous form paper is connected with the next. A feed mechanism pulls the paper through the printer using the holes on each side of the form. Perforations between each page allow a printed report to be folded and may be used to separate each page.

Printers for Small and Medium Computers

The increased popularity and use of personal computers has resulted in the development of a large number of printers that vary significantly in speed, quality, and price. Some of these printers are also used on larger systems. The following paragraphs describe the print devices most commonly used on small and medium-size computers.

Dot Matrix Printers

Dot matrix printers are used extensively because they are versatile and relatively inexpensive. The Epson printer shown in Figure 5-8 is a well-known dot matrix printer that is used with personal computers.

A **dot matrix printer** is an impact printer. Its print head consists of a series of small tubes containing pins that, when pressed against a ribbon and paper, print small dots. The combination of small dots printed closely together forms the character (Figure 5-9).

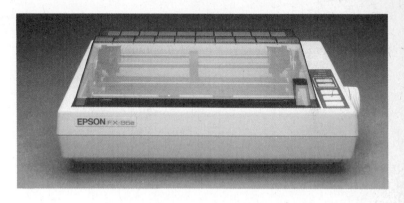

FIGURE 5-8

The Epson FX-86e printer is a dot matrix printer.

To print a character using a dot matrix printer, the character stored in main memory is sent to the printer's electronic circuitry. The printer circuitry activates the pins in the print head that correspond to the pattern of the character to be printed. The selected pins strike the ribbon and paper and print the character. Low-speed dot matrix printers utilize a movable print head that prints one character at a time. Medium- and high-speed dot matrix printers have print mechanisms at each print position and are able to print an entire line at one time.

Dot matrix printers can contain a varying number of pins, depending on the manufacturer and the printer model. Print heads consisting of nine and 24 pins are most common. Figure 5-10 illustrates the formation of the letter E using a nine-pin dot matrix printer.

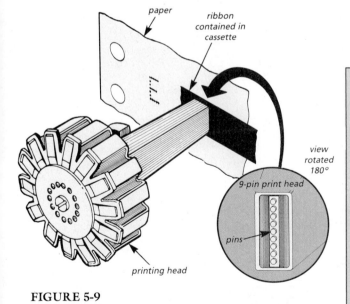

FIGURE 5-9

The print head for a dot matrix printer consists of a series of pins. When activated, the pins strike the ribbon that strikes the paper, creating a dot on the paper.

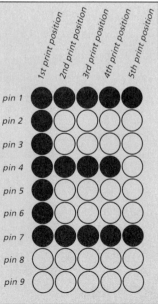

FIGURE 5-10

The letter E is formed with seven vertical and five horizontal dots. As the nine-pin print head moves from left to right, it fires one or more pins into the ribbon, which makes a dot on the paper. At print position 1, it fires pins 1 through 7. At print positions 2 through 4, it fires pins 1, 4, and 7. At print position 5, it fires pins 1 and 7. Pins 8 and 9 are used for lowercase characters such as p, q, y, g, and j that extend below the line.

A character produced by a dot matrix printer is made up of a series of dots. The quality of print produced is partly dependent on the number of pins used to form the character. A 24-pin print head produces better-looking characters than a nine-pin print head because the dots are closer together.

Several methods are used to improve the quality of dot matrix printers. On a nine-pin printer, one method is to print a line twice. Using this technique a line is printed, and then the print head is shifted very slightly and the line is printed again. This results in overlapping dots, which give the appearance of solid characters (Figure 5-11). The disadvantage, of course, is that the printing takes longer since each character is printed twice. Twenty-four-pin printers can produce the same print quality in a single pass.

Many dot matrix printers can also print characters in two or more sizes and densities. Typical sizes include condensed print, standard print, and enlarged print. In addition, each of the three print sizes can be printed with increased density or darkness, called bold print. Figure 5-12 illustrates condensed, condensed bold, standard, standard bold, enlarged, and enlarged bold print.

Most dot matrix printers have a graphics mode that enables them to print pictures and graphs. In graphics mode, the individual print head pins can be activated separately or in combination to form unique shapes or continuous lines. When special software packages are used, dot matrix printers can print in many different type styles and sizes (Figure 5-13). The flexibility of the dot matrix printer has resulted in widespread use of this type of printer by all types of computer users.

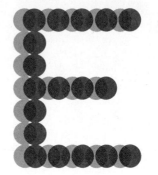

FIGURE 5-11

The letter E in this example is formed by overprinting, or printing the character twice. When it is printed the second time, the print head is slightly offset so that much of the space between the dots is filled in. This gives the character a better appearance and makes it easier to read.

```
CONDENSED PRINT - NORMAL CHARACTERS
CONDENSED PRINT - EMPHASIZED CHARACTERS

STANDARD PRINT - NORMAL CHARACTERS
STANDARD PRINT - EMPHASIZED CHARACTERS

ENLARGED   PRINT   -   NORMAL   CHARACTERS
ENLARGED   PRINT   -   EMPHASIZED   CHARACTERS
```

FIGURE 5-12

The three type sizes shown—condensed, standard, and enlarged—are printed using normal and emphasized (''bold'') print density.

Monaco	Chicago	Los Angeles
Venice	Geneva	Helvetica
Athens	London	San Francisco
Σψμβολ	Courier	New York

FIGURE 5-13

These letter styles illustrate the abilities of dot matrix printers to print graphics, depending on the software directing the printer.

Some dot matrix printers can print in multiple colors using ribbons that contain the colors red, green, and blue. Color output is obtained by repeated printing and repositioning of the paper, print head, and ribbon. Such printers can be useful in printing graphs and charts, but output quality is not comparable to color produced by other types of printers.

Daisy Wheel Printers

When users require printed output of high quality, such as for business or legal correspondence, a letter-quality printer is often used. The term **letter quality** refers to the quality of the printed character that is suitable for formal or professional business letters. A letter-quality printed character is a fully formed, solid character like those made by typewriters. It is not made up of a combination of dots, as by a dot matrix printer.

The letter-quality printer most often used with personal computers is the daisy wheel printer (Figure 5-14). The **daisy wheel printer** is an impact printer. It consists of a type element containing raised characters that strike the paper through an inked ribbon.

The daisy wheel element somewhat resembles the structure of a flower, with many long, thin petals (Figure 5-15). Each "petal" has a raised character at the tip. When printing occurs, the type element (daisy wheel) rotates so that the character to be printed is in printing position. A hammer extends, striking the selected character against the ribbon and paper, printing the character. Because of the time required to rotate the daisy wheel, the daisy wheel printer is normally slower than a dot matrix printer; however, the print quality is higher. Printing speeds vary from 20 to 80 characters per second.

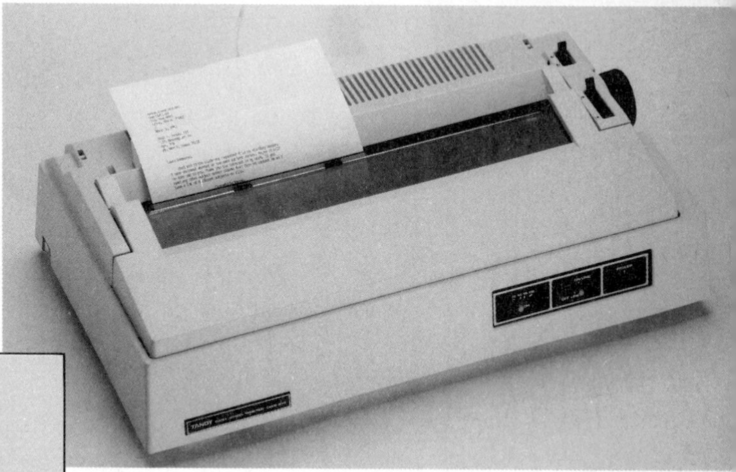

FIGURE 5-14

A daisy wheel printer produces letter-quality output comparable to that produced by a typewriter. Either continuous form or single-sheet paper can be used with most daisy wheel printers.

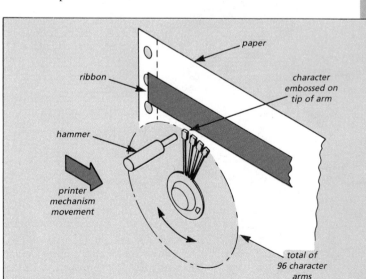

ribbon
paper
hammer
character embossed on tip of arm
printer mechanism movement
total of 96 character arms

FIGURE 5-15

The daisy wheel print element consists of a number of arms, each with a character at the end. When the printer is running the wheel spins until the desired character is lined up with the hammer. The hammer then strikes against the ribbon and paper, printing the character.

An additional feature of the daisy wheel printer is that the daisy wheel can be easily replaced. Daisy wheels come in a variety of sizes and fonts. A font, or typeface as they are sometimes called, is a complete set of characters in a particular style such as script, gothic, or roman. Therefore, whenever the user wishes to change fonts, he or she can remove one daisy wheel and put another wheel on the printer.

The disadvantage of a daisy wheel printer is that it is capable of printing only the characters that are on the wheel. It cannot, therefore, print graphic output.

Thermal Printers

Thermal printers use heat to produce fully formed characters, usually on special chemically treated paper. An advantage of thermal printers is that they are very quiet. Disadvantages are their need for special paper and their relatively slow printing speed. Thermal printers are not as commonly used as they once were.

Ink Jet Printers

A popular type of nonimpact printer is an **ink jet printer**. To form a character, an ink jet printer uses nozzles that spray ink onto the page. Ink jet printers produce relatively high-quality print and are very quiet because the paper is not struck as it is by dot matrix or daisy wheel printers. Disadvantages are that ink jet printers cannot produce multiple copies, and the ink sometimes smears on soft, porous paper. The ink jet printer in Figure 5-16 is designed for use with personal computers.

Laser Printers

The **laser printer** is a nonimpact printer that operates in a manner similar to a copying machine (Figure 5-17). The laser printer converts data from the computer into a laser beam that is directed by a mirror to a positively charged revolving drum. Each position on the drum touched by the laser beam becomes negatively charged and attracts the toner (powdered ink). The toner is transferred onto the

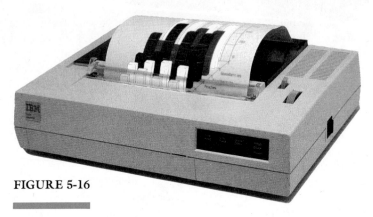

FIGURE 5-16

An ink jet printer by IBM

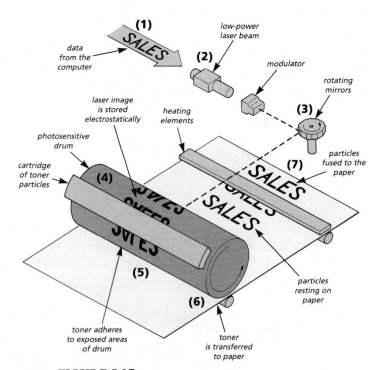

FIGURE 5-17

Laser printers use a process similar to a copying machine. Data from the computer (1), such as the word SALES, is converted into a laser beam (2) that is directed by a mirror (3) to a photosensitive drum (4). The sensitized drum attracts toner particles (5) that are transferred to the paper (6). The toner is fused to the paper with heat and pressure (7).

FIGURE 5-18

The output illustrated in this picture was produced by a laser printer. Note that the output contains a mixture of different sizes and styles of print.

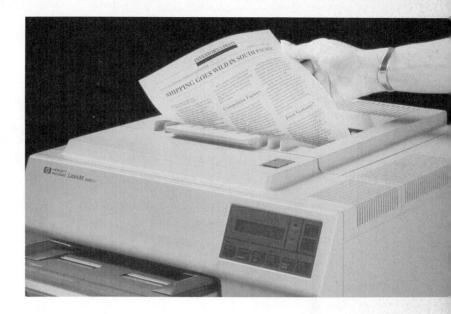

paper and then fused to the paper by heat and pressure. The end result is a high-quality printed image. As shown in Figure 5-18, laser printers can produce a variety of output.

Printers for Large Computers

Minicomputers and mainframes are frequently used to process and print large volumes of data. As the demand for printing information from a computer increases, the use of higher speed printers is required. The three types of printers often used on large computers are chain printers, band printers, and high-speed laser printers.

Chain Printers

The **chain printer** is a widely used high-speed printer. It contains numbers, letters of the alphabet, and selected special characters on a rotating chain (Figure 5-19). The chain consists of a series of type slugs that contain the character set. The character set on the type slugs is repeated two or more times on the chain mechanism. The chain rotates at a very high speed. Each possible print position has a hammer that can fire against the back of the paper, forcing the paper and ribbon against the character on the chain. As the chain rotates, the hammer fires when the character to be printed is in the proper position.

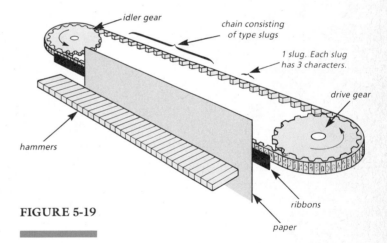

FIGURE 5-19

The chain printer contains a complete set of characters on several sections of a chain that rotates at a high, constant rate of speed. Print hammers are located at each horizontal print position. The paper and ribbon are placed between the hammers and the chain. As the chain rotates, the hammers fire when the proper characters are in front of their print positions.

The chain printer has proven to be very reliable. It produces good print quality at up to 3,000 lines per minute. The printers in the large computer installation in Figure 5-20 are chain printers.

FIGURE 5-20

These high-speed chain printers are used in a large computer installation to produce thousands of lines of printed output per minute.

Band Printers

Band printers, similar to chain printers, utilize a horizontal, rotating band containing characters. The characters are struck by hammers located behind the paper and a ribbon to create a line of print on the paper (Figure 5-21).

Interchangeable type bands can be used on band printers. The different type bands contain many different fonts or print styles. A band printer can produce up to six carbon copies, has good print quality, high reliability, and depending on the manufacturer and model of the printer, can print in the range of 300 to 2,000 lines per minute.

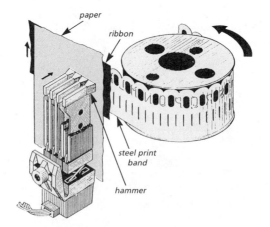

FIGURE 5-21

A band printer uses a metal band that contains solid characters. Print hammers at each print location strike the paper and the ribbon, forcing them into the band to print the character.

High-Speed Laser Printers

High-speed laser printers, also called **page printers**, can produce printed output at the rate of over 20,000 lines per minute, the equivalent of over 400 pages of 50 lines per page. As shown in Figure 5-22, these high-speed printers usually consist of a dedicated computer and tape drive to maximize the printing speed. When the device is printing, the paper moves so fast that it must be folded and stacked mechanically.

tape drive

console

printer

paper trays

FIGURE 5-22

This laser printer can operate at speeds up to 70 pages per minute. As shown in the picture, high-speed printers often use tape drives that contain the data to be printed.

Screens

The **screen**, also called the monitor, CRT (cathode ray tube), or VDT (video display terminal), is another important output device. Screens are used on both personal computers and terminals to display many different types of output. For example, responses obtained from user inquiries to a database are frequently displayed on a screen. A screen can also be used to display electronic spreadsheets, electronic mail, and graphs of various types.

Screen Features

Size The most widely used screens are equivalent in size to a 12- to 15-inch television screen. Although there is no standard number of displayed characters, screens are usually designed to display 80 characters on a line with a maximum of 25 lines displayed at one time. The 25th line is often reserved for messages or system status reports, not for data. This provides for a maximum of 2,000 characters on the screen at once. Some terminals can display up to 132 characters on a single horizontal line. The more characters that are displayed on a line, the smaller the size of the characters. Therefore, an important consideration when selecting a terminal is the number of characters displayed on the screen at one time and the *resolution* (clarity) of the characters displayed.

Color Most of the early screens displayed white characters on a black background. Research has indicated, however, that other color combinations are easier on the eyes. Today, many screens display either green or amber characters on a black background.

Cursor A **cursor** is a symbol that indicates where on the screen the next character entered will be displayed. It can also be used as a marker on a screen to identify the choices a user can make. Some of the symbols used to represent cursors are shown in Figure 5-23. Most cursors blink when they are displayed on the screen so the user can quickly find their location.

Scrolling **Scrolling** is a method of moving lines displayed on the screen up or down one line at a time. As a new line is added, for example, to the bottom of the screen, an existing one, from the top of the screen, is removed. The line removed from the screen remains in the computer's memory even though it is no longer displayed. When the screen is scrolled in the opposite direction (in this example, down), the line from the top that was removed reappears on the screen and the line at the bottom is removed.

Paging When **paging** is used, an entirely new "page" or screen of data can be displayed. This feature is useful in applications such as word processing when a user wants to use the screen to move quickly through pages of a long document.

Other Screen Features Screen features also include several options that can be used to emphasize displayed characters: reverse video, underlining, bold, blinking, and double size. **Reverse video** refers to the process of reversing the normal display on the screen. For example, it is possible to display a dark background with light characters or a light background with dark characters. Thus, if the normal screen had amber characters on a black background, reverse video shows black characters on an amber background. This feature permits single characters, whole words or lines, and even the entire screen to be reversed. The **underlining** feature allows characters, words, lines, or paragraphs to be underlined. Another feature used for emphasis is the ability to display some characters or words as bold. **Bold** means that characters are displayed at a greater brightness level

FIGURE 5-23

Three types of cursors are shown in this illustration—a rectangular cursor, an underline cursor, and an arrow cursor. Often, cursors blink to be easily identified.

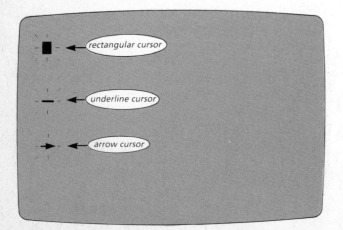

FIGURE 5-24

The memo shown on the screen uses both underlining and double-size characters to emphasize portions of the message.

```
TO: ALL SALES PERSONNEL
FR: REGINALD HAYES, V.P. SALES
RE: SALES BONUSES

    RUMORS HAVE BEEN CIRCULATING THAT
SALES BONUSES WILL NOT BE PAID THIS YEAR.
THIS RUMOR IS NOT TRUE! BONUSES WILL BE
PAID THE SAME AS IN PAST YEARS. GO FORTH!

SELL!        SELL!        SELL!
```

than the surrounding text. The **blinking** feature makes characters or words on a screen blink, thus drawing attention to them. The **double-size** feature means that certain characters or words are displayed at twice the size of normal characters and words. Figure 5-24 illustrates how underlining and double-size characters highlight data on the screen.

Types of Screens

Several types of screens are used with computers. The most common types are monochrome screens, color screens, plasma screens, and LCD screens. Plasma and LCD screens, which do not use the conventional cathode ray tube technology, are sometimes called **flat panel display screens** because of their relatively flat screens.

Monochrome screens specially designed for use with personal computers or for use as computer terminals usually display a single color, such as white, green, or amber characters on a black background. The characters are displayed without flicker and with very good resolution. Some monochrome screens have graphics capabilities.

The use of **color screens** is increasing in business and science applications, because numerous studies have found that color enables the user to more easily read and understand the information displayed on the screen.

A **plasma screen** produces a bright, clear image with no flicker (Figure 5-25). The screens are flat, so that they can be installed on desks or walls, taking up very little space.

With the development of truly portable computers that could be conveniently carried by hand or in a briefcase came a need for an output display that was equally as portable. Although several technologies have been developed, **liquid crystal displays (LCD)** are used as the output display for a number of laptop computers (Figure 5-26). LCD displays are also used in watches, calculators, and other electronic devices.

FIGURE 5-25

The high resolution of this plasma display allows the screen to display any combination of character fonts, line drawings, charts, sketches, and letters.

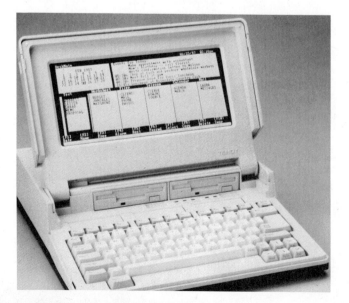

FIGURE 5-26

The liquid crystal display (LCD) screen used with this portable computer can display numbers, letters, and special characters, and even has some graphics capabilities.

Other Output Devices

Although printers and display devices provide the large majority of computer output, other devices are available for particular uses and applications. These include plotters, computer output microfilm devices, and voice output devices.

Plotters

A **plotter** is an output device used to produce high-quality line drawings, such as building plans, charts, or circuit diagrams. These drawings can be quite large; some plotters are designed to handle paper up to 40 by 48 inches, much larger than would fit in a standard printer. The plotter can also draw numbers and letters to add text to the output. Plotters can be classified by the way they create the drawing. The two types are pen plotters and electrostatic plotters.

As the name implies, **pen plotters** create images on a sheet of paper by moving one or more pens over the surface of the paper or by moving the paper under the tip of the pens.

Two different kinds of pen plotters are flatbed plotters and drum plotters. When a **flatbed plotter** is used to plot or draw, the pen or pens are instructed by the software to move to the down position so the pen contacts the flat surface of the paper. Further instructions then direct the movement of the pens to create the image. Most flatbed plotters have one or more pens of varying colors or widths. The plotter illustrated in Figure 5-27 is a flatbed plotter that can create color drawings. Another kind of flatbed plotter holds the pen stationary and moves the paper under the pen.

FIGURE 5-27

An example of a flatbed plotter

A **drum plotter** uses a rotating drum or cylinder over which drawing pens are mounted. The pens can move to the left and right as the drum rotates, creating an image (Figure 5-28). An advantage of the drum plotter is that the length of the plot is virtually unlimited, since roll paper can be used. The width of the plot is limited by the width of the drum.

With an **electrostatic plotter**, the paper moves under a row of wires (called styli) that can be turned on to create an electrostatic charge on the paper. The paper then passes through a developer and the drawing emerges where the charged wires touched the paper. The electrostatic printer image is composed of a series of very small dots, resulting in relatively high-quality output. In addition, the speed of plotting is faster than with pen plotters.

FIGURE 5-28

This drum plotter utilizes eight pens of different colors to create diagrams. As the paper moves forward and back, the pens move left and right and, under software control, draw where instructed.

Factors affecting the cost of a plotter are based on the resolution of the drawing and the speed of the plotting. Resolution is determined by the smallest movement a pen can make on the paper. Typical plotter movements may vary from .001 to .0005 inch. Plotting speeds of up to 36 inches per second are possible. Costs range from under $1,000 to over $100,000 for very high-speed plotters with extremely fine resolution.

Computer Output Microfilm

Computer output microfilm (COM) is an output technique that records output from a computer as microscopic images on roll or sheet film. The images stored on COM are the same as the images that would be printed on paper. The COM recording process reduces characters 24, 42, or 48 times smaller than would be produced on a printer. The information is then recorded on sheet film called **microfiche** or on 16mm, 35mm, or 105mm roll film.

The data to be recorded by the device can come directly from the computer (online) or from a magnetic tape that was previously produced by the computer (offline). After the COM film is processed, the user can view it.

To access data stored on microfilm, a variety of readers are available. They utilize indexing techniques to provide a quick reference to the data. Some microfilm readers can perform automatic data lookup, called **computer-assisted retrieval**, under the control of an attached minicomputer. With the powerful indexing software and hardware now available for microfilm, a user can usually locate any piece of data in a 200,000,000-character database in less than 10 seconds, at a far lower cost per inquiry than using an online inquiry system consisting of a computer system that stores the data on a hard disk.

Voice Output

The other important means of generating output from a computer is voice output. **Voice output** consists of spoken words that are conveyed to the user from the computer. Thus, instead of reading words on a printed report or monitor, the user hears the words over earphones, the telephone, or other devices from which sound can be generated.

The data that produces voice output is usually created in one of two ways. First, a person can talk into a device that will encode the words in a digital pattern. For example, the words "The number is" can be spoken into a microphone, and the computer software can assign a digital pattern to the words. The digital data is then stored on a disk. At a later time, the data can be retrieved from the disk and translated back from digital data into voice, so that the person listening will actually hear the words.

A second type of voice generation is new but holds great promise. Called a **voice synthesizer**, it can transform words stored in main memory into speech. The words are analyzed by a program that examines the letters stored in memory and generates sounds for the letter combinations. The software can apply rules of intonation and stress to make it sound as though a person were speaking. The speech is then projected over speakers attached to the computer.

You may have heard voice output used by the telephone company for giving number information. Automobile and vending machine manufacturers are also incorporating voice output into their products. The potential for this type of output is great and it will undoubtedly be used in many products and services in the future.

Chapter Summary

The output step of the information processing cycle uses a variety of devices to provide users with information. Some of the devices that were discussed in this chapter, including printers and screens, are summarized in Figure 5-29.

FIGURE 5-29

This table summarizes the most common output devices.

OUTPUT DEVICE	DESCRIPTION
Printers—Impact	
Dot matrix	Prints text and graphics using small dots.
Daisy wheel	Prints letter-quality documents—no graphics.
Chain	High-speed printer to 3,000 lines per minute—designed to print text.
Band	High-speed printer to 2,000 lines per minute—designed to print text.
Printers—Nonimpact	
Thermal	Uses heat to produce fully formed characters.
Ink jet	Sprays ink onto page to form text and graphic output—prints quietly.
Laser	Produces high-quality text and graphics.
High-speed laser	Can exceed 20,000 lines per minute.
Screens	
Monochrome	Displays white, green, or amber images on a black background.
Color	Uses multiple colors to enhance displayed information.
Plasma	A flat screen that produces bright, clear images with no flicker.
LCD	A flat screen used on many laptop computers.
Plotters	Produces hard copy graphic output.
COM	Records reduced-size information on sheet film called microfiche or on roll film.
Voice	Conveys information to the user from the computer in the form of speech.

The following list summarizes the remaining topics discussed in this chapter.

1. **Output** is data that has been processed into a useful form called information that can be used by a person or a machine (p. 5.1).
2. An **internal report** is used within an organization by people performing their jobs (p. 5.2).
3. An **external report** is used outside the organization (p. 5.2).
4. The major consideration for internal reports is that they be clear and easy to use. For external reports, the quality of the printed output may be important (p. 5.2).
5. In a **detail report**, each line on the report usually corresponds to one record read and processed (p. 5.2).

6. A **summary report** contains summarized data, consisting of totals from records read and processed (p. 5.2).

7. An **exception report** contains information that will help users to focus on situations that may require immediate decisions or specific actions (p. 5.2).

8. **Computer graphics** are used to present information so it can be quickly and easily understood (p. 5.3).

9. **Impact printing** devices transfer the image onto paper by some type of printing mechanism striking the paper, ribbon, and character together (p. 5.4).

10. Impact printers can be **front striking** or **hammer striking** (p. 5.4).

11. A **nonimpact printer** creates an image without having characters strike against a sheet of paper (p. 5.4).

12. Impact printing is noisy but multiple copies can be made (p. 5.4).

13. Nonimpact printers are quiet and some print very fast (p. 5.5).

14. Computer printers may be classified by the speed at which they print: low, medium, high, and very high speed (p. 5.5).

15. The printing rate of **low-speed printers** is expressed as the number of characters that can be printed in one second (p. 5.5).

16. The printing rate for **medium-speed printers** and **high-speed printers** is stated as the number of lines printed per minute (p. 5.5).

17. Medium- and high-speed printers are sometimes called **line printers** (p. 5.5).

18. **Very high-speed printers** are sometimes called **page printers** (p. 5.5).

19. Features of printers include carriage size, type of paper feed mechanism, and bidirectional printing (p. 5.5).

20. **Tractor feed mechanisms** transport continuous form paper by using sprockets inserted into holes on the sides of the paper (p. 5.6).

21. The pages of **continuous form paper** are connected for continuous flow through the printer (p. 5.6).

22. **Friction feed** mechanisms move paper through a printer by pressure between the paper and the carriage (p. 5.6).

23. **Bidirectional** means the print head on a printer can print while moving in either direction (p. 5.6).

24. Dot matrix printers have small pins that are contained in a print head. The pins strike the paper and ribbon to print a character (p. 5.7).

25. The quality of a dot matrix printer is partly dependent on the number of pins used to form the character (p. 5.8).

26. Most dot matrix printers can print condensed print, standard print, bold print, and enlarged print (p. 5.8).

27. Some dot matrix printers can print in color (p. 5.9).

28. A **letter-quality** printed character is a fully formed character that is easy to read (p. 5.9).

29. Speeds of a daisy wheel printer vary from 20 to 80 characters per second (p. 5.9).

30. **Thermal printers** use heat to produce fully formed characters, usually on chemically treated paper (p. 5.10).

31. An **ink jet printer** uses a nozzle to spray liquid ink drops onto the page. Some ink jet printers print in color (p. 5.10.)

32. **Chain printers** print up to 3,000 lines per minute (p. 5.11).

33. **Band printers** have interchangeable bands with many different styles of fonts (p. 5.12).

34. **Laser printers** are nonimpact printers that operate in a manner similar to a copying machine (p. 5.12).

35. Most screens utilize cathode ray tube (CRT) technology (p. 5.13).

36. Types of screens include monochrome screens, color screens, plasma screens, and LCD screens (p. 5.15).

37. **Monochrome** monitors usually display green, white, or amber characters on a black background (p. 5.15).

38. **Color screens** are being used more because color enables the user to more easily read and understand the information displayed on the screen (p. 5.15).

39. A **plasma** display can produce all kinds and sizes of type styles, charts, and drawings (p. 5.15).

40. **Liquid crystal displays** use a polarizing material and liquid crystal to form images (p. 5.15).

41. A **computer plotter** is an output device that can create drawings, diagrams, and similar types of output (p. 5.16).

42. **Computer output microfilm (COM)** is an output technique that records output from a computer as microscopic imprint on roll or sheet film (p. 5.17).
43. COM offers the advantages of faster recording speed, lower costs of recording the data, less space required for storing data, and lower costs of storing the data (p. 5.18).
44. **Voice output** consists of spoken words that are conveyed to the computer user from the computer (p. 5.18).
45. A **voice synthesizer** can transform words stored in main memory into human speech (p. 5.18).

Review Questions

1. Name and describe three types of commonly used reports.
2. What are the advantages of displaying information in a graphic form? What are the disadvantages? What are the three most commonly used types of charts?
3. What are the two major categories of printers? What are the differences between the two?
4. How does a dot matrix printer produce an image? What effect on the quality of print does this method have? What techniques are used on dot matrix printers to improve the print quality?
5. What does the term "letter quality" mean? What types of printers print with letter quality?
6. Describe some of the print capabilities of dot matrix printers with respect to graphics and character size and style.
7. How does an ink jet printer produce images? What are some advantages of ink jet printers?
8. Explain how a laser printer works. What are some advantages of laser printers?
9. List the three major types of high-speed printers used with large computers. List the characteristics such as speed and manner of printing for each one.
10. What types of screens are used with computers? List some screen features.
11. Describe some of the different types of plotters and the manner in which they produce drawings.
12. List several advantages of microfilm over printed reports.
13. Describe the two ways of creating voice output.

Auxiliary Storage

6

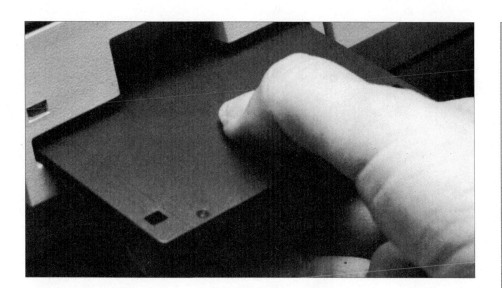

Objectives

- Define auxiliary storage.
- Identify the primary devices used for personal computer auxiliary storage.
- Describe the manner in which data is stored on disks.
- Describe the methods used to back up data stored on diskettes and hard disks.
- Identify the types of disk storage used with large computers.
- Explain how tape storage is used with large computers.
- List and describe three other forms of auxiliary storage: optical, solid state, and mass storage.

Storage is the fourth and final operation in the information processing cycle. Upon completion of this chapter you will be able to add the knowledge you acquire about storage operations to what you have learned in previous chapters about input, processing, and output operations. In addition, you will be familiar with the various types and capabilities of auxiliary storage devices that are used with computers.

What Is Auxiliary Storage?

Computer storage can be classified into two types: main memory and auxiliary storage. As you have seen, main memory temporarily stores programs and data that are being processed. **Auxiliary storage**, or **secondary storage**, stores programs and data when they are not being processed, just as a filing cabinet is used in an office to store records.

Records that are not being used are kept in the file cabinet until they are needed. In the same way, data and programs that are not being used on a computer are kept in auxiliary storage until they are needed. Auxiliary storage devices that are used with computers include devices such as magnetic disk and tape.

Auxiliary storage devices provide a more permanent form of storage than main memory because they are **nonvolatile**, that is, data and programs that have been placed on auxiliary storage devices are retained when the power is turned off. Main memory is volatile, which means that when power is turned off, whatever is stored in main memory is erased.

Auxiliary storage devices can be used as both input and output devices. When they are used to receive data that has been processed by the computer they are functioning as output devices. When data that they stored is transferred to the computer for processing, they are functioning as input devices.

In the next section we explain the auxiliary storage devices that are designed for users with personal computers. Later in the chapter, we discuss the devices that are used with larger computer systems.

Auxiliary Storage for Personal Computers

Personal computer users have several categories of auxiliary storage from which to choose. These include diskettes, hard disks, and removable disk cartridges.

Diskettes

In the early 1970s IBM introduced the floppy disk and the floppy disk drive as a new type of auxiliary storage. Today, **diskettes**, also called **floppy diskettes**, **floppies**, or just **disks**, are used as a principal auxiliary storage medium for personal computers (Figure 6-1). This type of storage is convenient, reliable, and relatively low in cost.

Diskettes are available in a number of different sizes. Many personal computers take diskettes that are 5 1/4 inches in diameter. Smaller diskettes, 3 1/2 inches in diameter and 2 inches in diameter, are also commonly used and are increasing in popularity (Figure 6-2).

FIGURE 6-1

In this picture, a user is inserting a diskette into the disk drive of an IBM microcomputer.

FIGURE 6-2

The most commonly used diskettes for personal computers are 5 1/4 and 3 1/2 inch diskettes.

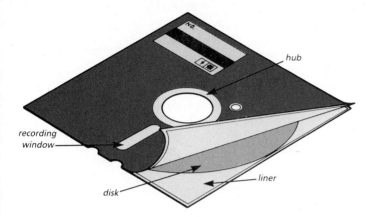

FIGURE 6-3

A 5 1/4 inch diskette, consists of the disk itself enclosed within a protective jacket, usually made of a vinyl material. The liner of the diskette is essentially friction-free so that the disk can turn freely, but the liner does contact the disk and keep it clean. The magnetic surface of the diskette, which is exposed through the window in the jacket, allows data to be read and stored. The large hole (hub) in the diskette is used to mount the diskette in the disk drive. The small hole is used by some disk drives as an indicator for where to store data.

A diskette consists of a circular piece of thin mylar plastic (the actual disk), which is coated with an oxide material similar to that used on magnetic tape. On a 5 1/4 inch diskette, the circular piece of plastic is enclosed in a flexible square protective jacket. The jacket has an opening so that a portion of the disk's surface is exposed for reading and recording (Figure 6-3). On a 3 1/2 inch diskette and a 2 inch diskette, the circular piece of plastic is enclosed in a rigid plastic cover and a piece of metal called the shutter covers the reading and recording area. When a 3 1/2 inch diskette or 2 inch diskette is inserted into a disk drive, the drive slides the shutter to the side to expose the disk surface (Figure 6-4).

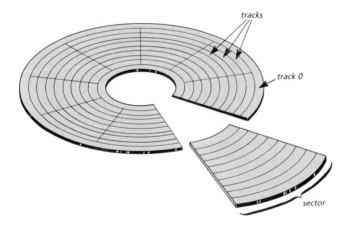

FIGURE 6-4

Each track on a disk is a narrow, circular band. On a disk containing 40 tracks, the outside track is called track 0 and the inside track is called track 39. The distance between track 0 and track 39 on a 5 1/4 inch diskette is less than one inch. The disk surface is divided into sectors. This example shows a disk with nine sectors.

How Is a Diskette Formatted? Before a diskette can be used on a microcomputer for auxiliary storage, it must be formatted. The **formatting** process includes defining the tracks and sectors on the surface of a disk (Figure 6-4). A **track** is a narrow recording band forming a full circle around the disk. Each track on the disk is divided into sectors. A **sector** is a section of a track. It is the basic storage unit of a diskette. When data is read from a diskette, a minimum of one full sector is read. When data is stored on a diskette, at least one full sector is written. The number of tracks and sectors that are placed on a disk when it is formatted varies based on the capacity of the disk, the capabilities of the disk drive being used, and the specifications in the software that does the formatting. Many 5 1/4 inch diskettes and all 2 inch diskettes are formatted with 40 tracks and 9 sectors on the surface of the disk. The 3 1/2 inch diskettes are usually formatted with 80 tracks and 9 sectors on each side. A 3 1/2 inch diskette has more tracks than a 5 1/4 inch diskette because even though it is smaller in size it has a larger storage capacity. When 40 tracks are recorded on a diskette, the tracks are numbered from 0 to 39. When 80 tracks are used, the tracks are numbered from 0 to 79.

What Is the Storage Capacity of a Diskette? Knowing the storage capacity of a diskette gives a user an idea of how much data or how many programs can be stored on it. The number of characters that can be stored on a diskette depends on three basic factors: (1) the number of sides of the disk used; (2) the recording density of the bits on a track; and (3) the number of tracks on the disk.

Some disks and drives are designed so that data can be recorded on only one side of the disk. These drives are called **single-sided drives**. Similarly, disks on which data can be recorded on one side only are called **single-sided disks**. Today, most disk drives are designed to record and read data on both sides of the disk. Drives that can read and write data on both sides of the disk are called **double-sided drives** and the disks are called **double-sided disks**. The use of double-sided drives and disks doubles the number of characters that can be stored on the disk. The term cylinder is sometimes used with double-sided disks. A **cylinder** is defined as all tracks of the same number. For example, track 0 on side 1 of the disk and track 0 on side 2 of the disk are collectively called cylinder 0.

Another factor in determining the storage capacity of a disk is the recording density provided by the drive. The **recording density** is the number of bits that can be recorded on one inch of the innermost track on the disk. This measurement is referred to as **bits per inch (bpi)**. The higher the recording density, the higher the storage capacity of the disk.

The third factor that influences the number of characters that can be stored on a disk is the number of tracks onto which data can be recorded. This measurement is referred to as **tracks per inch (tpi)**. As we saw earlier in this chapter, the number of tracks depends on the size of the disk, the drive being used, and how the disk was formatted.

While the capacity of diskettes can vary, a common capacity for a 5 1/4 inch diskette is approximately 360K and for a 3 1/2 inch diskette, 720K. With high-density disk drives, 3 1/2 inch diskettes can store 1.44 megabytes (million characters) of data. The capacity of a 2 inch diskette is 360K.

How Is Data Stored on a Diskette?

Regardless of the type of diskette or the formatting scheme that is used, the method of storing data on it is essentially the same. When a diskette is inserted in a disk drive, the center hole fits over a hub mechanism that positions the disk in the unit (Figure 6-5).

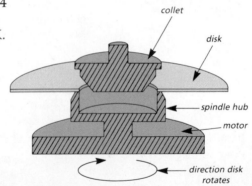

collet
disk
spindle hub
motor
direction disk
rotates

FIGURE 6-5

When a diskette is inserted in a drive, the center hole is positioned between the collet and the hub. After the door to the disk drive is closed and the disk is engaged, it begins rotating within the protective jacket at approximately 300 RPM.

The circular plastic disk rotates within its cover at approximately 300 revolutions per minute. Data is stored on tracks character by character, using the same code (ASCII or EBCDIC) that is used to store characters in main memory. Electronic impulses are placed along a track to represent the bit pattern for each character. To do this, a recording mechanism in the drive called the **read/write head** rests just above the surface of the rotating disk, generating electronic impulses representing the bits to be recorded (Figure 6-6). To access different tracks on the disk, the drive moves the read/write head from track to track.

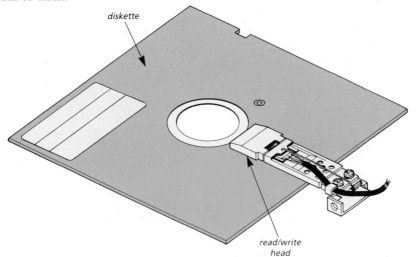

diskette

read/write head

FIGURE 6-6

The read/write head moves back and forth over the opening in the protective jacket to read or write data on the disk.

What Is Access Time?   Data stored in sectors on a diskette must be retrieved and placed in main memory to be processed. The time required to access and retrieve the data is called the **access time**.

The access time for a disk drive depends on four factors:

1. **Seek time**, the time it takes to position the read/write head over the proper track.
2. **Latency**, the time it takes for the sector containing the data to rotate under the read/write head.
3. **Settling time**, the time required for the read/write head to be placed in contact with the disk.
4. **Data transfer rate**, the time required to transfer the data from the disk to main memory.

The access time for diskettes varies from about 175 milliseconds (one millisecond equals 1/1000 of a second) to approximately 300 milliseconds. What this means to the user is that, on the average, data stored in a single sector on a diskette can be retrieved in approximately 1/5 to 1/3 of a second.

The Care of Diskettes   With reasonable care, diskettes provide an inexpensive and reliable form of storage. In handling diskettes, take care to avoid exposing them to heat, magnetic fields, and contaminated environments. One advantage of the 3 1/2 inch diskette and 2 inch diskette is that they have a rigid plastic cover that provides more protection for the data stored on the plastic disk inside than the flexible cover on a 5 1/4 inch diskette. Figure 6-7 shows ways to care for diskettes properly.

Hard Disks

Hard disks used on personal computers are sometimes called **fixed disks** because the platters used to store the data are permanently mounted inside the computer and are not removable like diskettes. On fixed disks, the metal disks, the read/write heads, and the mechanism for moving the heads across the surface of the disk are enclosed in a sealed case. This helps to ensure a clean environment for the disk.

The **hard card** is a circuit board that has a hard disk built onto it. Hard cards provide an easy way to expand the storage capacity of a personal computer because the board can be installed into an expansion slot of the computer (Figure 6-8).

How Is Data Stored on a Hard Disk? Storing data on hard disks is similar to storing data on diskettes. Hard drives contain a spindle on which one or more disk platters are mounted. The spindle rotates the disk platters at a high rate of speed, usually 3,600 revolutions per minute. In order to read or write data on the surface of the spinning disk platter, the disk drives are designed with **access arms**, or **actuators**. The access arms or

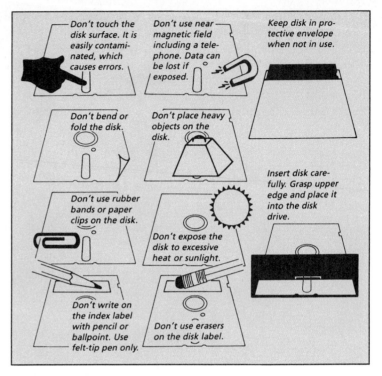

FIGURE 6-7

Guidelines for the proper care of diskettes

FIGURE 6-8

A hard card is a hard disk on a circuit board that can be mounted in a computer's expansion slot. In the picture above, the protective cover for the disk has been removed.

FIGURE 6-9

This picture of a hard disk drive illustrates the access arm and the read/write heads, which are over the surface of the disks. These heads are extremely stable. They can read and write tracks very close together on the surface of the disk.

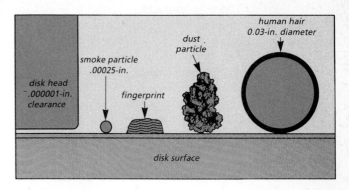

FIGURE 6-10

The clearance between a disk head and the disk surface is about 1 millionth of an inch. With these tolerances, contamination such as a smoke particle, fingerprint, dust particle, or human hair could render the drive unusable. Sealed disk drives are designed to minimize contamination.

actuators contain one or more read/write heads per disk surface (Figure 6-9). These read/write heads "float" on a cushion of air and do not actually touch the surface of the disk. The distance between the head and the surface varies from approximately one-millionth of an inch to 1/2 millionth of an inch. As shown in Figure 6-10, the close tolerance leaves no room for any type of contamination. If some form of contamination is introduced or if the alignment of the read/write heads is altered by something accidentally jarring the computer, the disk head can collide with and damage the disk surface, causing a loss of data. This event is known as a **head crash**. Because of the time needed to repair the disk and to reconstruct the data that was lost, head crashes can be extremely costly for users.

When reading data from the disk, the read/write head senses the magnetic spots that are recorded on the disk along the various tracks and transfers the data to main memory. When writing, the read/write head transfers data from main memory and stores it as magnetic spots on the tracks on the recording surface of one or more of the disks. As the disk rotates at a high rate of speed, the read/write heads move across its surface.

The number of platters permanently mounted on the spindle in the drive can vary. For 5 1/4 inch drives, the number varies between one and four platters. On many drives, each surface of a platter can be used to store data. Thus, if one platter is used in the drive, two surfaces are available for data. If two platters are used, four surfaces are available for data, and so on. Naturally, the more platters, the more data that can be stored on the drive.

The storage capacity of hard drives is measured in megabytes or millions of bytes (characters) of storage. Common sizes for personal computers range from 10MB to 300MB of storage and even larger sizes are available. As an idea of how much data these storage capacities represent, 10MB of storage is equivalent to approximately 5,000 double-spaced typewritten pages.

In addition to a larger storage capacity, hard disks provide faster access time than diskettes. The typical access time of a hard disk for a personal computer is between 25 and 80 milliseconds.

The use of a hard disk drive on a personal computer provides many advantages for users. Because of its large storage capacity, a hard disk can store many software application programs and data files. When a user wants to run a particular application or access a particular data file on a hard disk, it is always available. The user does not have to find the appropriate diskette and insert it into the drive. In addition, the faster access time of a hard disk reduces the time needed to load programs and access data.

Disk Cartridges   Another variation of disk storage available for use with personal computers is the removable **disk cartridge**. Disk cartridges, which can be inserted and removed from a computer (Figure 6-11), offer the storage and fast access features of hard disks and the portability of diskettes. Disk cartridges are often used when data security is an issue. At the end of a work session, the disk cartridge can be removed and locked up, leaving no data on the computer.

Protecting Data Stored on a Disk

Regardless of whether you are using diskettes, hard disks, or removable disk cartridges on a personal computer, you must protect the data you store on the disk from being lost. Disk storage is reusable and data that is stored on a disk may be overwritten and replaced with new data. This is a desirable feature allowing users to remove or replace unwanted files. However, it also raises the possibility of accidentally removing or replacing a file that you really wanted to keep. To protect programs and data stored on disks, there are several things you can do.

How Is the Write-Protect Notch Used?   One way to protect the data and programs stored on a diskette is to use the write-protect notch. On the 5 1/4 inch diskettes, this notch is located on the right side. To prevent writing to a disk, a user covers this notch with a small piece of removable tape. Before writing data onto a disk, the disk drive checks the notch. If the notch is open the drive will proceed to write on the disk. If the notch is covered, the disk drive will not write on the disk (Figure 6-12).

On 3 1/2 inch and 2 inch diskettes, the situation is reversed. The write-protect notch is a small window in the lower left corner of the diskette. A piece of plastic in the window can be moved to open and close the window. If the write-protect window is closed, the drive can write on the diskette. If the window is open, the drive will not write on the diskette.

Backup Storage   Another way to protect programs and data stored on diskettes is by creating backup storage. Backup storage means creating a duplicate copy of important programs and data on a separate diskette. To back up diskettes, simply copy the data on one diskette to another. When using hard disks, however, the user is faced with a more difficult problem. The amount of data that can be stored on a hard disk can fill many diskettes. For example, to back up a hard disk containing 10 million characters,

FIGURE 6-11

This photo shows a removable hard disk cartridge, which allows a user to remove and transport the entire hard disk from computer to computer or to lock it up in a safe.

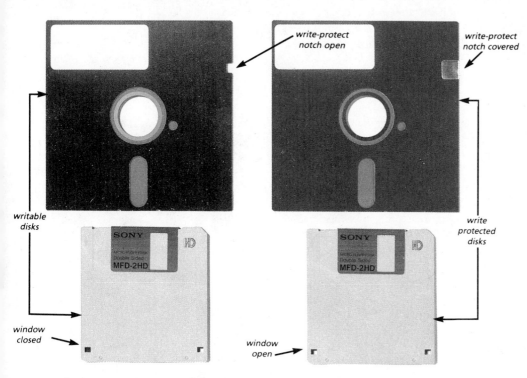

writable
disks

write-protect
notch open

write-protect
notch covered

write
protected
disks

window
closed

window
open

FIGURE 6-12

The write-protect notch of the
5 1/4 inch diskette on the left is
open and therefore data could be
written to the diskette. The notch
of the 5 1/4 inch diskette on the
right, however, is covered. Data
cannot be written to this diskette.
The reverse situation is true for
the 3 1/2 inch diskette. Data cannot be written on the 3 1/2 inch
diskette on the right because the
small black piece of plastic is not
covering the window in the lower
left corner. Plastic covers the window of the 3 1/2 inch diskette on
the left, so data can be written on
this diskette.

approximately thirty 5 1/4 inch diskettes that could each store
360,000 characters would be required. For this reason, cartridge
tape is sometimes used to back up hard disk storage.

Cartridge Tape   A device commonly used to back up hard
disks on personal computers is the **cartridge tape drive** (Figure
6-13). When these devices are available on a personal computer,
the data and programs that are stored on a hard disk can be
copied onto the tape cartridge for backup storage.

   Some cartridge tape drives can operate in a **streaming mode**,
without the normal stopping and starting usually associated
with tape operations. Tape streaming results in more data being
recorded in less time. Using the streaming method, a cartridge
tape unit can completely copy a 20 million byte hard disk in
approximately four minutes.

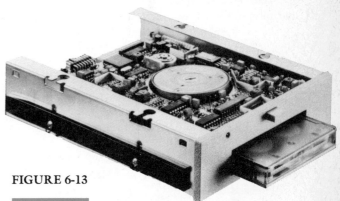

FIGURE 6-13

Cartridge tape drives are an effective way to back up and
store data that would otherwise require numerous diskettes.

Auxiliary Storage for
Medium and Large Computers

A wide variety of devices are available for use as auxiliary storage on medium and large
computers. Most of these devices use storage techniques that are similar, if not identical,

to the devices that we discussed for personal computers. As you would expect, however, storage devices used for medium and large computers provide greater storage capacity and faster retrieval rates than devices used with small systems. For discussion purposes, we group storage devices for medium and large computers into three categories: magnetic disk, magnetic tape, and other storage devices.

Magnetic Disk

Magnetic disk is the most common type of auxiliary storage device for medium and large computers. Disks for medium and large computers are similar to devices used on personal computers but have larger capacities, usually as a result of having more recording surfaces. Some disk devices used on large computers can store billions of characters of information. Because of their ability to retrieve data directly from a specific location on the disk, disk devices for medium and large computers are sometimes referred to as **direct-access storage devices (DASD)**.

One difference between auxiliary storage for a personal computer and for larger computers is that many more disk devices can be attached to larger computers. While most personal computers are limited to two to four disks, medium computers can support 8 to 16 disk devices and large computers can support over 100 high-speed disk devices (Figure 6-14).

Disk devices for medium and large computers fall into two categories: fixed disks and removable disks.

Fixed Disks Fixed disks, the most commonly used disks for medium and large computers, can be either mounted in the same cabinet as the computer or enclosed in their own stand-alone cabinet (Figure 6-15). As with fixed disks in personal computers, fixed disks on medium and large computers contain nonremovable platters that are enclosed in airtight cases to prevent contamination.

Removable Disks Removable disk units were introduced in the early 1960s and were the most prevalent type of disk storage for nearly 20 years. During the 1980s, however, removable disks began to be replaced by fixed disks that offered larger storage capacities and higher reliability.

Removable disk devices consist of the drive unit, which is usually in its own cabinet, and the removable recording media, called a **disk pack**. Removable disk packs consist of 5 to 11 metal platters that are used on both sides for recording data. The recording capacity of these packs varies from 10 to 300 megabytes of data. One advantage of removable disk packs is that the data on a disk drive can be quickly changed by removing one pack and replacing it with another.

FIGURE 6-14

A large installation of removable disk drives showing the protective disk pack cases on top of the drive units.

FIGURE 6-15

A high-speed, high-capacity fixed disk drive in a stand-alone cabinet.

This can be accomplished in minutes. When removable disk packs are not mounted in a disk drive they are stored in a protective plastic case. When the packs are being used, the plastic case is usually placed on top of the drive unit. Figure 6-14 shows a large installation of removable disk devices with the empty protective disk pack cases on top of the drives.

How Is Data Physically Organized on a Disk?   Depending on the type of disk drive, data is physically organized in one of two ways on disks used with medium and large computers. One way is the sector method and the other is the cylinder method.

As with the diskette drives and hard disks used with personal computers, the **sector method** for physically organizing data on disks divides each track on the disk surface into individual storage areas called sectors (Figure 6-16). Each sector can contain a specified number of bytes. Data is referenced by indicating the surface, track, and sector where the data is stored.

With the **cylinder method**, all tracks of the same number on each recording surface are considered part of the same cylinder (Figure 6-17). For example, if each platter contained 200 tracks, the tenth track on all surfaces would be considered part of the tenth

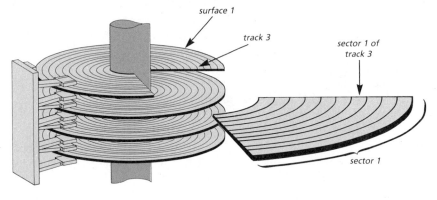

FIGURE 6-16

The sector method of disk addressing divides each track into a number of sectors. To locate data, the surface, track, and sector where the data is stored are specified.

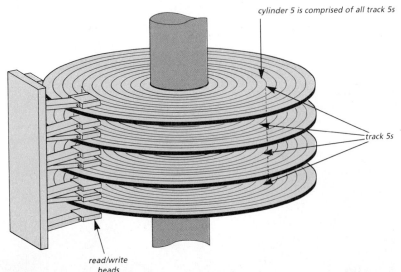

FIGURE 6-17

The cylinder method reduces the movement of the read/write head (thereby saving time) by writing information "down" the disk on the same track of successive surfaces.

cylinder. All twentieth tracks would be part of the twentieth cylinder, and so on. When the computer requests data from a disk using the cylinder method, it must specify the cylinder, recording surface, and record number. Because the access arms containing the read/write heads all move together, they are always over the same track on all surfaces. Thus, using the cylinder method to record data "down" the disk surfaces reduces the movement of the read/write head during both reading and writing of data.

Magnetic Tape

During the 1950s and early 1960s, prior to the introduction of removable disk pack drives, magnetic tape was the primary method of storing large amounts of data. Today, even though tape is no longer used by medium and large computers as the primary method of auxiliary storage, it still functions as a cost-effective way to store data that does not have to be accessed immediately. In addition, tape serves as the primary means of backup for most medium and large systems and is often used when data is transferred from one system to another.

   Magnetic tape consists of a thin ribbon of plastic. The tape is coated on one side with a material that can be magnetized to record the bit patterns that represent data. The most common types of magnetic tape devices are reel-to-reel and cartridge. Reel-to-reel tape is usually 1/2 inch wide and cartridge tape is 1/4 inch wide (Figure 6-18).

Reel-to-Reel Tape Devices   **Reel-to-reel** tape devices use two reels: a supply reel to hold the tape that will be read or written on, and the take-up reel to temporarily hold portions of the supply reel tape as it is being processed. At the completion of processing, tape on the take-up reel is wound back onto the supply reel. As the tape moves from one reel to another, it passes over a read/write head (Figure 6-19), an electromagnetic device that can read or write data on the tape.

   Older style tape units (Figure 6-20) are vertical cabinets with vacuum columns that hold five or six feet of slack tape to prevent breaking during sudden start or stop operations.

FIGURE 6-18 ▬▬▬

A standard 10 1/2 inch reel of magnetic tape

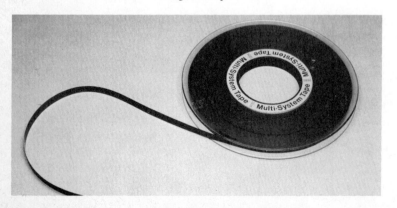

FIGURE 6-19 ▬▬▬

The tape read/write head senses and records the electronic bits that represent data.

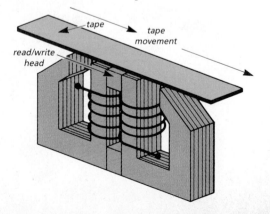

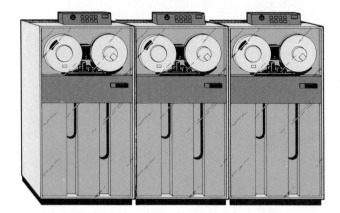

FIGURE 6-20

Older style reel-to-reel magnetic tape storage devices

Newer style tape units (Figure 6-21) allow a tape to be inserted through a slot opening similar to the way videotapes are loaded in a videocassette recorder. This front-loading tape drive takes less space and can be cabinet mounted. The drive automatically threads the end of the tape onto an internal take-up reel.

Reels of tape usually come in lengths of 300, 1,200, 2,400, and 3,600 feet and can store up to 100 megabytes of data.

Cartridge Tape Devices Cartridge tape devices for medium and large computers are identical to units previously discussed for personal computers. They are becoming increasingly popular because they can store more data and take less space than the traditional 10 1/2 inch diameter reels of tape (Figure 6-22).

FIGURE 6-21

Newer style tape drives allow the user to slide the tape into a slot at the front of the unit. The drive automatically threads the tape.

FIGURE 6-22

The 4 × 5-inch tape cartridge can hold 20% more data than the 10 1/2 inch reel of tape.

How Is Data Stored on Magnetic Tape? Data is recorded on magnetic tape in the form of magnetic spots that can be read and transferred to main memory. The magnetic spots on the tape are organized into a series of horizontal rows called channels. The presence or absence of magnetic spots representing bits is used to represent a given character on the tape.

Several different coding structures are used with magnetic tape, including both ASCII and EBCDIC. The coding structure for EBCDIC divides half-inch tape into nine horizontal channels. A combination of bits in a vertical column that consists of the nine horizontal channels is used to represent characters and the error-checking parity bit on the tape (Figure 6-23).

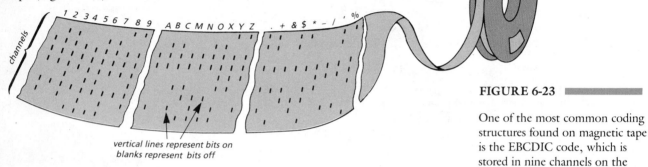

vertical lines represent bits on
blanks represent bits off

FIGURE 6-23

One of the most common coding structures found on magnetic tape is the EBCDIC code, which is stored in nine channels on the tape. Eight channels are used to store the bits representing a character. The ninth channel is a parity error-checking channel.

Tape density is the number of characters or bytes that can be stored on an inch of tape. As on disk drives, tape density is expressed in bytes per inch or bpi. Commonly used tape densities are 800, 1,600, 3,200, and 6,250 bpi. Some of the newer cartridge tape devices can record at densities of over 38,000 bpi. The higher the density, the more data that can be stored on a tape.

Tape is considered a **sequential storage** media because the computer must read tape records one after another until it finds the one it wants. Tapes do not have fixed data storage location addresses like disk drives that allow direct access of a record.

In order to allow some room for starting and stopping, tapes use **interblock gaps (IBG)**, also called **interrecord gaps (IRG)** (Figure 6-24). These spaces are usually about .6 inch long. To increase recording efficiency, **blocked records** are normally used.

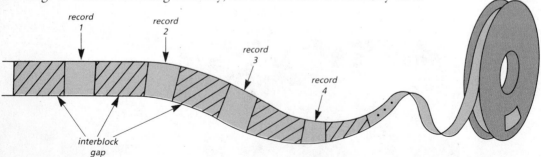

record 1 *record 2* *record 3* *record 4*

interblock gap

FIGURE 6-24

Records stored on tape are stored sequentially, separated by an interblock gap that allows for the starting and stopping of the tape drive.

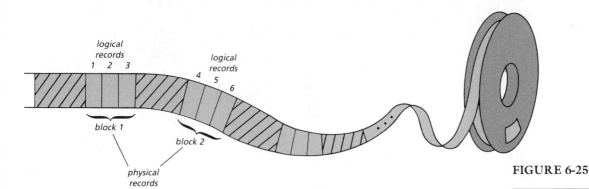

FIGURE 6-25

Blocking refers to placing two or more individual records, called **logical records**, into a block to form a **physical record** (Figure 6-25). A logical record refers to the amount of data that a program uses when it processes one record. A physical record refers to the amount of data that is physically transferred into memory from the tape. For example, there could be three employee payroll (logical) records contained within one block (physical record) on a tape. Using blocking has two advantages. First, the tape is used more efficiently. More data can be stored because the gap between each logical record is eliminated. Second, because an entire physical record is read into memory each time data is read from the tape, reading data takes place faster. Two or more logical records are read each time data is transferred from the tape to main memory.

Three logical records are stored in each block or physical record in this diagram. An entire block of records is brought into main memory each time the tape file is read.

Other Forms of Auxiliary Storage

While the conventional disk and tape devices previously described comprise the majority of auxiliary storage devices and media, several other means for storing data are used. These include optical storage technology, solid-state devices, and mass storage devices.

Optical Storage Technology

Optical storage technology is one of the newest and most promising methods of data storage. Enormous quantities of information can be stored on **optical disks** by using a laser to burn microscopic holes on the surface of a hard plastic disk (Figure 6-26) on the next page. A lower power laser reads the disk by reflecting light off the disk surface. The reflected light is converted into a series of bits that the computer can process.

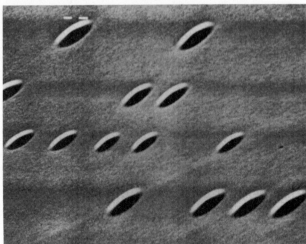

A full-size 12 inch optical disk can store several billion characters. The smaller disks, just under 5 inches in diameter, can store over 800 million characters or approximately 2,500 times the data that can be stored on a 5 1/4 inch diskette. That's enough space to store approximately 400,000 pages of typed data. The smaller optical disks are called **CDROM**, for compact disk read-only memory (Figure 6-26). They use the same laser technology that is used for the CDROM disks that have become popular for recorded music.

The disadvantage of optical disks now available is that they cannot be modified once the data is recorded. Most optical disks are prerecorded but some devices provide for one-time recording. These units are called **WORM** devices, for write once read many. Recently announced optical disk devices will be able to erase and rerecord data.

Even as read-only devices, optical disks have great potential. Because of their tremendous storage capacities, entire catalogs or reference materials can be stored on a single disk. Some people predict that optical disks will soon be used in place of film media such as microfiche.

FIGURE 6-26

To record data on an optical disk (shown left being inserted into an optical disk player), a laser burns microscopic holes on the surface (right).

Solid-State Devices

To the computer, solid-state storage devices look and act just like disk drives, only faster. As their name suggests, they contain no moving parts, only electronic circuits. **Solid-state storage devices** use the latest in random-access memory (RAM) technology to provide high-speed data access and retrieval. Rows of RAM chips (Figure 6-27) provide megabytes of memory that can be accessed much faster than the fastest conventional disk drives. Solid-state storage devices are significantly more expensive than conventional disk drives offering the same storage capacity.

FIGURE 6-27

Solid-state storage devices use megabytes of RAM chips to simulate a conventional disk drive.

Mass Storage Devices

Mass storage devices provide for the automated retrieval of data from a "library" of storage media such as cartridge tapes or diskettes. Mass storage is ideal for extremely large databases that require all information to be readily accessible even though any one portion of the database may be infrequently required. Mass storage systems take less room than conventional tape storage and can retrieve and begin accessing records within seconds. Figure 6-28 shows a mass storage system that uses tape cartridges.

FIGURE 6-28

This mass storage system can access any one of thousands of tape cartridges in an average of 11 seconds. Each cartridge is a 4 × 4 inch square and about 1 inch thick.

Chapter Summary

Auxiliary storage is used to store programs and data that are not currently being processed by the computer. This chapter discussed the various types of auxiliary storage used with computers. The chart in Figure 6-29 provides a summary of the auxiliary storage devices. What you have learned about these devices and storage operations in general can now be added to what you have learned about the input, processing, and output operations of the information processing cycle.

FIGURE 6-29

A summary of some of the more common auxiliary storage devices

DEVICE	DESCRIPTION
Personal Computers	
Diskette	Plastic storage media that is reliable and low in cost.
Hard disk	Fixed metal storage media that provides large storage capacity and fast access.
Hard card	Fixed disk that is built on a circuit board and installed in an expansion slot of a personal computer.
Disk cartridge	Combines storage and access features of hard disk and portability of diskettes.
Tape cartridge	Used to back up hard disks on personal computers.
Medium and Large Computers	
Fixed disk	Large multiplatter fixed disk with high storage capacity and fast access.
Removable disk	Disk drives with removable disk packs.
Reel tape	Magnetic tape device using the reel-to-reel method of moving tape.
Tape cartridge	Magnetic tape device using cartridge method of holding tape.
Other Storage Devices	
Optical storage	Uses lasers to record and read data on a hard plastic disk. High quality and large storage capacity.
Solid state	Uses RAM chips to provide high-speed data access and retrieval.
Mass storage	Automated retrieval of storage media such as tape cartridges and diskettes.

The following list summarizes the key topics discussed in this chapter.

1. **Auxiliary storage** is used to store data and programs that are not being processed on the computer (p. 6.1).

2. Most personal computers use a diskette 5 1/4 inches in diameter. Smaller diskettes (approximately 3 1/2 inches in diameter and 2 inches in diameter) are also available and are increasing in popularity (p. 6.2).

3. A diskette consists of a plastic disk enclosed within a square protective jacket. A portion of the surface of the disk is exposed so data can be stored on it (p. 6.3).

4. Data is stored on a disk in tracks. A **track** is a narrow recording band forming a full circle around the diskette (p. 6.3).

5. The number of tracks most often found are 40 tracks or 80 tracks per diskette (p. 6.4).

6. Each track on a disk is divided into **sectors**, the basic unit of disk storage. A minimum of one full sector of data is read from a diskette; a minimum of one sector is written on a diskette (p. 6.3).

7. The factors affecting disk storage capacity are the number of sides of the disk used, the recording density of the bits, and the number of tracks on the disk (p. 6.4).

8. **Single-sided drives** read and record data on only one side of a disk. **Double-sided drives** read and record data on both sides of the disk (p. 6.4).

9. The **recording density** is stated as the number of bits that can be recorded on one inch of the innermost track on a disk. The measurement is referred to as **bits per inch (bpi)** (p. 6.4).

10. To read or write data on a disk, the diskette is placed in the disk drive. Within its protective covering the disk rotates at about 300 revolutions per minute. The **read/write head** rests just above the disk and senses or generates electronic impulses representing bits (p. 6.5).

11. The time required to access and retrieve data stored on a diskette is called the **access time** (p. 6.5).

12. Access time depends on four factors: (1) **seek time**, the time it takes to position the read/write head on the correct track; (2) **latency time**, the time it takes for the data to rotate under the read/write head; (3) **settling time**, the time required for the head to be placed in contact with the disk; and (4) **data transfer rate**, the amount of data that can be transferred from the disk to main memory (p. 6.5).

13. Diskettes should not be exposed to heat or magnetic fields. With proper care, diskettes provide an inexpensive and reliable form of storage (p. 6.5).

14. A **hard disk** consists of one or more rigid metal platters coated with a metal oxide material (p. 6.6).

15. On **hard disks**, the metal disks, read/write heads, and access arm are enclosed in a sealed case (p. 6.6).

16. To read and write data on a hard disk, an **access arm** moves read/write heads in and out. The heads float very close to the surface of the disk, generating or sensing electronic impulses that represent bits (p. 6.6).

17. The number of platters in a hard disk for a microcomputer can vary from one to four. On many disks, both sides of the platters can be used for storing data (p. 6.7).

18. The typical access time for a microcomputer hard disk is between 25 and 85 milliseconds (p. 6.7).

19. The write-protect notch on diskettes can be used to protect the data stored on a disk from being overwritten (p. 6.8).

20. To back up storage means to create a duplicate copy of important programs and data on a separate disk or tape (p. 6.8).

21. The normal method for diskette backup is to copy the data onto another diskette. For hard disk, the disk is often copied to a **cartridge tape** (p. 6.9).

22. **Fixed disks** are sealed in an enclosure and permanently mounted in the disk drive (p. 6.10).

23. **Disk packs** contain between 5 and 11 platters that can be mounted and removed from the disk drive (p. 6.11).

24. The **sector method** (identifying the surface, track, and sector number) or the **cylinder method** (identifying the cylinder, recording surface, and record number) can be used to physically organize and address data stored on disk (p. 6.11).

25. The tracks that can be referenced at one position of the access arm are called a **cylinder** (p. 6.11).

26. **Magnetic tape** is used primarily for backup purposes in large computer installations (p. 6.12).

27. Data is recorded on **magnetic tape** as a series of magnetic spots along a series of horizontal channels. Each spot represents a bit in a coding scheme. Large computers commonly use the EBCDIC coding scheme on nine-track tape (p. 6.14).

28. **Tape density** is the number of characters or bytes that can be stored on one inch of tape. Common densities are 800, 1,600, 3,200, and 6,520 bytes per inch (p. 6.14).

29. **Sequential storage** means records are stored one after the other on the tape (p. 6.14).

30. An **interblock gap** separates records stored on tape (p. 6.14).

31. **Blocked records** mean two or more **logical records** are stored in a **physical record** on the tape (p. 6.15).

32. **Optical disks** use a laser beam recording and reading method and can store enormous quantities of data (p. 6.15).

Review Questions

1. Differentiate between the uses of main memory and auxiliary storage.
2. Draw a diagram of a diskette and label the main parts.
3. What does formatting a disk mean?
4. What are the three factors influencing the storage capacity of a disk? Briefly describe each of them.
5. Describe the care and handling of diskettes.
6. Identify the factors that influence the access time of a disk drive.
7. Describe the characteristics of a fixed disk drive. What sizes are commonly used with personal computers?
8. What is disk backup? How are diskettes normally backed up? How are hard disks backed up?
9. Describe the differences between fixed disks and removable disks on large computers.
10. Describe the sector method of disk organization and the cylinder method of disk organization.
11. How is data stored on magnetic tape? What are typical tape densities?
12. Describe optical storage technology. Why is it one of the most promising methods of data storage?

File Organization and Databases

7

Objectives

- Describe sequential files, indexed files, and direct (or relative) files.
- Explain the difference between sequential retrieval and random retrieval of records from a file.
- Describe the data maintenance procedures for updating files, including adding, changing, and deleting data in a file or database.
- Discuss the advantages of a database management system (DBMS).
- Describe a relational database system.
- Describe a hierarchical database system.
- Describe a network database system.
- Explain the use of a query language.
- Describe the responsibilities of a database administrator.

The data and information that a company accumulates is a valuable asset. For data and information to provide maximum benefit to a company, they must be carefully organized, used, and managed. While you are now familiar with the auxiliary storage devices used to store data and information, it is equally important that you understand the various ways in which the data and information stored on these devices is organized, used, and managed. The purpose of this chapter is to explain (1) how files on auxiliary storage are organized, retrieved, and maintained (kept current); and (2) the advantages, organization, use, and management of databases.

As you read this chapter, you will notice that several of the file and database concepts that are discussed were introduced earlier in the text. With the computer knowledge that you now have, especially about auxiliary storage devices, you are ready for a more in-depth look at these topics. The first part of this chapter concentrates on how files are organized and used. The second part of this chapter discusses the advantages, organization, and use of databases. Learning this information will help you to better understand how data and information is stored and managed on a computer.

What Is a File?

A **file** is a collection of related records that is usually stored on an auxiliary storage device. A **record** is a collection of related fields and a **field**, also called a **data item** or **data element**, is a fact (Figure 7-1). Files contain data that pertains to one topic. For example, a business can have separate files that contain data related to personnel, inventory, customers, vendors, and so forth. Most companies have hundreds, sometimes thousands of files that contain the data pertaining to their business. Files that are stored on auxiliary storage devices can be organized in several different ways and there are advantages and disadvantages to each of these types of file organization.

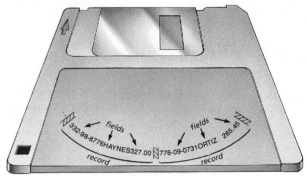

FIGURE 7-1

This payroll file stored on a diskette contains payroll records. Each payroll record contains a social security field, a name field, and a paycheck amount field.

Types of File Organization

Three types of file organization are used on auxiliary storage devices: sequential, indexed, and direct.

Sequential File Organization

Sequential file organization means that records are stored one after the other, normally in ascending or descending order, based on a value in each record called the key. The **key** is a field that contains data, such as a social security number, that is used to sequence the records in a file (Figure 7-2). Files that are stored on tape are always sequential files. Files on disk may be sequential, indexed, or direct.

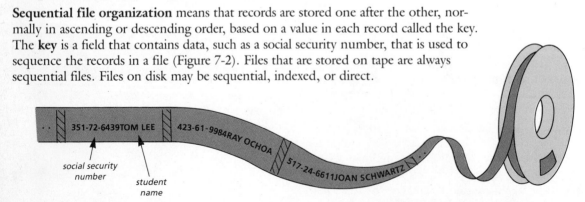

FIGURE 7-2

The student records in this file are stored sequentially in ascending order using the social security number as the key field. The records in this file can only be retrieved sequentially.

Records that are stored using sequential file organization are also retrieved sequentially. **Sequential retrieval**, also called **sequential access**, means that the records in a file are retrieved one record after another in the same order that the records are stored. For example, in Figure 7-2, the file contains student records stored in sequence by social security number. The data in the file is retrieved one record after another in the same sequence that it is stored in the file.

Sequential retrieval has a major disadvantage—since records must be retrieved one after another in the same sequence as they are stored, the only way to retrieve a record is to read all preceding records first. Therefore, in Figure 7-2, if the record for Joan Schwartz must be retrieved, the records for Tom Lee and for Ray Ochoa must be read before retrieving the Joan Schwartz record. Because of this, sequential retrieval is not used when fast access to a particular record is required. However, sequential retrieval is appropriate when records are processed one after another.

A common use of sequential files in a computer center is as backup files, where data from a disk is copied onto a tape or another disk so that if the original data becomes unusable, the original file can be restored from the backup file.

Indexed File Organization

A second type of file organization is called **indexed file organization**. Just as in a sequential file, records are stored in an indexed file in an ascending or descending sequence based on the value in the key field of the record.

An indexed file, however, also contains an index. An **index** consists of a list containing the values of the key field and the corresponding disk address for each record in a file (Figure 7-3). In the same way that an index for a book points to the page where a particular topic is covered, the index for a file points to the place on a disk where a particular record is located. The index is stored on disk along with the data file when it is created. The index is retrieved from the disk and placed in main memory whenever the file is processed.

Records can be accessed in an indexed file both sequentially and randomly. As previously discussed, sequential retrieval means that the records in a file are retrieved one record after another in the same order that the records are stored. **Random retrieval**, also called **random**

FIGURE 7-3

The index in an indexed file contains the record key value and the corresponding disk address for each record in the file. In this example, the index contains the employee number, which is the key for the employee file, and the disk address for the corresponding employee record.

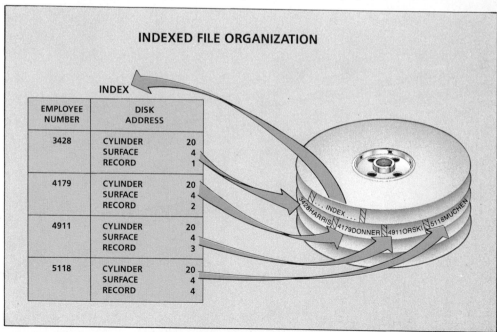

INDEXED FILE ORGANIZATION

INDEX

EMPLOYEE NUMBER	DISK ADDRESS	
3428	CYLINDER	20
	SURFACE	4
	RECORD	1
4179	CYLINDER	20
	SURFACE	4
	RECORD	2
4911	CYLINDER	20
	SURFACE	4
	RECORD	3
5118	CYLINDER	20
	SURFACE	4
	RECORD	4

access, means any record in a file can be directly accessed (retrieved) regardless of where it is stored in the file. For example, the 50th record in a file can be retrieved first, followed by the 3rd record, and then the 20th record. Random retrieval is used when fast access to a record is required, as in an airline reservation system. For random retrieval to be used, files must be stored on disk.

To randomly access a record in an indexed file, the index is searched until the key of the record to be retrieved is found. The address of the record (also stored in the index) is then used to retrieve the record directly from the file without reading any other records. For example, if an inquiry was received from the personnel office asking the name of employee number 5118, the index is searched until key 5118 is found (Figure 7-4). The corresponding disk address (cylinder 20, surface 4, record 4) is then used to read the record from disk into main memory.

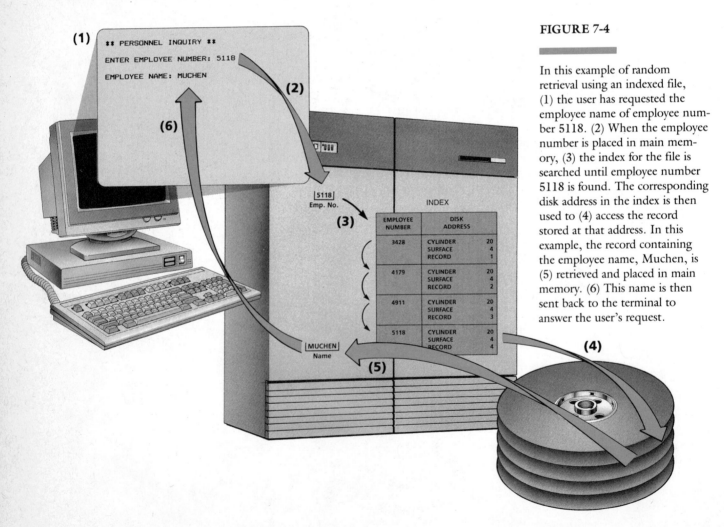

FIGURE 7-4

In this example of random retrieval using an indexed file, (1) the user has requested the employee name of employee number 5118. (2) When the employee number is placed in main memory, (3) the index for the file is searched until employee number 5118 is found. The corresponding disk address in the index is then used to (4) access the record stored at that address. In this example, the record containing the employee name, Muchen, is (5) retrieved and placed in main memory. (6) This name is then sent back to the terminal to answer the user's request.

Direct or Relative File Organization

A **direct file** or **relative file** (occasionally called a random file) contains records that are stored and retrieved according to either their disk address or their position within a file. This means that the program that stores and accesses records in a direct file must specify either the exact physical address of a record in the file (for example, cylinder, surface, and track number, or track and sector number), or the relative location (position) where a record is stored in the file, such as the first, tenth, or fiftieth record (Figure 7-5).

The location where a record is stored is based on a key value found in the record. For example, a program could establish a file that has nine locations where records can be stored. These locations are sometimes called **buckets**. If the key in the record is a one-digit value (1–9), then the value in the key would specify the relative location within the file where the record is stored. For example, the record with key 3 is placed in relative location or bucket 3; the record with key 6 is placed in relative location 6, and so on.

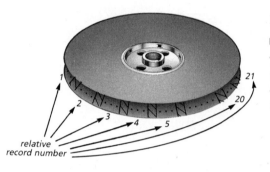

FIGURE 7-5

The relative address of a record is the same as the numeric position of the record in the file. The fifth record has a relative address of 5.

Usually the storage of records in a file is not so simple. For instance, what if the maximum number of records to be stored in a direct file is 100 and the key for the record is a four-digit number? In this case, the key of the record is not used to specify the relative or actual location of the record because the four-digit key results in up to 9,999 records. In cases such as these, an arithmetic formula must be used to calculate the relative or actual location in the file where the record is stored. The process of using a formula and performing the calculation to determine the location of a record is called **hashing** (Figure 7-6).

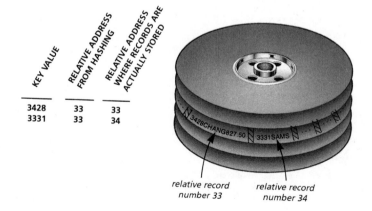

relative record
number 33

relative record
number 34

FIGURE 7-6

Sometimes the hashing computation produces synonyms, or records that have the same relative address. In this example, both records have a relative address of 33. When the computer tries to store the second record and finds that location 33 is already full, it stores the second record at the next available location. In this example, record 3331 is stored in location 34.

Once a record is stored in its relative location within a direct file, it can be retrieved either sequentially or randomly. The method normally used with direct files is random retrieval. In order to randomly retrieve a record from a direct file three steps are performed:

1. The program must obtain the key of the record to be retrieved. The value of the key is entered into the computer by the user.
2. The program determines the location of the record by performing the same hashing process as when the record was initially stored.
3. The software then directs the computer to the proper bucket to retrieve the record.

Sequential retrieval from a direct file can be accomplished by indicating that the record from the first relative location is to be retrieved, followed by the record from the second relative location, and so on. All the records in the file are retrieved based on their relative location in the file.

Summary of File Organization Concepts

Files are organized as either sequential, indexed, or direct files. Sequential file organization can be used on tape or disk and requires that the records in the file be retrieved sequentially. Indexed files must be stored on disk and the records can be accessed either sequentially or randomly. Direct files are stored on disk and are usually accessed randomly (Figure 7-7).

FILE TYPE	TYPE OF STORAGE	ACCESS METHOD
Sequential	Tape or Disk	Sequential
Indexed	Disk	Random* or Sequential
Direct (Relative)	Disk	Random* or Sequential

* Primarily accessed as random files

FIGURE 7-7

The chart shows the type of storage and the access methods that can be used with each of the three file types.

How Is Data in Files Maintained?

Data stored on auxiliary storage must be kept current to produce accurate results when it is processed. To keep the data current, the records in the files must be updated. **Updating** records within a file consists of adding records to the file, changing records within the file, and deleting records from the file.

Adding Records

Records are added to a file when additional data is needed to make the file current. For example, if a customer opens a new account at a bank, a record containing the data for the new account must be added to the bank's account file. The process that takes place to *add* this record to the file is shown in Figure 7-8.

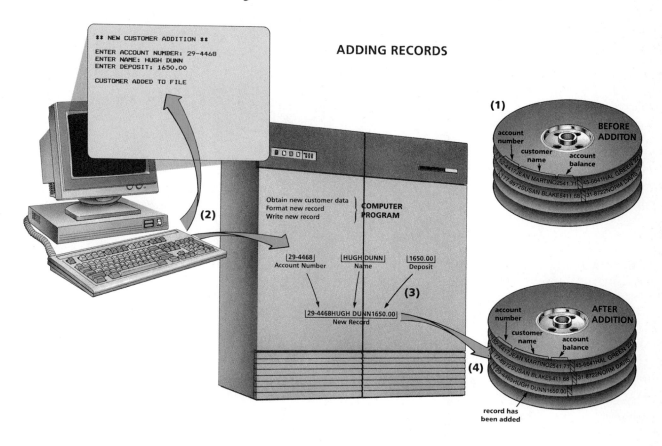

ADDING RECORDS

** NEW CUSTOMER ADDITION **

ENTER ACCOUNT NUMBER: 29-4468
ENTER NAME: HUGH DUNN
ENTER DEPOSIT: 1650.00

CUSTOMER ADDED TO FILE

1. A bank teller enters the new customer data into the computer through a terminal. The data includes the account number, the customer name, and the deposit that will become the account balance.
2. The update program moves the data entered by the user into the new record area in main memory.
3. The update program writes the new record to the file. The location on the disk where the record is written is determined by the program. In some cases, a new record is written between other records in the file. In other cases, such as illustrated in this example, the added record is added to the end of the file.

   Whenever data is stored on auxiliary storage for subsequent use, the ability to add records must be present in order to keep the data current.

FIGURE 7-8

In this example of adding records, (1) the file first exists without the new account. (2) The teller enters the account number, customer name, and deposit. (3) This data is used to create a record that is then (4) added to the file.

Changing Records

The second task that must be accomplished when updating data is to *change* data that is currently stored in a record. Changes to data stored on auxiliary storage take place for two primary reasons: (1) to correct data that is known to be incorrect, and (2) to update data when new data becomes available.

As an example of the first type of change, assume in Figure 7-9 that instead of entering HUGH DUNN as the name for the customer, the teller enters HUGH DONE. The error is not noticed and the customer leaves the bank. Later in the day, when the customer returns to question the transaction, the name stored in the file must be changed so that it contains the correct spelling. Therefore, the teller enters HUGH DUNN as a change to the name field in the record. This change is made to replace data known to be incorrect with data known to be correct.

The bank account example also illustrates the second reason for change—to update data when new data becomes available. This type of change is made when a customer deposits or withdraws money. In Figure 7-9, Jean Martino has withdrawn $500.00. The record for Jean Martino must be changed to reflect her withdrawal. The following steps occur:

1. The teller enters Jean Martino's account number 52-4417 and the amount 500.00.

FIGURE 7-9

When Jean Martino withdraws $500.00, the bank's records must be changed to reflect her new account balance. In this example, (1) the teller enters Jean Martino's account number and withdrawal amount, (2) the account number is used to retrieve Jean's account balance record, and (3) the account balance is reduced by the amount of the withdrawal ($500.00). (4) The record is then rewritten back onto the disk.

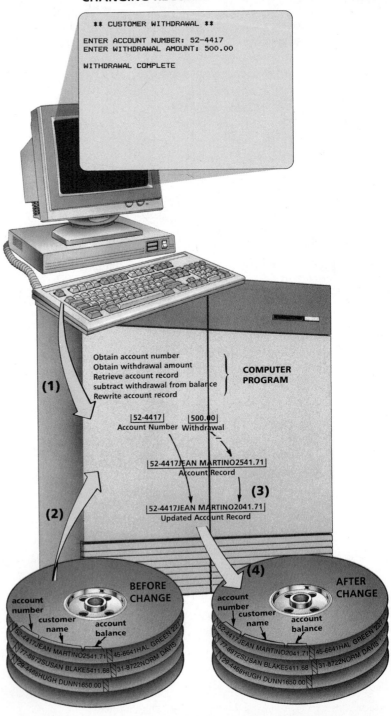

CHANGING RECORDS

```
** CUSTOMER WITHDRAWAL **

ENTER ACCOUNT NUMBER: 52-4417
ENTER WITHDRAWAL AMOUNT: 500.00

WITHDRAWAL COMPLETE
```

Obtain account number
Obtain withdrawal amount
Retrieve account record
subtract withdrawal from balance
Rewrite account record

COMPUTER PROGRAM

52-4417 500.00
Account Number Withdrawal

52-4417JEAN MARTINO2541.71
Account Record

52-4417JEAN MARTINO2041.71
Updated Account Record

BEFORE CHANGE

account number
customer name
account balance

52-4417JEAN MARTINO2541.71
77-8972SUSAN BLAKE5411.68
29-4468HUGH DUNN1650.00
45-6641HAL GREEN 227
31-8722NORM DAVIS

AFTER CHANGE

account number
customer name
account balance

52-4417JEAN MARTINO2041.71
77-8972SUSAN BLAKE5411.68
29-4468HUGH DUNN1650.00
45-6641HAL GREEN 227
31-8722NORM DAVIS

2. The update program retrieves the record for account number 52-4417 and stores the record in main memory.
3. The program subtracts the withdrawal amount from the account balance in the record. This changes the account balance to reflect the correct balance in the account.
4. After the balance has been changed in memory, the record is written back onto the disk. After the change, the account balance has been updated, and the record stored on auxiliary storage contains the correct account balance.

Changing data stored on auxiliary storage to reflect the correct and current data is an important part of the updating process that is required for data.

Deleting Records

The third major type of activity that must occur when updating data is to delete records stored in a file or database. Records are deleted when they are no longer needed as data. Figure 7-10 on the next page shows the updating procedures to *delete* a record for Hal Gruen who has closed his account. The following steps occur:

1. The teller enters Hal Gruen's account number (45-6641).
2. The update program retrieves the record from the disk using the account number as the key. The record is placed in main memory.
3. The actual processing that occurs to delete a record from a file depends on the type of file organization being used and the processing requirements of the application. Sometimes the record is removed from the file. Other times, as in this example, the record is not removed from the file. Instead, the record is *flagged*, or marked, in some manner so that it will not be processed again. In this example, the first three characters of the account number are changed from the actual number to the letters DEL (short for delete).
4. After the letters DEL are placed in the first three characters of the account number, the record is written back to the file. The application program will not process the record again because it begins with DEL instead of a valid account number. Even though the record is still physically stored on the disk, it is effectively deleted because it will not be retrieved for processing.

Deleting records from auxiliary storage is important because it provides a way of either removing or flagging records that are no longer needed for processing. This is necessary to keep data accurate.

Summary of How Data Is Maintained

Data maintenance is updating (adding, changing, and deleting) data stored on auxiliary storage. The maintenance of data is critical if information derived from the processing of that data is to be reliable. When updating data, it does not matter if the data is stored as a single file or if it is part of a series of files organized into a database. The concept of adding, changing, and deleting data to keep it current remains the same.

FIGURE 7-10

DELETING RECORDS

In this example, (1) the account number entered by the teller is used to (2) retrieve Hal Green's account record. (3) The account record is marked as deleted by placing the letters DEL in the first three positions of the account number. (4) The record is then rewritten back to the file. With DEL in the account number, the record will not be retrieved in the future by the application program.

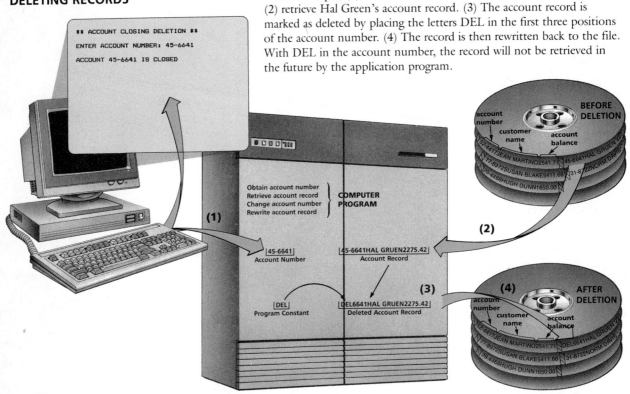

Databases: A Better Way to Manage Data and Information

As stated at the beginning of this chapter, more and more businesspeople realize that next to the skills of their employees, data (and the information it represents) is one of a company's most valuable assets. They recognize that the information accumulated on sales trends, competitors' products and services, employee skills, and production processes is a valuable resource that would be difficult if not impossible to replace.

Unfortunately, in many cases this resource is located in different files in different departments throughout the organization, often known only to the individuals who work with their specific portion of the total information. In these cases, the potential value of the information goes unrealized because it is not known to people in other departments who may need it or it cannot be accessed efficiently. In an attempt to organize their information resources and provide for timely and efficient access, many companies have implemented databases.

What Is a Database?

Previously in this chapter, we've discussed how data elements (characters, fields, and records) can be organized in files. In file-oriented systems, each file is independent. In a **database**, the data is organized in multiple related files. These related files are not independent of one another and it is possible for them to obtain data from one another. A **database management system (DBMS)** is the software that allows the user to create, maintain, and report the data and file relationships. Note that a **file management system**, sometimes mistakenly referred to as a database management system, is software that only allows the user to create, maintain, and access a single file at a time.

Why Use a Database?

The following example (Figure 7-11) illustrates some of the advantages of a database system as compared to a file-oriented system. Assume that a business periodically mails catalogs to its customers. If the business is using a file-oriented system, it would probably have a file used for the catalog mailing application that contains information about the catalog plus customer information, such as customer account number, name, and address. Files that are used in a file-oriented system are independent of one another. Therefore, other applications, such as the sales application, that also need to have customer information would each have files that contain the same customer information stored in the catalog mailing file. Thus in a file-oriented system, the customer data would be duplicated several times in different files. This duplication of data wastes auxiliary storage space. In addition, it makes maintaining the data difficult because when a customer record must be updated, all files containing that data must be individually updated.

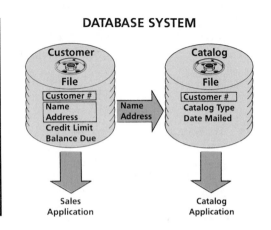

FIGURE 7-11

In a file-oriented system, each file contains the customer name and address. In the database system, only the customer file contains the name and address. Other files, such as the catalog file, use the customer number to retrieve the customer name and address when it is needed for processing.

In a database system, however, only one of the applications would have a file containing the customer name and address data. That is because in a database system, files are integrated; related files are linked together by the database software either through predefined relationships or through common data fields. In this example, the link is the customer account number. Since the sales file contains the customer account number, name, and address, the catalog mailing file need only contain the customer's account number plus the other catalog information. When the catalog application software is executed, the customer's name and address is obtained from the sales file. The advantage of the database is that because the files are integrated, the customer name and address need only be stored once. This saves auxiliary storage space. It also allows data to be maintained more easily because update information need only be entered once.

As the previous example illustrates, a database system offers a number of advantages over a file-oriented system. These advantages and several others are summarized in the following list:

1. **Reduced data redundancy.** Redundant or duplicate data is greatly reduced in a database system. Frequently used data elements such as names, addresses, and descriptions are stored in one location. Having such items in one instead of many locations lowers the cost of maintaining the data.
2. **Improved data integrity.** Closely related to reduced data redundancy is the database advantage of improved data integrity. Because data is only stored in one place, it is more likely to be accurate. When it is updated, all applications that use the data will be using the most current version.
3. **Integrated files.** As demonstrated by the catalog mailing example (Figure 7-11), a key advantage of a database management system is its ability to "integrate" or join together data from more than one file for inquiry or reporting purposes.
4. **Improved data security.** Most database management systems allow the user to establish different levels of security over information in the database. For example, a department manager may have "read only" privileges on certain payroll data: the manager could inquire about the data but not change it. The payroll supervisor would have "full update" privileges: the supervisor could not only inquire about the data but could also make changes. A nonmanagement employee would probably have no access privileges to the payroll data and could neither inquire about nor change the data.

Now that we've discussed some of their advantages, let's discuss the different types of databases.

Types of Database Organization

There are three major types of database organization: relational, hierarchical, and network. The relational database structure is the most recent of the three methods and is considered a trend for the future. The relational database structure takes advantage of large-capacity direct-access storage devices that were not available when the hierarchical and network methods were developed.

Relational Database

In a **relational database**, data is organized in tables that in database terminology are called **relations**. The tables are further divided into rows (called **tuples**) and fields (called **attributes**). The tables can be thought of as sequential files and the rows as records. The description or name of a particular attribute is called a **domain**. Figure 7-12 illustrates these terms with a student name and address file.

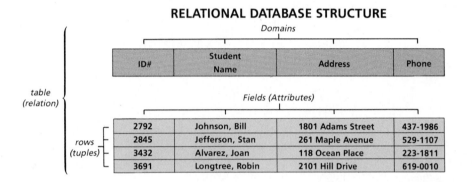

RELATIONAL DATABASE STRUCTURE

FIGURE 7-12

This example illustrates the terms used to identify the data in a relational database. A relational database is made up of multiple tables that can be thought of as files. In this example, other tables would probably exist for student grades, courses, faculty, and other logical groups of data.

As previously mentioned, a key advantage of a database is its ability to link multiple files together. A relational database accomplishes this by using a common field, sometimes called a **link**, that exists in each file. For example, in a database for a college, the link between files containing student information could be the student identification number. Hierarchical and network databases can also extract data from multiple files, but in these database structures, the data relationships that will enable the multiple file combination must be defined *when the database is created*. The advantage of a relational database is that the data relationships do not have to be predefined. The relational database only needs a common field in both data files to make a relationship between them. Because it is sometimes difficult to know ahead of time how data will be used, the flexibility provided by a relational database is an important advantage.

Another advantage of a relational database is its ability to add new fields. All that needs to be done is to define the fields in the appropriate table. With hierarchical and network database systems, the entire database has to be "redefined": existing relationships have to be reestablished to include the new fields.

Hierarchical Database

In a **hierarchical database** (Figure 7-13), data is organized in a series like a family tree or organization chart (the term hierarchy means an organized series). Like a family tree, the hierarchical database has branches made up of parent and child records. Each **parent record** can have multiple child records. However, each **child record** can only have one parent. The parent record at the top of the database is referred to as the **root** record.

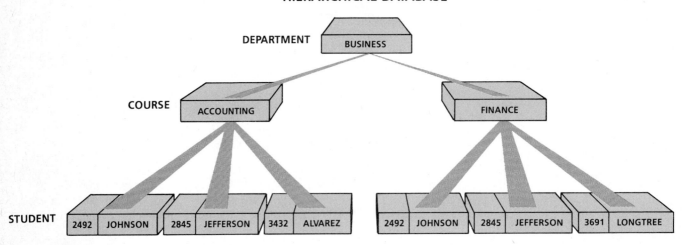

HIERARCHICAL DATABASE

Hierarchical databases are the oldest form of database organization and reflect the fact that they were developed when the disk and memory capacity of computers was limited and most processing was done in batch mode. Data access is sequential in the sense that an inquiry begins at the root record and proceeds down the branch until the requested data is found. All parent-child relationships must be established before the user can access the database. These relationships are defined by the person who is responsible for designing the database and are established when the database is created in a separate process that is sometimes called "generating the database."

After the database is created, access must be made through the established relationships. This points out two disadvantages of hierarchical databases. First, records located in separate branches of the database cannot be accessed easily at the same time. Second, adding new fields to database records or modifying existing fields, such as adding the four-digit zip code extension, requires the redefinition of the entire database. Depending on the size of the database, this redefinition process can take a considerable amount of time. The advantage of a hierarchical database is that because the data relationships are predefined, access to and updating of data is very fast.

FIGURE 7-13

In this hierarchical database, Johnson, Jefferson, and Longtree are the children of Finance and Finance is their parent. Finance and Accounting are the children of Business and Business is their parent. These relationships must be established before the database can be used.

Network Database

A **network database** (Figure 7-14) is similar to a hierarchical database except that each child record can have more than one parent. In network database terminology, a child record is referred to as a **member** and a parent record is referred to as an **owner**. Unlike the hierarchical database, the network database is able to establish relationships between different branches of the data and thus offers increased access capability for the user. However, like the hierarchical database, these data relationships must be established prior to the use of the database and must be redefined if fields are added or modified.

NETWORK DATABASE

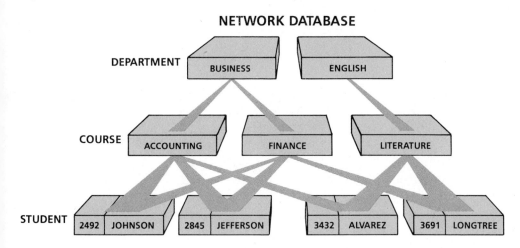

FIGURE 7-14

In a network database, lower level (member) records can be related to more than one higher level (owner) record. For example, Longtree's owners are Finance and Literature. Accounting has three members, Johnson, Jefferson, and Alvarez. As in a hierarchical database, these relationships must be established before the database can be used.

Database Management Systems

Database management systems, the software that manages the creation, maintenance, and reporting of data in a database, have a number of common features. These features include:

1. **Data dictionary.** The **data dictionary** defines each data field that is contained in the database files. The dictionary is used to record the field name, size, description, type of data (for example, text, numeric, or date), and relationship to other data elements.
2. **Utilities.** Database management system utility programs provide for a number of maintenance tasks including creating files and dictionaries, monitoring performance, copying data, and deleting unwanted records.
3. **Security.** Most database management systems allow the user to specify different levels of user access privileges. The privileges can be established for each user for each type of access (retrieve, update, and delete) to each data field. Note that without some type of access security, the data in a database is more subject to unauthorized access than in a decentralized system of individual files.

4. Query language. The query language is one of the most valuable features of a database management system. It allows the user to retrieve information from the database based on the criteria and in the format specified by the user.

Query Languages: Access to the Database

A **query language** is a simple English-like language that allows users to specify what data they want to see on a report or screen display. Although each query language has its own grammar, syntax, and vocabulary, these languages can generally be learned in a short time by persons without a programming background.

A Query Example

Figure 7-15 shows how a user might query a relational database. This example illustrates the relational operations that may be performed when a relational database inquiry is made. These three **relational operations** are select, project, and join. They allow the user to manipulate the data from one or more files to create a unique "view" or subset of the total data.

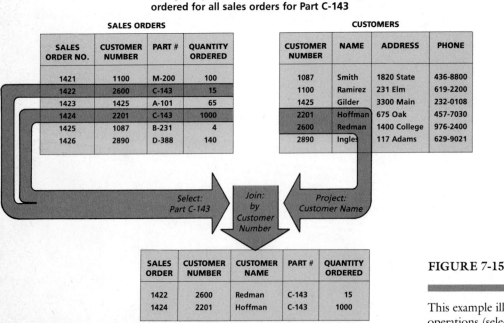

FIGURE 7-15

This example illustrates the three relational operations (select, project, and join) that are used to produce a response to the query.

The **select relational operation** selects certain records (rows or tuples) based on user-supplied criteria. In the example, the user queries the database to select records from the sales order file that contain part number C-143. Selection criteria can be applied to more than one field and can include tests to determine if a field is greater than, less than, equal to, or not equal to a value specified by the user. Connectors such as AND and OR can also be used.

The **project relational operation** specifies the fields (attributes) that appear on the query output. In the example, the user wants to see the names of the customers who placed orders for part number C-143.

The **join relational operation** is used to combine two files (relations or tables). In the example, the link used to join the two files is the customer number, a field contained in each file.

After the query is executed, most query languages allow the user to give the query a unique name and save it for future use.

Structured Query Language: An Emerging Standard

One of the most widely used query languages is **Structured Query Language**, often referred to as **SQL**. Originally developed during the 1970s by IBM, SQL has been incorporated into a number of relational database software packages including ORACLE by Oracle Corporation and INGRES by Relational Technology. IBM actively supports SQL and incorporates it into their two major relational database system products, SQL/DS and DB2. SQL received increased support as the emerging relational database management system query language when, in 1985, the American National Standards Institute formed a committee to develop industry standards for SQL. The standards were issued in 1987. Today, it is difficult to pick up a computer industry publication and not read about at least one database software vendor announcing plans to incorporate SQL into its product. The standardization of SQL will further accelerate its implementation on a wide range of computer systems from micros to supercomputers. This fact, coupled with the increasing dominance of relational databases, will mean that SQL will be used by many computer users.

Database Administration

The centralization of an organization's data into a database requires a great deal of cooperation and coordination on the part of the database users. In file-oriented systems, if a user wanted to keep track of some data he or she would just create another file, often duplicating some data that was already being tracked by someone else. In a database system, the user must first check to see if some or all of the data is already on file and if not, how it can be added to the system. The role of coordinating the use of the database belongs to the database administrator.

The Database Administrator

The **database administrator**, or **DBA**, is the person responsible for coordinating all database activities (Figure 7-16). In small organizations, this person usually has other responsibilities such as the overall management of the computer resources. In medium and large organizations, the role of DBA is a full-time job for one or more people. The job of DBA usually includes the following responsibilities:

1. **Database design.** The DBA determines the initial design of the database and specifies where to add additional data files and records when they are needed.

2. **User coordination.** The DBA is responsible for letting users know what data is available in the database and how the users can retrieve it. The DBA also reviews user requests for additions to the database and helps establish priorities for their implementation.

3. **Backup and recovery.** The centralization of data in a database makes an organization particularly vulnerable to a computer system failure. It is often the responsibility of the DBA to minimize this risk, making sure that all data is regularly backed up and that contingency plans are prepared (and periodically tested) for a prolonged equipment or software malfunction.

4. **System security.** It is the DBA's responsibility to establish and monitor system access privileges to prevent the unauthorized use of an organization's data.

5. **Performance monitoring.** The performance of the database, usually measured in terms of response time to a user request, can be affected by a number of factors such as file sizes and the types and frequency of inquiries during the day. Most database management systems have utility programs that enable the DBA to monitor these factors and make adjustments to provide for more efficient database use.

In addition to the DBA, the user also has a role in a database management system.

FIGURE 7-16

The database administrator plays a key role in the managing of a company's data. The DBA should possess good technical as well as good management skills.

The Responsibility of the User in a Database Management System

One of the user's first responsibilities is to become familiar with the data in the existing database. First-time database users are often amazed at the wealth of information available to help them perform their jobs more effectively.

Another responsibility of the user, in organizations of any size, is to play an active part in the specification of additions to the database. The maintenance of an organization's database is an ongoing task that must be constantly measured against the overall goals of the organization. Therefore users must participate in designing the database that will be used to help them achieve those goals and measure their progress.

Managing Data on a Personal Computer

A variety of data management systems are available for personal computers, ranging from simple file management programs to full relational database management systems. As with large system packages, many personal computer software vendors are developing or modifying existing packages to support Structured Query Language (SQL). The advantage of SQL packages for personal computers is that they can directly query mainframe databases that support SQL.

The increased computing power of the latest personal computers has also allowed database management packages originally written for mainframe computers to be modified to run on the smaller systems. ORACLE (Oracle Corporation) and INGRES (Relational Technology) are two SQL-based packages that have been adapted to personal computers.

Perhaps the best known and most widely used personal computer-based database management system is the dBASE series from Ashton-Tate Corporation. dBASE III PLUS offers a relational database manager, a programming language, and application development tools. dBASE IV includes a complete implementation of SQL.

With so many data management packages available, it's difficult to decide which one to choose. For those with simple needs, a file management package is probably all that is necessary. For larger databases with multiple files, one of the more popular database management systems will offer increased capability and growth potential. For complex database requirements, the packages originally developed on mainframes should provide all the database resources required. If you need to select a database software package for your personal computer, you may want to refer to the section in Chapter 2 that discusses how to choose software packages for a personal computer.

Chapter Summary

Databases provide a better way of organizing data by relating items in multiple files. With databases, redundant data is minimized and data integrity improved. Database query languages allow data to be retrieved according to the criteria and in the format specified by the user.

Understanding the database and file concepts that have been presented in this chapter will help you to have a better understanding of how data and information are organized and managed on the auxiliary storage of a computer. Whether you are a home computer user who wants to store personal data on diskettes or a hard drive, or a mainframe user accessing the database of the company where you are employed, a fundamental knowledge of how data is organized and managed will be useful to you.

The following list summarizes the key topics discussed in this chapter.

1. A file is a collection of related records that is usually stored on an auxiliary storage device. The three types of file organization are sequential, indexed, and direct or relative (p. 7.2).
2. When **sequential file organization** is used, records are stored one after the other, normally in ascending or descending order by the value in the **key** field (p. 7.2).
3. **Sequential retrieval** means that the records on a tape or disk file are retrieved (accessed) one after another in the same order that the records are stored on the tape or disk (p. 7.3).
4. With **indexed file organization**, the records are stored on the disk in an indexed file in ascending or descending sequence based on a key field. An index is used to retrieve records (p. 7.3).

5. An **index** consists of entries containing the key to the records and the disk addresses of the records (p. 7.3).

6. **Random retrieval**, or random access, allows the records in a disk file to be accessed in any order based on the value in a key field or on the location of a record in a file. Random retrieval is used when fast access to a record is required (p. 7.3).

7. Random access and sequential access can be used with indexed files (p. 7.4).

8. A **direct file** or **relative file** contains records that are stored and retrieved according to their disk address or their physical location within the file (p. 7.5).

9. The locations on a disk where records in a direct file can be stored are called **buckets** (p. 7.5).

10. **Hashing** means using a formula or performing a calculation in a program to determine the location (position) where a record will be placed on a disk (p. 7.5).

11. Data maintenance refers to the process of **updating** files and databases by adding, changing, or deleting data from a file (p. 7.6).

12. A **database** uses multiple related files to organize data (p. 7.11).

13. A **database management system (DBMS)** is the software that allows the user to create, maintain, and generate reports using the data and file relationships in a database (p. 7.11).

14. By contrast, a **file management system** allows a user to access only one file at a time (p. 7.11).

15. **Reduced data redundancy** (data that is duplicated in several different files), **improved data integrity** (data accuracy), **integrated files** (joining data from more than one file), and **improved data security** (ensuring that the data is accessible only to those with the proper authorization) are the major advantages of using a database (p. 7.12).

16. A **relational database** is organized into tables called **relations**. The relations are divided into **tuples** (rows) and **attributes** (fields). Each attribute is given a unique name, called the **domain** (p. 7.13).

17. In a relational database, a common attribute or **link** is used to connect multiple files (p. 7.13).

18. The advantage of a relational database is that the data relationships do not need to be predefined (p. 7.13).

19. A **hierarchical database** is organized in a top to bottom series of parent-child relationships. Each **parent record** can have multiple child records. However, each **child record** can have only one parent. The parent record at the top of the hierarchy is called the **root** record (p. 7.14).

20. A **network database** is organized similar to a hierarchical database except each child record (called a **member**) may have more than one parent record (called an **owner**) (p. 7.15).

21. Data relationships in both the hierarchical database and the network database must be established prior to the use of the database (p. 7.15).

22. The database management system consists of a **data dictionary** that defines each data field to be used in the database; utility programs (usually referred to as utilities) that provide a number of special functions (such as copying data, creating files, and deleting records); security levels that control access to the data; and a **query language** that allows users to specify what data they wish to view (p. 7.15).

23. The **relational operations** of a relational database include the select relational operation, the project relational operation, and the join relational operation (p. 7.16).

24. The **select relational operation** selects specific records based on the specifications provided by the user (p. 7.17).

25. The **project relational operation** specifies the fields to be displayed (p. 7.17).

26. The **join relational operation** is used to combine two files (p. 7.17).

27. A widely used query language is **Structured Query Language (SQL)** (p. 7.17).

28. The **database administrator (DBA)** is the person who coordinates all use of the database (p. 7.17).

29. The database administrator is responsible for database design, user coordination, backup and recovery, system security, and database performance monitoring (p. 7.18).

30. Users should become familiar with the data in their organization's database and should actively participate in the specification of additions to the database that will affect their jobs (p. 7.18).

Review Questions

1. Describe sequential file organization. How are records in sequential files retrieved?
2. What is an indexed file? Describe how the index is used to retrieve records from an indexed file.
3. How is the location where a record is stored in a direct file determined?
4. List the three data maintenance procedures that are used to update files. Give an example of each.
5. Write a definition for the term database.
6. What is the difference between a database management system and a file management system?
7. What are the advantages of a database management system over a file-oriented system?
8. In a relational database, how are different files related to one another?
9. What is the difference between the structures of a hierarchical and a network database?
10. How is a data dictionary used?
11. Why is access security important in a database system?
12. How is a database query used?
13. What are the responsibilities of a database administrator?
14. What are the responsibilities of the user in a database management system?

Data
Communications   8

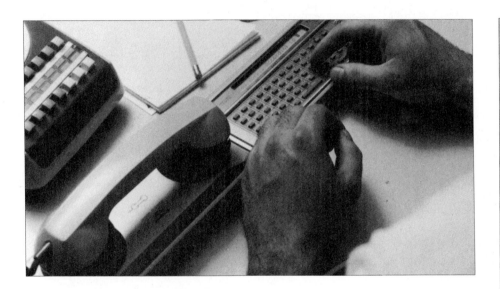

Objectives

- Define data communications.
- Describe the basic components of a data communications system.
- Describe the various transmission media that are used for communication channels.
- Describe the different types of line configurations.
- Describe how data is transmitted.
- Identify and explain the communications equipment that can be used in a data communications system.
- Describe the functions that communications software can perform.
- Explain the two major categories of networks and describe the common network configurations.
- Discuss how personal computers can use data communications.

Computers are well recognized as important computing devices. They should also be recognized as important communication devices. It is now possible for a computer to communicate with other computers anywhere in the world. This capability allows users to quickly and directly access data and information that otherwise would have been unavailable or that probably would have taken considerable time to acquire. Banks, retail stores, airlines, hotels, and many others businesses use computers for communication purposes. Personal computer users communicate with other personal computer users and also access special databases available on larger machines to quickly and conveniently obtain information such as weather reports, stock market data, airline schedules, news stories, or even theater and movie reviews.

This chapter provides an overview of data communications and explains some of the terminology, equipment, procedures, and applications that relate to computers and their use as communication devices.

What Is Data Communications?

Data communications is the transmission of data over a communication channel, such as a standard telephone line, between one computer (or a terminal) and another computer.

Figure 8-1 shows the basic components of a data communications system. These components include:

1. A computer or a terminal.
2. Data communications equipment that sends (and can usually receive) data.
3. The communication channel over which the data is sent.
4. Data communications equipment that receives (and can usually send) data.
5. Another computer.

As you will see, the basic model of a data communications system illustrated in Figure 8-1 can be applied to virtually all data communications systems.

FIGURE 8-1

A basic model of a data communications system.

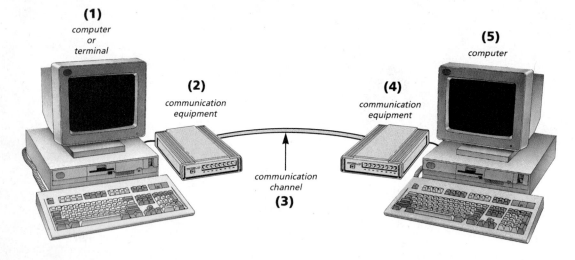

(1)
*computer
or
terminal*

(2)
*communication
equipment*

(4)
*communication
equipment*

(5)
computer

*communication
channel*
(3)

Communication Channels

A **communication channel** is the link or path that the data follows as it is transmitted from the sending equipment to the receiving equipment in a data communications system. These channels are made up of one or more **transmission media**, including twisted pair wire, coaxial cable, fiber optics, microwaves, and communication satellites.

Twisted Pair Wire

Twisted pair wire (Figure 8-2) consists of pairs of copper wires that are twisted together. To insulate and identify the wires, each wire is covered with a thin layer of colored plastic. Twisted pair wire is commonly used for telephone lines. It is an inexpensive transmission medium, and it can be easily strung from one location to another. The disadvantage of twisted pair wire is that it is susceptible to outside electrical interference generated by fans or air conditioners. This interference can garble the data as it is sent over the line, causing transmission errors to occur.

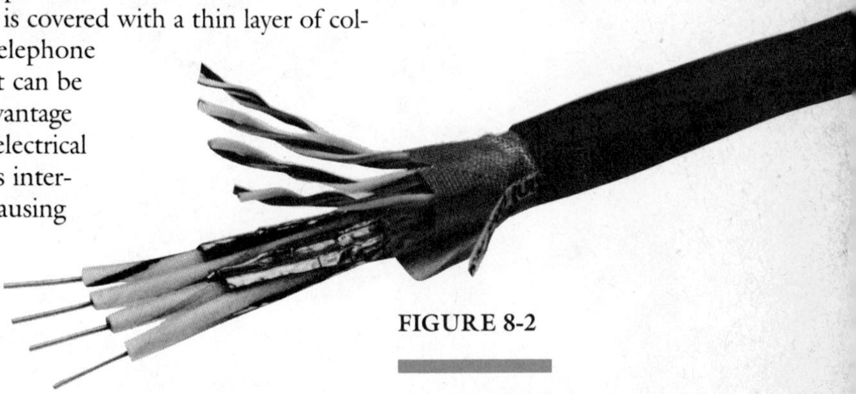

Coaxial Cable

A **coaxial cable** is a high-quality communication line that is used in offices, laid under the ground and under the ocean. Coaxial cable consists of a wire or central conductor surrounded by a nonconducting insulator that is in turn surrounded by a woven metal shielding layer, and finally a plastic outer coating (Figure 8-3). Because of its more heavily insulated construction, coaxial cable is not susceptible to electrical interference and can transmit data at higher data rates over longer distances than twisted pair telephone wire.

There are two types of coaxial cable, named for the transmission techniques they support: baseband and broadband. **Baseband** coaxial cable carries one signal at a time. The signal, however, can travel very fast—in the area of ten million bits per second for the first 1,000 feet. The speed drops off significantly as the length of cable increases and special equipment is needed to amplify (boost) the signal if it is transmitted more than approximately one mile.

Broadband coaxial cable can carry multiple signals at one time. It is similar to cable TV where a single cable offers a number of channels to the user. A particular advantage of broadband channels is that data, audio, and video transmission can take place over the same line.

Fiber Optics

Fiber optics (Figure 8-4 on the next page) is a technology that may eventually replace conventional wire and cable in communication systems. This technology is based on the ability of smooth hair-thin strands of material to conduct light with high efficiency. The major advantages of fiber optics over wire cables include substantial weight and size savings and increased speed of transmission. A single fiber-optic cable can carry several hundred thousand voice communications simultaneously. Fiber optics is frequently being used in new installations and promises to dramatically increase data communication capabilities.

FIGURE 8-2

Twisted pair wire is most commonly used as telephone wire. It is inexpensive but susceptible to electrical interference that can cause errors in data transmission.

FIGURE 8-3

This photograph shows several types of coaxial cable that can be used to transmit data.

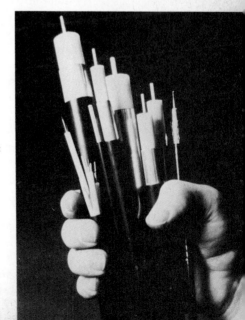

FIGURE 8-4

The two-strand fiber-optic cable can transmit as much information as the 1500-pair copper cable.

Microwaves

Microwaves are a type of radio waves that can be used to provide high-speed transmission of both voice and data. Data is transmitted through the air from one microwave station to another in a manner similar to the way radio signals are transmitted. A disadvantage of microwaves is that they are limited to line-of-sight transmission. This means that microwaves must be transmitted in a straight line and that there can be no obstructions, such as buildings or mountains, between microwave stations. For this reason, microwave stations are characterized by antennas positioned on tops of buildings, towers, or mountains (Figure 8-5). Because of the curvature of the earth, the maximum distance between microwave stations is about 30 miles.

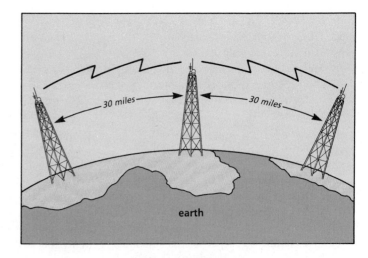

FIGURE 8-5

Data is transmitted through the air from one microwave station to another. Because of the curvature of the earth, such antennas cannot transmit farther than about 30 miles.

Communication Satellites

Communication satellites have the ability to receive signals from earth, amplify the signals, and retransmit the signals back to the earth. **Earth stations** (Figure 8-6) are communication facilities that use large dish-shaped antennas to transmit and receive data from satellites. The transmission to the satellite is called an **uplink** and the transmission from the satellite to a receiving earth station is called a **downlink**. Communication satellites are normally placed about 22,000 miles above the earth in a geosynchronous orbit. This means that the satellite rotates with the earth, so that the same dish antennas on earth that are used to send and receive signals can remain fixed on the satellite at all times.

An Example of a Communication Channel

When data is transmitted over long distances, it is likely that a number of different types of transmission media will be used to make a complete communication channel. The diagram in Figure 8-7 illustrates some of the various transmission media that could be used to transmit data from a personal computer on the west coast of the United States to a large computer on the east coast. The steps that could occur are:

1. An entry is made on the personal computer. The data is sent over telephone lines from the computer to a microwave station.
2. The data is then transmitted between microwave stations that are usually located no more than 30 miles apart.
3. The data is transmitted from the last microwave station to an earth station.
4. The earth station transmits the data to the communications satellite.
5. The satellite relays the data to another earth station on the other side of the country.
6. The data received at the earth station is transmitted to microwave stations.
7. The data is sent by the telephone lines to the large computer.
8. The computer processes the data.

FIGURE 8-6

Earth stations use large dish antennas to communicate with satellites and microwave antennas.

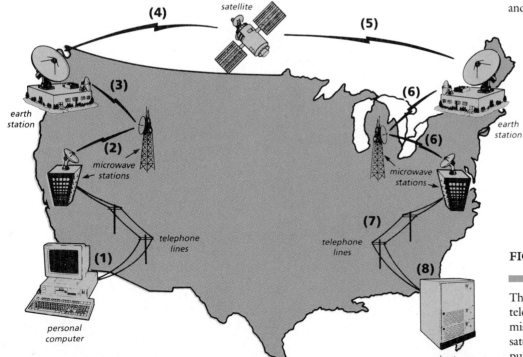

FIGURE 8-7

This diagram illustrates the use of telephone wires, microwave transmission, and a communication satellite to allow a personal computer to communicate with a large host computer.

The entire transmission process just described would take less than one second.

Not all data transmission is as complex as this example, but such sophisticated communication systems do exist to satisfy the needs of some users.

Line Configurations

There are two major **line configurations** (types of line connections) that are commonly used in data communications: point-to-point lines and multidrop or multipoint lines.

Point-to-Point Lines

A **point-to-point line** is a direct line between a sending and a receiving device. It may be one of two types: a switched line or a dedicated line (Figure 8-8).

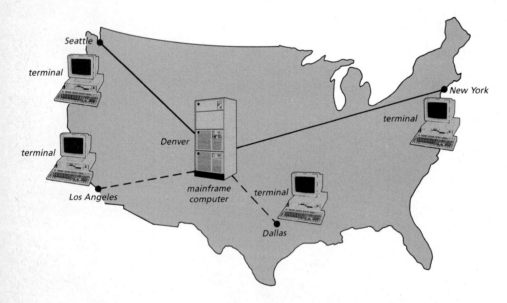

FIGURE 8-8

This diagram illustrates a point-to-point line configuration using both switched phone (dial up) lines (- - - -) and dedicated leased lines (_____) connected to a main computer in Denver. The leased lines are always connected whereas the switched lines have to be connected each time they are used.

Switched Line A **switched line** uses a regular telephone line to establish a communication connection. Each time a connection is made, the line to be used for the call is selected by the telephone company switching stations (hence the name switched line). Using a switched line is the same as one person using a phone to call another person. The communication equipment at the sending end dials the phone number of the communication equipment at the other end. When the communication equipment at the receiving end answers the call, a connection is established and data can be transmitted.

Dedicated Line A **dedicated line** is a line connection that is always established (unlike the switched line where the line connection is reestablished each time it is used). The communication device at one end is always connected to the device at the other end. A user can create a dedicated line connection by running a wire or cable between two points, such as between two offices or buildings, or the dedicated line can be provided by an outside organization such as the phone company or some other communication service company. If the dedicated line is provided by an outside organization, it is sometimes called a **leased line** or a **private line**. Because a dedicated line is always established, the quality and consistency of the connection is better than on a switched line.

Multidrop Lines

The second major line configuration is called a **multidrop line** or **multipoint line**. This type of line configuration is commonly used to connect multiple devices, such as terminals or personal computers, on a single line to a main computer, sometimes called a **host computer** (Figure 8-9). For example, a ticket agent in San Diego could use a terminal to enter an inquiry requesting flight information from a database stored on a main computer in Denver. While the request is being transmitted to the main computer, other terminals on the same line are not able to transmit data. The time required for the data to be transmitted to the main computer, however, is short—most likely less than one second. As soon as the inquiry is received by the computer, a second terminal can send an inquiry. With such short delays, it appears to the users that no other terminals are using the line, even though multiple terminals may be sharing the same line.

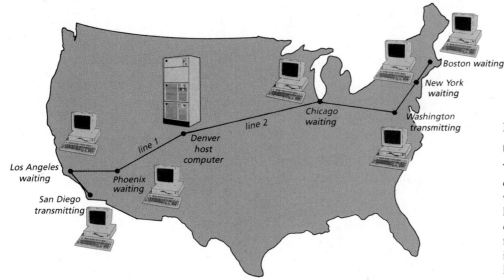

FIGURE 8-9

This diagram illustrates two multidrop lines connecting several cities with a computer in Denver. Each line is shared by terminals at several locations. Multidrop line configurations are less expensive than individual lines to each remote location.

Characteristics of Communication Channels

The communication channels we have discussed can be categorized by a number of characteristics, including the type of signal, transmission mode, transmission direction, and transmission rate.

Types of Signals: Digital and Analog

Computer equipment is designed to process data as **digital signals**, individual electrical pulses that can represent the bits that are grouped together to form characters. However, telephone equipment was originally designed to carry only voice transmission, which is comprised of a continuous electrical wave called an **analog signal** (Figure 8-10). Therefore, in order to use voice phone lines to carry data, a special piece of equipment called a **modem** is used to convert the digital signals into analog signals. We discuss modems in more detail later in this chapter.

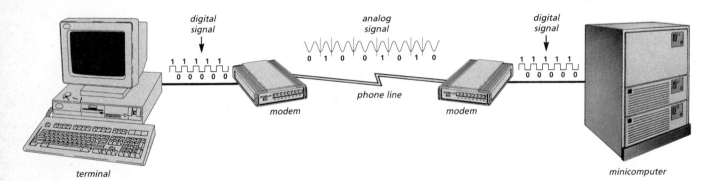

FIGURE 8-10

Individual electrical pulses of the digital signal are converted into analog (electrical wave) signals for transmission over voice phone lines. At the main computer receiving end, another modem converts the analog signals back into digital signals that can be processed by the computer.

Transmission Modes: Asynchronous and Synchronous

In **asynchronous transmission mode** (Figure 8-11), individual characters (made up of bits) are transmitted at irregular intervals, for example, as they are entered by a user. To distinguish where one character stops and another starts, the asynchronous communication mode uses a start and a stop bit. An additional bit called a **parity bit** is sometimes included at the end of each character to provide a way of checking against data loss. The parity bit is turned on or off depending on the error detection method being used. As you recall from the discussion on memory in Chapter 4, parity bits are used to detect if one of the data bits has been changed during transmission. The asynchronous transmission mode is used for lower speed data transmission and is used with most communication equipment designed for personal computers.

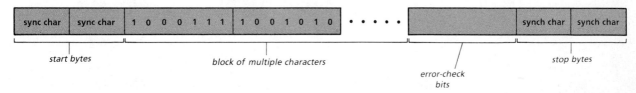

Asynchronous Transmission Mode

Synchronous Transmission Mode

FIGURE 8-11

In the **synchronous transmission mode** (also shown in Figure 8-11), large blocks of data are transmitted at regular intervals. Timing signals synchronize the communication equipment at both the sending and receiving ends and eliminate the need for start and stop bits for each character. Error-checking bits and start and end indicators called sync bytes are also transmitted. Synchronous transmission requires more sophisticated and expensive equipment but does give much higher speeds and accuracy than asynchronous transmission.

In asynchronous transmission mode, individual characters are transmitted. In synchronous transmission mode, multiple characters are sent in a block. Synchronous transmission is faster and more accurate.

Direction of Transmission: Simplex, Half-Duplex, and Full-Duplex

The direction of data transmission is classified as either simplex, half-duplex, or full-duplex. In **simplex transmission**, data flows in only one direction. Simplex is used only when the sending device, such as a temperature sensor, never requires a response from the computer. For example, if a computer is used to control the temperature of a building, numerous sensors are placed throughout it. Each sensor is connected to the computer with a simplex transmission line because the computer only needs to receive data from the temperature sensors and does not need to send data back to the sensors.

In **half-duplex transmission**, data can flow in both directions but in only one direction at a time. An example is a citizens band radio. The user can talk or listen but not do both at the same time. Half-duplex is often used between terminals and a central computer.

In **full-duplex transmission**, data can be sent in both directions at the same time. A normal phone line is an example of full-duplex transmission. Both parties can talk at the same time. Full-duplex transmission is used for most interactive computer applications and for computer-to-computer data transmission.

Transmission Rate

The transmission rate of a communication channel is determined by its bandwidth and its speed. The **bandwidth** is the range of frequencies that a channel can carry. Since transmitted data can be assigned to different frequencies, the wider the bandwidth, the more frequencies, and the more data that can be transmitted at the same time. Figure 8-12 summarizes the bandwidths of the communication channels we have discussed.

The speed at which data is transmitted is usually expressed as bits per second or as a baud rate.

COMMUNICATION CHANNEL	BANDWIDTH	RELATIVE CARRYING CAPACITY
Twisted pair	10–100,000 hertz	1
Coaxial cable	1–1,000 megahertz	1,000
Microwave	1–10 gigahertz	10,000
Satellite	2–40 gigahertz	40,000
Fiber optics	100–1,000 terahertz	1,000,000,000

FIGURE 8-12

Bandwidth and relative carrying capacity of communication channels. Bandwidth is measured in hertz or cycles per second. A megahertz is one million cycles per second; a gigahertz is one billion cycles per second; and a terahertz is one trillion cycles per second.

Bits per second (bps) is the number of bits that can be transmitted in one second. Using a 10-bit byte to represent a character (7 data bits, 1 start, 1 stop, and 1 parity bit), a 2,400 bps transmission can transmit 240 characters per second. At this rate, a 20-page single-spaced report can be transmitted in approximately five minutes.

The **baud rate** is the number of times per second that the signal being transmitted changes. With each change, one or more bits can be transmitted. At speeds up to 2,400 bps, usually only one bit is transmitted per signal change and thus the bits per second and the baud rate are the same. To achieve speeds in excess of 2,400 bps, more than one bit is transmitted with each signal change and thus the bps will exceed the baud rate.

Communications Equipment

If a terminal or a personal computer is within approximately 1,000 feet of another computer, the two devices can usually be directly connected by a cable. Over 1,000 feet, however, the electrical signal weakens to the point that some type of special communications equipment is required to increase or change the signal to transmit it farther. A variety of complex communications equipment exists to perform this task, but the equipment that a user is most likely to encounter is a modem, a multiplexor, and a front-end processor.

Modems

A **modem** converts the digital signals of a terminal or computer to analog signals that can be transmitted over phone equipment. The word modem comes from a combination of the words *mo*dulate, which means to change into a sound or analog signal, and *dem*odulate, which means to convert an analog signal into a digital signal. A modem must be present at both the sending and receiving ends of a communication channel.

An **external modem** (Figure 8-13) is a separate or stand-alone device that is attached to the computer or terminal by a cable and to the phone outlet by a standard phone cord. An advantage of an external modem is that it may be moved from one terminal or computer to another.

FIGURE 8-13

An external modem is connected to a terminal or computer and to a phone outlet.

An **internal modem** (Figure 8-14) is a circuit board that is installed inside a computer or terminal. Internal modems are generally less expensive and take up no desk space. However, they are not as easy to move from one terminal or computer to another.

An **acoustic modem**, also called an **acoustic coupler**, is designed to be used with a phone handset (Figure 8-15). The acoustic coupler converts the digital signals generated by the terminal or personal computer into a series of audible tones, which are picked up by the mouthpiece in the headset in the same manner that a telephone picks up a person's voice. The analog signals are then transmitted over the communication channel.

FIGURE 8-15

The acoustic coupler in the lower left corner of this picture allows a portable computer user to communicate with another computer over telephone lines. Note that the telephone handset is placed in the molded rubber cups on the acoustic coupler.

FIGURE 8-14

An internal modem is mounted inside a personal computer.

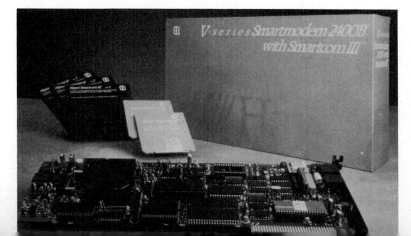

An acoustic coupler provides portability but is generally less reliable than an internal or external modem, because small outside sounds can be picked up by the acoustic coupler and cause transmission errors. Acoustic couplers are not common and are primarily used for special applications, such as with portable computers.

Modems can transmit data at rates from 300 to 38,400 bits per second (bps). Most personal computers would use either a 1,200 or 2,400 bps modem. Business or heavier volume users would use faster and more expensive modems.

Multiplexors

A **multiplexor** combines more than one input signal into a single stream of data that can be transmitted over a communication channel (Figure 8-16). The multiplexor at the sending end codes each character it receives with an identifier that is used by the multiplexor at the receiving end to separate the combined data stream into its original parts. A multiplexor may be connected to a separate modem or may have a modem built in. By combining the individual data streams into one, a multiplexor increases the efficiency of communications and saves the cost of individual communication channels.

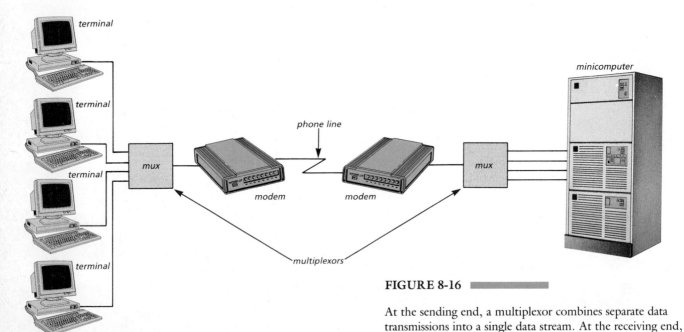

FIGURE 8-16

At the sending end, a multiplexor combines separate data transmissions into a single data stream. At the receiving end, the multiplexor separates the single stream into its original parts.

Front-End Processors

A **front-end processor** is a computer that is dedicated to handling the data communications requirements of a larger computer. Relieved of these tasks, the activity of the large computer is dedicated to processing data, while the front-end processor communicates the data. Tasks that the front-end processor would handle include **polling** (checking the connected terminals or computers to see if they have data to send), error checking and correction, and access security to make sure that a connected device or the user of the connected device is authorized to access the computer.

Communications Software

Sometimes communications equipment is preprogrammed to accomplish its designed communication tasks. In other cases, the user must load a program before beginning data transmission. These programs, referred to as **communications software**, can perform a number of tasks including dialing (if a switched phone line is used), terminal emulation, and data encryption.

Dialing software allows the user to store, review, select, and dial phone numbers of computers that can be called. The software provides a variety of meaningful messages to assist the user in establishing a connection before transmitting data.

Terminal emulation software allows a personal computer to imitate or appear to be a specific type of terminal so that the personal computer can connect to another computer. Most mini and mainframe computers are designed to work with a limited number of terminals that have specific characteristics such as speed and parity. Terminal emulation software performs the necessary speed and parity conversion.

Data encryption is used to protect confidential data during transmission. **Data encryption** is the conversion of data at the sending end into an unrecognizable string of characters or bits and the reconversion of the data at the receiving end. Without knowing how the data was encrypted, someone who intercepted the transmitted data would have a difficult time interpreting the data.

Communication Networks

A communication **network** is a collection of terminals, computers, and other equipment that use communication channels to share data. Networks can be classified as either local area networks or wide area networks.

Local Area Networks (LANs)

A **local area network** or **LAN** is a communications network that is privately owned and that covers a limited geographic area, such as an office, a building, or a group of buildings.

The LAN consists of a communication channel that connects either a series of computer terminals together with a minicomputer or, more commonly, a group of personal computers to one another. Very sophisticated LANs may connect a variety of office devices, such as word processing equipment, computer terminals, video equipment, and personal computers.

Three common applications of local area networks are hardware resource sharing, information resource sharing, and software resource sharing. **Hardware resource sharing** allows each personal computer in the network to access and use devices that would be too expensive to provide for each user or would not be justified for each user because of only occasional use. For example, when a number of personal computers are used on the network, each may need to use a laser printer. Using a LAN, a laser printer could be purchased and made a part of the network. Whenever a user of a personal computer on the network needs the laser printer, it can access it over the network.

The drawing in Figure 8-17 depicts a simple local area network consisting of four personal computers linked together by a cable. Computer 4 is used as a **network control unit**, sometimes called a **server**, which is dedicated to handling the communication needs of the other computers in the network.

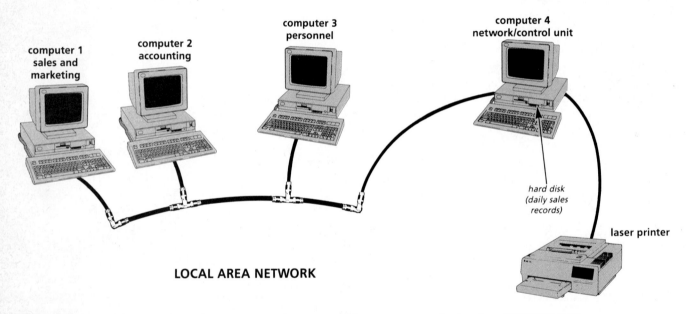

LOCAL AREA NETWORK

FIGURE 8-17

A local area network (LAN) consists of multiple personal computers or terminals connected to one another. The LAN allows users to share hardware and information.

Information resource sharing allows anyone using a personal computer on the local area network to access data stored on any other computer in the network. In actual practice, hardware resource sharing and information resource sharing are often combined. For example, in Figure 8-17, the daily sales records could be stored on the hard disk associated with the control unit personal computer. Anyone needing access to the sales records could use this information resource. The ability to access and store data on common auxiliary storage is an important feature of many local area networks.

Software resource sharing is another advantage available with a local area network. For example, if all users need access to word processing software, the software can be stored on the hard disk and accessed by all users as needed. This is much more convenient and faster than having the software stored on a diskette and available at each computer. For software written in-house, this is a common approach. Note, however, that the licensing agreement from many software companies does not permit the purchase of a single software package for use by all the computers in a network; therefore, it may be necessary to obtain a special agreement, called a **site license**, if a commercial software package is to be stored on hard disk and accessed by many users. Many software vendors now sell a network version of their packages.

Wide Area Networks (WANs)

A **wide area network** or **WAN** is one that is geographic in scope (as opposed to local) and uses phone lines, microwaves, satellites, or a combination of communication channels. Public wide area network companies include so-called "common carriers" such as the telephone companies. In recent years, telephone company deregulation has encouraged a number of companies to build their own wide area networks and others, such as MCI, to build WANs to compete with the telephone companies. Some common carriers are now offering **Integrated Services Digital Network (ISDN)** services. ISDN establishes an international standard for the digital transmission of data using different channels and communication companies.

Network Configurations

Communication networks are usually configured or arranged in one or a combination of three patterns, sometimes called a **topology**. These configurations are star, bus, and ring networks. Although these configurations can also be used with wide area networks, we illustrate them with local area networks.

Star Network

A **star network** (Figure 8-18) contains a central computer and one or more terminals or personal computers connected to it, forming a star. A pure star network consists of only point-to-point lines between the terminals and the computer, but most star networks, such as the one shown in Figure 8-18, include both point-to-point lines and multidrop lines. A star network configuration is often used when the central computer contains all the data required to process the input from the terminals, such as an airline reservation system. For example, if inquiries are being processed in the star network, all the data to answer the inquiry would be contained in the database stored on the central computer.

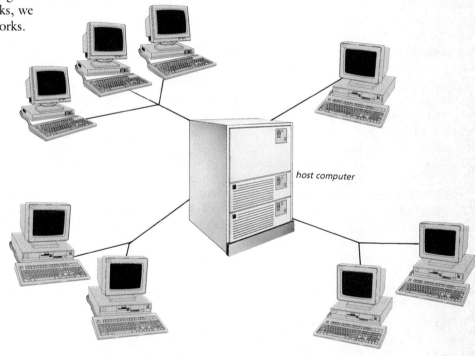

host computer

FIGURE 8-18

A star network contains a single, centralized host computer with which all the terminals or personal computers in the network communicate. Both point-to-point and multidrop lines can be used in a star network.

A star network can be relatively efficient and close control can be kept over the data processed on the network. Its major disadvantage is that the entire network is dependent on the central computer and the associated hardware and software. If any of these elements fail, the entire network is disabled. Therefore, in most large star networks, backup systems are available in case the primary system fails.

Bus Network

When a **bus network** is used, all devices in the network are connected to and share a single cable. Information is transmitted in either direction from any one personal computer to another. Any message can be directed to a specific device. An advantage of the bus network is that devices can be attached or detached from the network at any point without disturbing the rest of the network. In addition, if one computer on the network fails, this does not affect the other users of the network. Figure 8-17 illustrates a simple bus network.

Ring Network

A **ring network** does not utilize a centralized host computer. Rather, a series of computers communicate with one another (Figure 8-19). A ring network can be useful when all the processing is not done at a central site, but at local sites. For example, computers could be located in three departments: the accounting department, the personnel department, and the shipping and receiving department. The computers in each of these departments could perform the processing required for each of the departments. On occasion, however, the computer in the shipping and receiving department could communicate with the computer in the accounting department to update certain data stored on the accounting department computer. Ring networks have not been extensively implemented for data communications systems that are used for long-distance communication; they are used more for local communications.

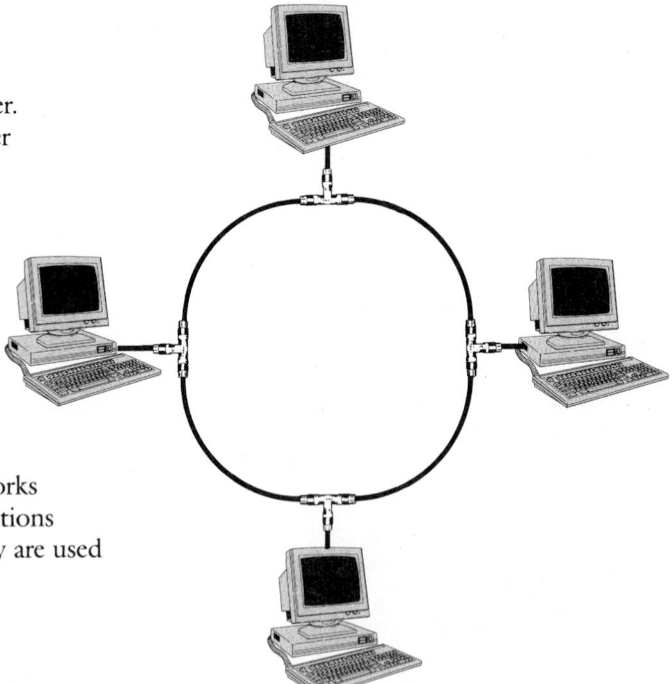

The Personal Computer and Data Communications

The increased use of personal computers and the decreasing cost of communications equipment has resulted in a number of services that are now available to the individual personal computer user. To use these services, all that is required is a personal computer, a modem, communications software, and a phone line. These services include home banking, electronic shopping, commercial databases, and electronic bulletin boards.

FIGURE 8-19

In a ring network, all computers are connected in a continuous loop. Data flows around the ring in only one direction.

Home banking, sometimes called electronic banking, allows a user to schedule payments to creditors, make transfers from one account to another, review bank statements and cleared checks, and inquire about current account balances.

Electronic shopping allows a user to select from a catalog of merchandise that the service offers for sale. The catalog is displayed on the user's screen.

Commercial databases offer a wealth of information in hundreds of subject areas. These services are literally electronic libraries containing information on such topics as economics, education, science, law, and a variety of business subjects. One service, NEXIS, offers access to the complete text of the *Encyclopaedia Britannica*. CompuServe offers a variety of databases that include information on world and business news, travel, and weather. Dow Jones provides business and financial information including access to the full text of the *Wall Street Journal*. To access commercial databases, users generally pay an initial subscription fee and additional charges based on the amount of use.

Electronic bulletin boards, like their physical counterparts, allow users to post messages on virtually any subject. These bulletin boards are usually maintained by computer clubs or vendors for local users although some have been established for wider use. Some bulletin boards offer members access to public domain software, programs that are available free to anyone who wants to use them.

Chapter Summary

Data communications will continue to have an increasing impact on the way people work and the way they use computers. Individuals and organizations are no longer limited to local data resources but instead, with communication capabilities, can obtain information from anywhere in the world at electronic speed. With data communications technology rapidly changing, today's businesses are challenged to find ways to adapt the technology to provide better products and services for their customers and make their operations more efficient. For individuals, the new technology offers increased access to worldwide information and services, and provides new opportunities for education.

The following list summarizes the key topics discussed in this chapter.

1. The transmission of data from one computer (or terminal) to another computer over communication channels is called **data communications** (p. 8.2).

2. The basic components of a data communications system are: (1) a personal computer or terminal; (2) data communications equipment that sends (and can usually receive) data; (3) the communication channel over which data is sent; (4) data communications equipment that receives (and can usually send) data; and (5) another computer (p. 8.2).

3. A **communication channel** is the link or path that the data follows as it is transmitted from the sending device to the receiving device in a data communications system (p. 8.2).

4. A communication channel can consist of various **transmission media** including twisted pair wire, coaxial cable, fiber optics, microwaves, and communication satellites (p. 8.2).

5. **Twisted pair wire** is the color-coded copper wires that are twisted together and commonly used as telephone wire (p. 8.3).

6. **Coaxial cable** is high-quality underground or sub-oceanic communication lines consisting of a central conductor or wire that is surrounded by a nonconducting insulator and encased in a woven metal shield (p. 8.3).

7. Coaxial cable can be either **baseband**, carrying one signal at a time at very high rates of speed, or **broadband**, carrying multiple signals at a time (p. 8.3).

8. **Fiber optics** uses technology based on the ability of smooth, hair-thin strands of material that conduct light waves to rapidly and efficiently transmit data (p. 8.3).

9. **Microwaves** are high-speed radio transmissions sent through the air between microwave stations (p. 8.4).

10. **Communication satellites** are human-made space devices that receive, amplify, and retransmit signals from earth (p. 8.4).

11. **Earth stations** are communication facilities that contain large dish-shaped antennas used to transmit data to and receive data from communication satellites (p. 8.4).

12. **Line configurations** can be either point-to-point lines or multidrop lines (p. 8.6).

13. A **point-to-point line** is a direct line between a sending and receiving device. It may be either a **switched line** (a connection established through regular telephone lines) or a **dedicated line** (a line whose connection between devices is always established) (p. 8.6–8.7).

14. A **multidrop line**, also known as a **multipoint line**, uses a single line to connect multiple devices to a main computer (p. 8.7).

15. Computer equipment processes data as **digital signals**, which are individual electrical pulses representing the bits that are grouped together to form characters (p. 8.8).

16. **Analog signals** are continuous electrical waves that are used to transmit data over standard telephone lines (p. 8.8).

17. A **modem** is a special piece of equipment that converts the digital signals used by computer equipment into analog signals that are used by telephone equipment (p. 8.8).

18. There are two modes of transmitting data: **asynchronous transmission mode**, which transmits one character at a time at irregular intervals using start and stop bits, and **synchronous transmission mode**, which transmits blocks of data at regular intervals using timing signals to synchronize the sending and receiving equipment (p. 8.8–8.9).

19. Transmissions may be classified according to the direction in which the data can flow on a line: sending only (**simplex transmission**); sending or receiving, but in only one direction at a time (**half-duplex transmission**); and sending and receiving at the same time (**full-duplex transmission**) (p. 8.9).

20. The transmission rate of a communication channel depends on the **bandwidth** and its speed. The wider the bandwidth, the greater the number of signals that can be carried on the channel at one time, and the more data that can be transmitted (p. 8.10).

21. **Bits per second (bps)** is the number of bits that can be transmitted in one second (p. 8.10).

22. There are three basic types of modems: an **external modem**, which is a separate stand-alone device attached to the computer or terminal by a cable and to the phone outlet by a standard phone cable; an **internal modem**, which is a circuit board installed inside a computer or terminal; and an **acoustic modem** or **acoustic coupler**, which is a device used with a phone handset (p. 8.11).

23. A **multiplexor** combines more than one input signal into a single stream of data that can be transmitted over a communication channel (p. 8.12).

24. A **front-end processor** is a computer dedicated to handling the data communications requirements of a larger computer (p. 8.12).

25. **Communications software** consists of programs that perform tasks such as dialing (software that stores, selects, and dials phone numbers); **terminal emulation** (software that allows the personal computer to imitate or appear to be a specific type of terminal so that the personal computer can connect to specific types of computers); and **data encryption** (software that can code and decode transmitted data for security purposes) (p. 8.13).

26. A **network** is a collection of terminals, computers, and other equipment that use communication channels to share data (p. 8.13).

27. A **local area network (LAN)** is a communications network that covers a limited geographic area and is privately owned (p. 8.13).

28. Three common uses of local area networks are **hardware resource sharing**, which allows all network users to access a single piece of equipment rather than each user having to be connected to his or her own device, **information resource sharing**, which allows the network users to access data stored on other computers in the network, and **software resource sharing**, which allows network users to access commonly used software (p. 8.13–8.14).

29. A **wide area network** or **WAN** is a network that covers a large geographical area (p. 8.15).

30. Network **topology** describes the pathways by which devices in a network are connected to each other (p. 8.15).

31. A **star network** contains a central computer and one or more terminals or computers connected to it, forming a star (p. 8.15).

32. In a **bus network** all devices in the network are connected to and share a single cable (p. 8.16).

33. A **ring network** has a series of computers connected to each other in a ring (p. 8.16).

34. For a personal computer to access other computers through data communications, it must have a modem, communications software, and a phone line (p. 8.16).

35. Some of the data communications services available to personal computer users are home banking, electronic shopping, commercial databases, and electronic bulletin boards (p. 8.16).

Review Questions

1. Define data communications. What are the basic components of a data communications system?
2. List five kinds of transmission media used for communication channels.
3. Describe the two major types of line configurations. What are the advantages and disadvantages of each?
4. List and describe the three types of data transmission (direction) that are used.
5. Why is a modem used? Describe some of the types of modems available.
6. Describe some of the tasks that communications software can perform.
7. Compare and contrast a local area network and a wide area network.
8. Discuss the reasons for using a local area network.
9. Name three topologies or configurations that are used with networks. Draw a diagram of each.
10. Describe several data communications services that are available to personal computer users.

Operating Systems and System Software

9

Objectives

- Define the terms operating system and system software.
- Describe the various types of operating systems and explain the differences in their capabilities.
- Describe the functions of an operating system, including allocating system resources, monitoring system activities, and using utilities.
- Explain the difference between proprietary and portable operating systems.
- Name and briefly describe the major operating systems that are being used today.

When most people think of software they think of applications software such as the word processing, spreadsheet, and database software that we discuss in this text. However, for applications software to run on a computer, another type of software is needed to interface between the user, the applications software, and the equipment. This software consists of programs that are referred to as the operating system. The operating system is part of what is called the system software.

What Is System Software?

System software consists of all the programs including the operating system that are related to controlling the operations of the computer equipment. System software differs from applications software. Application software tells the computer how to produce information, such as how to calculate the correct amount to print on a paycheck. In contrast, some of the functions that system software perform are: starting up the computer; loading, executing, and storing application programs; storing and retrieving files; and performing a variety of utility functions such as formatting disks, sorting data files, and translating program instructions into machine language. The most important part of the system software is the operating system.

What Is an Operating System?

All computers utilize an operating system. An **operating system (OS)** consists of one or more programs that manage the operations of a computer. These programs function as an interface between the user, the application programs, and the computer equipment (Figure 9-1).

For a computer to operate, the essential and most frequently used instructions in the operating system must be stored in main memory. This portion of the operating system is called by many different names: the **supervisor**, **monitor**, **executive**, **master program**, **control program**, and **kernel**. The remaining part of the operating system is usually stored on disk and can be loaded into main memory whenever it is needed.

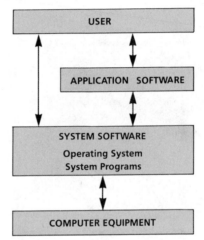

FIGURE 9-1

The operating system and other system programs act as an interface between the user, the application software, and the computer equipment.

Loading an Operating System

The process of loading an operating system into main memory is called **booting** the system. Figure 9-2 shows the steps that occur when an operating system is loaded on a personal computer. While this process is not identical to that used on large computers, the functions performed are similar.

Once the operating system is loaded into main memory, it usually remains there until the computer is turned off. The operating system controls the loading and manages the execution of each application program that is requested by the user. When an application program completes its task, the operating system queries the user by displaying the system prompt. The prompt indicates that the operating system is ready to receive a command specifying the next program or operation that is to be performed.

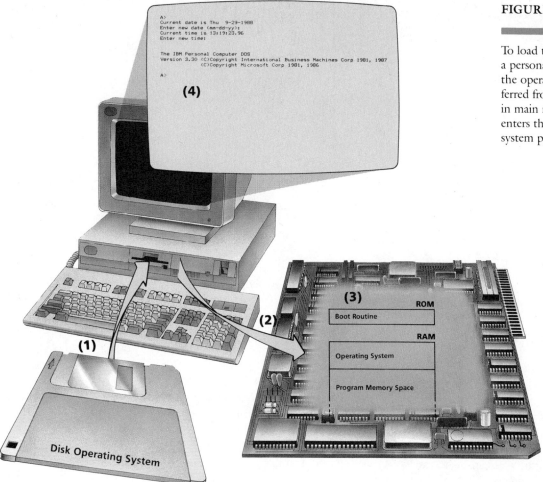

```
A>
Current date is Thu  9-29-1988
Enter new date (mm-dd-yy):
Current time is 13:19:23.96
Enter new time:

The IBM Personal Computer DOS
Version 3.30 (C)Copyright International Business Machines Corp 1981, 1987
          (C)Copyright Microsoft Corp 1981, 1986

A>
```

(4)

(3)

ROM

Boot Routine

RAM

Operating System

Program Memory Space

(2)

(1)

Disk Operating System

FIGURE 9-2

To load the operating system into a personal computer, (1) a copy of the operating system is (2) transferred from the disk and (3) stored in main memory. After the user enters the date and time, (4) the system prompt (A>) displays.

Types of Operating Systems

The various types of operating systems include single program, multiprogramming, multiprocessing, and virtual machine operating systems. These operating systems can be classified by two criteria: (1) whether or not they allow more than one user to use the computer at the same time and (2) whether or not they allow more than one program to run at the same time (Figure 9-3 on the next page).

	SINGLE PROGRAM	MULTI-PROGRAMMING	MULTI-PROCESSING	VIRTUAL MACHINE
NUMBER OF PROGRAMS RUNNING	One	More than one	More than one on each CPU	More than one under each operating system
NUMBER OF USERS	One	One or more than one	More than one on each CPU	More than one under each operating system

FIGURE 9-3

Operating systems can be classified by whether they allow more than one user and more than one program to be operating at one time.

Single Program

Single-program operating systems allow only a single user to run a single program at one time. This was the first type of operating system developed. Today, many personal computers use this type of operating system.

Multiprogramming

Multiprogramming operating systems, also called **multitasking** operating systems, allow more than one program to be run at the same time. Even though the CPU is only able to work on one program instruction at a time, its ability to switch back and forth between programs makes it appear that all programs are running at the same time. For example, with a multiprogramming operating system the computer can perform a complex spreadsheet calculation and at the same time download a file from another computer while the user is writing a memo with the word processing program.

Multiprogramming operating systems on personal computers can usually support a single user running multiple programs. Multiprogramming operating systems on some personal computers and most mini and mainframe computers can support more than one user running more than one program. This version of a multiprogramming operating system is sometimes called a **multiuser-multiprogramming** operating system. Most of these operating systems also allow more than one user to be running the same program. For example, a wholesale distributor may have dozens of terminal operators entering sales orders using the same order entry program.

Multiprocessing

Computers that have more than one CPU are called **multiprocessors**. A **multiprocessing** operating system coordinates the operations of multiprocessor computers. Because each CPU in a multiprocessor computer can be executing one program instruction, more than one instruction can be executed simultaneously. Besides providing an increase in performance, most multiprocessors offer another advantage. If one CPU fails, work can be shifted to the remaining CPUs. The ability to continue processing when a major component fails is called **fault tolerance**.

Virtual Machine

A **virtual machine (VM)** operating system, available on some large computers, allows a single computer to run two or more different operating systems. The VM operating system allocates system resources to each operating system. To users it appears that they are working on separate systems. The advantage of this approach is that an organization can concurrently (at the same time) run different operating systems that are best suited to different tasks. For example, some operating systems are best for interactive processing and others are best for batch processing. With a VM operating system both types of operating systems can be run at the same time.

Functions of Operating Systems

The operating system performs a number of functions that allow the user and the applications software to interact with the computer. These functions apply to all operating systems but become more complex for operating systems that allow more than one program run at a time. The functions can be grouped into three areas: allocating system resources, monitoring system activities, and utilities (Figure 9-4).

ALLOCATING RESOURCES	MONITORING ACTIVITIES	UTILITIES
CPU management Memory management Input/output management	System performance System security	File management Sorting

FIGURE 9-4

Operating system functions.

Allocating System Resources

The primary function of the operating system is to allocate the resources of the computer system. These resources include the CPU, main memory, and the input and output devices such as disk and tape drives and printers. Like a police officer directing traffic, the operating system decides what resource will currently be used and for how long.

CPU Management   Because a CPU can only work on one program instruction at a time, a multiprogramming operating system must keep switching the CPU among the different instructions of the programs that are waiting to be performed. A common way of allocating CPU processing is time slicing. A **time slice** is a fixed amount of CPU processing time, usually measured in milliseconds (thousandths of a second). With this technique, each user in turn receives a time slice.

Because some work is more important than other work, most operating systems have ways to adjust the amount of time slices a user receives, either automatically or based on user-specified criteria. One technique for modifying time slices is to have different priorities assigned to each user. The highest priority would receive several consecutive time slices for each time slice received by the lowest priority.

Memory Management   During processing, memory is used to store a variety of items including the operating system, application program instructions for one or more programs, data waiting to be processed, and workspace used for calculations, sorting, and other temporary tasks. Data that has just been read or is waiting to be sent to an output device is stored in reserved areas of memory called **buffers**. It is the operating system's job to keep track of all this data by allocating memory.

All operating systems allocate at least some portion of memory into fixed areas called **partitions** (Figure 9-5). Some operating systems allocate all memory on this basis while others use partitions only for the operating system instructions and buffers.

Input and Output Management   At any one time, a number of different input devices can be trying to send data to the computer. At the same time, the CPU could be ready to send data to an output device such as a terminal or printer or a storage device such as a disk. It is the operating system's responsibility to manage these input and output processes.

The operating system keeps track of disk read and write requests, stores these requests in buffers along with the associated data for write requests, and usually processes them sequentially.

OPERATING SYSTEM
Partition 1 Program A
Partition 2 Program B
Partition 3 Program C Data
Partition 4 (Available)

FIGURE 9-5

Some computer systems allocate memory into fixed blocks called partitions. The CPU then keeps track of programs and data by assigning them to a specific partition.

Monitoring System Activities

Another function of the operating system is monitoring the system activity. This includes monitoring system performance and system security.

System Performance   System performance can be measured in a number of ways but is usually gauged by the user in terms of response time. **Response time** is the amount of time from the moment a user enters data until the computer responds. Response time can vary based on what the user has entered. If the user is simply entering data into a file, the response time is usually within a second or two. However, if the user has just completed a request for a display of sorted data from several files, the response time could be minutes.

A more precise way of measuring performance is to run a program that is designed to record and report system activity. Among other information, these programs usually report **CPU utilization**, the amount of time that the CPU is working and not idle, waiting for data to process.

Another measure of performance is to compare the CPU utilization with the disk input and output rate, referred to as disk I/O. We previously discussed how a virtual memory management operating system swaps pages or segments from disk to memory as they are needed. Systems with heavy workloads and insufficient memory or CPU power can get into a situation called **thrashing**, where the system is spending more time moving pages to and from the disk than processing the data. System performance reporting can indicate this problem.

System Security   Most multiuser operating systems provide for a logon code, a user ID, and a password that must all be entered correctly before a user is allowed to use an application program (Figure 9-6). Each is a word or series of characters. A **logon code** usually identifies the application that will be used, such as accounting, sales, or manufacturing. A **user ID** identifies the user, such as Jeffrey Ryan or Mary Gonzales. The **password** is usually confidential; often it is known only to the user and the data processing manager. The logon code, user ID, and password must match entries in an authorization file. If they don't match, the user is denied access to the system. Both successful and unsuccessful logon attempts are often recorded in a file so that managers can review who is using or attempting to use the system. These logs can also be used to allocate data processing expenses based on the percentage of system use by an organization's various departments.

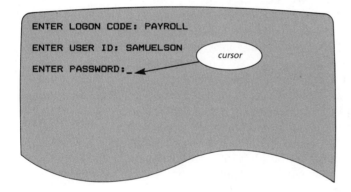

FIGURE 9-6

The logon code, user ID, and password must all be entered correctly before the user is allowed to use the computer. Because the password is confidential, it is usually not displayed on the screen when the user types it in.

Utilities

In addition to allocating system resources and monitoring system activities, most operating systems contain programs called **utilities** that can perform functions such as file management, sorting, and editing. Some of the functions that the file management utility programs can perform include formatting disks, deleting files from a disk, copying files from one auxiliary storage device to another, and renaming stored files. Sort utilities are used to place the data stored in files into ascending or descending order based on a value stored in the key field of each record in a file. For example, a sort utility program could be used to sort the records in a personnel file in alphabetical order by the employees' last names. **Editors** allow users to make direct changes to programs and data. An editor would be used by a programmer to change a program instruction that was incorrect or had to be modified.

Popular Operating Systems

Many computer users are supporting the move away from **proprietary operating systems** (meaning privately owned) and toward **portable operating systems** that will run on many manufacturers' computers. The advantage of portable operating systems is that the user is not tied to a particular manufacturer. Using a portable operating system, a user could change computer systems, yet retain existing software and data files, which usually represents a sizable investment in time and money. One of the most popular portable operating systems is UNIX, which we will discuss along with the popular personal computer operating system, MS-DOS, and IBM's latest personal computer operating system, O/S 2.

UNIX

The **UNIX** operating system was developed in the early 1970s by scientists at Bell Laboratories. It was specifically designed to provide a way to manage a variety of scientific and specialized computer applications. Because of federal regulations, Bell Labs (a subsidiary of AT&T) was prohibited from actively promoting UNIX in the commercial marketplace. Instead, for a low fee Bell Labs licensed UNIX to numerous colleges and universities where it obtained a wide following. With the deregulation of the telephone companies in the 1980s, AT&T was allowed to enter the computer system marketplace. With AT&T's increased promotion and the trend toward portable operating systems, UNIX has aroused tremendous interest. One of the advantages of UNIX is its extensive library of over 400 instruction modules that can be linked together to perform almost any programming task. Today, most major computer manufacturers offer a multiuser version of the UNIX operating system to run on their computers.

With all its strengths, however, UNIX has not yet obtained success in the commercial business systems marketplace. Some people attribute this to the fact that UNIX has never been considered "user friendly." For example, most of the UNIX program modules are identified by obscure names such as MAUS, SHMOP, and BRK. Other critics contend that UNIX lacks the file management capabilities to support the online interactive databases that more and more businesses are implementing. With the support of most major computer manufacturers, however, these problems are being worked on and UNIX has a good chance of becoming one of the major operating systems of the coming years.

MS-DOS

The Microsoft Disk Operating System or **MS-DOS** was released by Microsoft Corporation in 1981. MS-DOS was originally developed for IBM for their first personal computer system. IBM calls their equivalent version of the operating system **PC-DOS**. Because so many personal computer manufacturers followed IBM's lead and chose MS-DOS for their computers, MS-DOS quickly became an industry standard. Other personal computer operating systems exist, but by far the majority of personal computer software is written for MS-DOS. This single-user operating system is so widely used that it is often referred to simply as **DOS**.

OS/2

In 1988, IBM released the **OS/2** operating system for its new family of PS/2 personal computers (Figure 9-7). Microsoft Corporation, which developed OS/2 for IBM, also released their equivalent version, called MS-OS/2. OS/2 is designed to take advantage of the increased computing power of the 80286, 80386, and 80486 microprocessors and will only run on systems that use these chips. OS/2 also requires a lot more computing power to operate. For example, OS/2 requires 5MB of hard disk and a minimum of 2MB of main memory just to run the operating system. Additional features offered by OS/2 include the ability to run larger and more complex programs and the ability to do multiprogramming. OS/2 can have up to 12 programs running at the same time.

There are two versions and two editions of OS/2. One of the versions includes the *Presentation Manager*, a graphic windowing environment similar to that available on the Apple Macintosh. The difference between the Standard Edition and the Extended Edition of OS/2 is that the Extended Edition includes database management and communications capabilities.

Other Operating Systems

A number of other popular operating systems exist in addition to the ones just discussed. The Apple Macintosh multiprogramming operating system, currently available only on Apple systems, provides a unique graphic interface that uses icons (figures) and windows (Figure 9-8) that many people find easy to learn and use. The ProDos operating system is used on many of Apple's other computer systems. The PICK operating system is another portable operating system that runs on personal, mini, and mainframe computers. The PICK operating system incorporates a relational database manager and has had much success in the business data processing marketplace. Most mainframe operating systems are unique to a particular make of computer or are designed to be compatible with one of IBM's operating systems such as DOS/VS, MVS, or VM, IBM's virtual machine operating system.

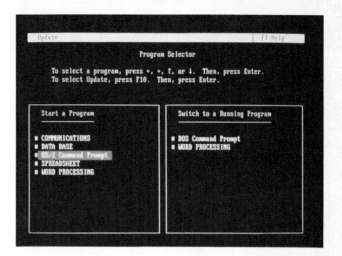

FIGURE 9-7

IBM's OS/2 operating system takes advantage of the increased processing power of the latest personal computer systems.

FIGURE 9-8

The Macintosh operating system offers a unique graphic interface and the ability to display information in separate "windows."

Chapter Summary

System software and the operating system are essential parts of any computer system and should be understood by users who want to obtain the maximum benefits from their computer. This is especially true for the latest personal computer operating systems that include features such as virtual memory management and multiprogramming. Understanding and being able to use these and other features will give users even more control over their computer resources.

The following list summarizes the key topics discussed in this chapter.

1. **System software** consists of all the programs including the operating system that are related to managing the operations of the computer (p. 9.1).

2. An **operating system** consists of one or more programs that manage the operations of a computer (p. 9.2).

3. Operating systems function as an interface between the user, the application programs, and the computer equipment (p. 9.2).

4. The essential and most frequently used instructions in an operating system are sometimes called the **supervisor** and must be stored in the main memory of a computer for the computer to operate (p. 9.2).

5. **Booting** the system is the process of loading the operating system into main memory (p. 9.2).

6. **Single-program** operating systems allow a single user to run a single program at one time (p. 9.4).

7. **Multiprogramming** operating systems, also called **multitasking** operating systems, allow more than one program to be run at the same time (p. 9.4).

8. A multiprogramming operating system that allows multiple users is called a **multiuser-multiprogramming** operating system (p. 9.4).

9. A **multiprocessor** computer has more than one CPU. **Multiprocessor** operating systems coordinate the operations of these computers (p. 9.4).

10. A **virtual machine (VM)** operating system allows a single computer to run two or more different operating systems (p. 9.5).

11. The functions of an operating system include allocating system resources, monitoring system activities, and utilities (p. 9.5).

12. The system resources that the operating system allocates include the CPU, main memory, and the input/output devices (p. 9.5).

13. **Time slicing** is a common way for an operating system to allocate the CPU (p. 9.5).

14. Data that has been read or is waiting to be sent to an output device is stored in **buffers** (p. 9.6).

15. All operating systems allocate at least some portion of memory into fixed areas called **partitions** (p. 9.6).

16. The operating system is responsible for managing the input and output processes of the computer (p. 9.6).

17. **Response time** is the amount of time from the moment a user enters data until the computer responds (p. 9.6).

18. System performance can be measured by the response time and by comparing the **CPU utilization** with the disk I/O to determine if the system is **thrashing** (p. 9.6–9.7).

19. System security is monitored by the operating system through the use of **passwords** (p. 9.7).

20. Most operating systems contain programs called **utilities** that can perform functions such as file management and sorting (p. 9.7).

21. Many computer users are supporting the move away from **proprietary operating systems** and toward **portable operating systems** (p. 9.8).

22. Some of the popular operating systems being used today include UNIX, MS-DOS, and OS/2 (p. 9.8–9.9).

Review Questions

1. Define system software. List some of the functions of system software.
2. Describe how to boot an operating system on a personal computer.
3. List the various types of operating systems and briefly describe their capabilities.
4. The functions of an operating system can be grouped into three areas. What are they?
5. How does an operating system use time slicing?
6. What is virtual memory management?
7. Describe how system performance can be measured.
8. What are three types of authorizations that an operating system uses to provide system security?
9. List several functions that the utilities of an operating system provide.
10. Explain the difference between proprietary and portable operating systems. Name and briefly describe three popular operating systems.

The System Development Life Cycle

10

Objectives

- Describe the six elements of an information system: equipment, software, data, personnel, users, and procedures.

- Define the term information system and describe the different types of information systems.

- Explain the five phases of the system development life cycle: analysis, design, development, implementation, and maintenance.

- Explain the importance of documentation and project management in the system development life cycle.

- Describe how various analysis and design tools, such as data flow diagrams, are used.

- Explain how program development is part of the system development life cycle.

- Explain several methods that can be used for a conversion to a new system.

- Discuss the maintenance of an information system.

Every day, factors such as competition and government regulations cause people to face new challenges in obtaining the information they need to perform their jobs. A new product, a new sales commission plan, or a change in tax rates are just three examples of events that require a change in the way an organization develops information. Sometimes these challenges can be met by existing methods but other times, meeting the challenge requires an entirely new way of processing data. In these cases, a new or modified information system is needed. As a computer user, either as an individual or within your organization, it is very likely that someday you will participate in the development or modification of such a system. This chapter discusses information systems and how they are developed.

What Is an Information System?

An **information system** is a collection of elements that provide accurate, timely, and useful information. As discussed in Chapter 1, an information system is comprised of six elements: equipment, software, data, personnel, users, and procedures. Each element is important in order to obtain quality information from an information system.

The term information system is frequently used to describe the entire computer operation of an organization, as in a computer information system or the information system(s) department. The term is also used to mean an individual application or "system" that is processed on the computer. For example, an accounting system or an inventory control system can each be thought of as an information system.

Types of Information Systems

The types of information systems that use a computer fall into four broad categories: (1) operational systems; (2) management information systems; (3) decision support systems; and (4) expert systems.

Operational Systems

An **operational system** is designed to process data generated by the day-to-day business transactions of a company. Examples of operational systems are accounting systems, billing systems, inventory control systems, and order entry systems (Figure 10-1).

Management Information Systems

When computers were first used for processing business applications, the information systems developed were primarily operational systems. Usually, the purpose was to "computerize" an existing manual system. This approach often resulted in faster processing, reduced clerical costs, and improved customer service.

Managers soon realized, however, that computer processing could be used for more than just day-to-day transaction processing. The computer's ability to perform rapid calculations and compare data could be used to produce meaningful information for management. This led to the concept of management information systems.

Although the term management information system has been defined in a number of ways, today a **management**

FIGURE 10-1

Operational systems process the day-to-day transactions of an organization, such as the tax forms that are shown being entered into an IRS computer.

information system (MIS) refers to a computer-based system that generates timely and accurate information to support the low, middle, and top-levels of management in their decision-making activities (Figure 10-2). Lower-level management utilizes detail reports to control the day-to-day operations to ensure that specific jobs are done. Middle-level management relies more on summary reports and exception reports to organize, schedule, and do short-term planning. Top-level management counts on historical information and an analysis of data trends for strategic planning. In the management information system, the focus is on the information that management needs to do its job.

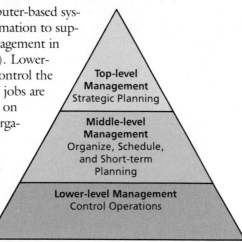

Top-level
Management
Strategic Planning

Middle-level
Management
Organize, Schedule,
and Short-term
Planning

Lower-level Management
Control Operations

FIGURE 10-2

The function of a management information system is to provide timely and accurate information to support the three levels of management in their decision-making activities.

Decision Support Systems

Frequently management needs information that is not routinely provided by operational and management information systems. For example, a vice president of finance may want to know the effect on company profits if sales increase by 10% and costs increase by 5%. This type of information is not usually provided by operational or management information systems. To provide this information, decision support systems have been developed.

A **decision support system** is a system designed to help someone reach a decision by summarizing or comparing data from either or both internal and external sources. Internal sources include data from an organization's database such as sales, manufacturing, or financial data. Data from external sources could include information on interest rates, population trends, or new housing construction. Decision support systems often include query languages, statistical analysis capabilities, spreadsheets, and graphics to help the user evaluate the decision data. More advanced decision support systems also include capabilities that allow users to create a model of the factors affecting a decision. A simple model for determining the best product price would include factors for the expected sales volume at each price level. With a model, users can ask "what if" questions by changing one or more of the factors and seeing what the projected results would be. Many people use electronic spreadsheets for simple modeling tasks.

Expert Systems

Expert systems combine the knowledge on a given subject of one or more human experts into a computerized system that simulates the human experts' reasoning and decision making processes. Thus, the computer also becomes an "expert" on the subject. Expert systems are made up of the combined subject knowledge of the human experts, called the **knowledge base**, and the **inference rules** that determine how the knowledge is used to reach decisions. Although they may appear to "think," the current expert systems actually operate within narrow preprogrammed limits and cannot make decisions based on "common sense" or on information outside of their knowledge base. Expert systems have been successfully applied to problems as diverse as diagnosing illnesses, searching for oil, and making soup. These systems are part of an exciting branch of computer science called **artificial intelligence**, the application of human intelligence to computer systems.

The Integration of Information Systems

With today's sophisticated software, it can be difficult to classify a system as belonging uniquely to one of the four types of information systems. For example, much of today's applications software provides both operational and management information and some of the more advanced software even includes some decision support capabilities. Although expert systems still operate primarily as separate systems, the trend is clear: to combine all of an organization's information needs into a single integrated information system.

To develop the information systems they need, many organizations use the system development life cycle.

What Is the System Development Life Cycle?

The **system development life cycle (SDLC)** is an organized approach to developing an information system.

Regardless of the type or complexity of an information system, the structured process of the system development life cycle should be followed whenever an information system is developed. Although some experts group them differently, this chapter divides the activities of the system development life cycle into five phases.

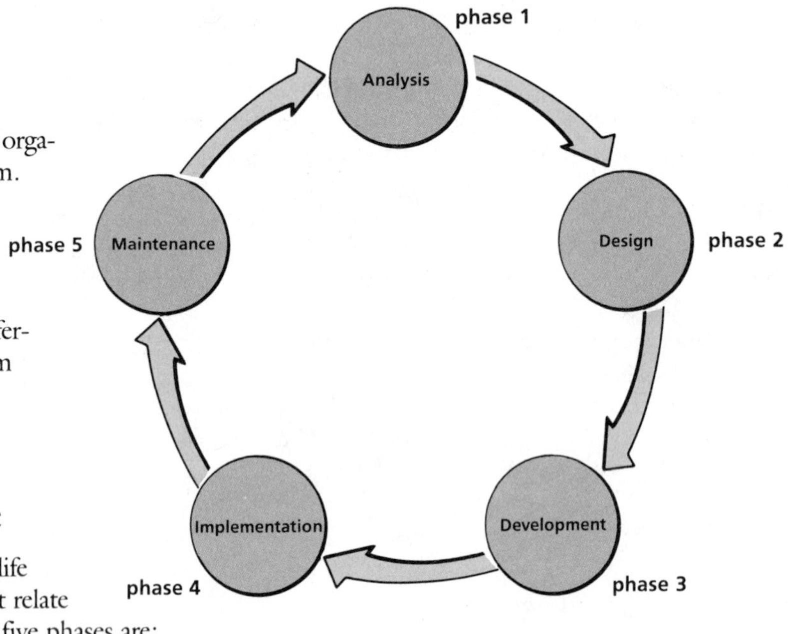

The Five Phases of the System Development Life Cycle

Each of the five phases of the system development life cycle (Figure 10-3) includes important activities that relate to the development of an information system. The five phases are:

Phase 1 Analysis   Phase 4 Implementation
Phase 2 Design   Phase 5 Maintenance
Phase 3 Development

FIGURE 10-3

The five phases of the system development life cycle.

Before explaining each of the phases, we will discuss project management and documentation because these two activities are ongoing processes that are performed throughout the cycle. In addition, we will identify the information system specialists and users who participate in the various phases of the SDLC.

Project Management

Project management involves planning, scheduling, reporting, and controlling the individual activities that make up the system development life cycle. These activities are usually recorded in a **project plan** on a week-by-week basis that includes an estimate of the time to complete the activity and the start and finish dates. As you might expect, the start of many activities depends on the successful completion of other activities. For example, implementation (Phase 4) activities can't begin until you have completed at least some, if not all, of the development activities (Phase 3). An effective way of showing the relationship of project activities is with a **Gantt chart** (Figure 10-4).

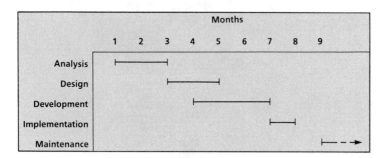

   Project management is a task that should be done *throughout* the development process. In most projects, activities need frequent rescheduling. Some activities will take less time than originally planned and others will take longer. To measure the impact of the actual results and revised estimates, they should be recorded regularly and a revised project plan issued. A number of project management software packages are available to assist in this task.

Documentation

Documentation refers to written materials that are produced as part of the system development life cycle, such as a report describing the overall purpose of the system or layout sheets that are used to design reports and screens. Documentation should be identified and agreed on prior to beginning the project. Well-written, thorough documentation makes it easier for users and others to understand why particular decisions are made. Too often, documentation is put off until the completion of a project and is never adequately finished. Documentation should be an ongoing part of the entire development process and should not be thought of as a separate phase.

Who Participates in the System Development Life Cycle?

Every person who will be affected by the new system should have the opportunity to participate in its development. The participants fall into two categories: users and information system personnel such as systems analysts and computer programmers. As discussed in Chapter 1, the systems analyst works closely with both the users and the programmers. The systems analyst's job is challenging, requiring good communication, analytical, and diplomatic skills to keep the development process on track and on schedule. Good communication skills are especially important during analysis, the first phase of the system development life cycle.

Phase 1—Analysis

Analysis is the separation of a system into its parts to determine how the system works. In addition, the analysis phase of a development project also includes the identification of a proposed solution to the problems identified in the current system.

A system project can originate in several ways, but a common way is for the manager of a user department, such as accounting or personnel, to contact the information systems department with a request for assistance. The initial request may be oral, but it is eventually written on a standard form that becomes the first item of documentation (Figure 10-5). In most organizations, requests for new system projects exceed the capacity of the information systems department to implement them. Therefore, the manager of the systems department must review each request and make a preliminary determination as to the potential benefit for the company. Requests for large development projects, such as an entirely new system, are often reviewed by committees made up of both user and information systems personnel and representatives of top management. When the managers of both the user and information systems departments determine that a request warrants further review, one or more systems analysts will be assigned to begin a preliminary investigation, the first step in the analysis phase.

REQUEST FOR SYSTEM SERVICES

ISD CONTROL #: 2143

I. To Be Completed By Person Requesting Services

SUBMITTED BY: MIKE CHARLES DEPT AUTO PARTS SALES DATE: 1-22-92

REQUEST TYPE: ☐ MODIFICATION ☑ NEW SYSTEM

NEED: ☐ ASAP ☑ IMMEDIATE ☐ LONG RANGE

BRIEF STATEMENT OF REQUEST (attach additional material, if necessary)

NEED AUTOMATED ORDER ENTRY AND INVOICING CAPABILITY. MANUAL PROCEDURES CAN NO LONGER KEEP UP WITH INCREASED SALES VOLUME.

☐ ADDITIONAL MATERIAL ATTACHED

II. To Be Completed By Information Systems Department

REQUEST INVESTIGATED BY: FRANK PEACOCK DATE: 2-4-92

COMMENTS: MANUAL INVOICING RUNNING 3 DAYS BEHIND SHIPMENTS. RECOMMEND DETAILED SYSTEM ANALYSIS FOR DEVELOPMENT OF COMPUTERIZED SYSTEM

III. Disposition

☑ REQUEST APPROVED FOR IMMEDIATE IMPLEMENTATION

☐ Analyst assigned: MARY RUIZ

☐ REQUEST APPROVED FOR IMPLEMENTATION AS SOON AS POSSIBLE

☐ REQUEST REJECTED

COMMENTS:

SIGNED: George Lang DATE: 2-15-92

FIGURE 10-5

The system development project usually starts with a request from a user. The request should be documented on a form such as the one shown here to provide a record of the action taken.

The Preliminary Investigation

The purpose of the **preliminary investigation** is to determine if a request justifies further detailed investigation and analysis. The most important aspect of the preliminary investigation is **problem definition**, the identification of the true nature of the problem. Often the stated problem and the real problem are not the same. For example, the investigation of a request for a new accounts receivable report may reveal that the real problem is that customer payments are not being recorded in a timely manner. The existing accounts receivable reports may be fine if the payments are recorded when received instead of once a week. The purpose of the preliminary investigation is to determine the real source of the problem.

The preliminary investigation begins with an interview of the manager who submitted the request. Depending on the scope of the request, other users may be interviewed as well.

The duration of the preliminary investigation is usually quite short when compared to the remainder of the project. At the conclusion of the investigation, the analyst presents the findings to both user and information system management and recommends the next course of action. Sometimes the results of a preliminary investigation indicate an obvious solution that can be implemented at minimal cost. Other times, however, the only thing the preliminary investigation does is confirm that there is a problem that needs further study. In these cases, detailed system analysis is recommended.

Detailed System Analysis

Detailed system analysis involves both a thorough study of the current system and at least one proposed solution to any problems found.

The study of the current system is important for two reasons. First, it helps increase the analyst's understanding of the activities that the new system will perform. Second, and perhaps most important, studying the current system builds a relationship with the user. The analyst will have much more credibility with users if the analyst understands how the users currently do their job. This may seem an obvious point, but surprisingly, many systems are created or modified without studying the current system or without adequately involving the users.

The basic fact-gathering techniques used during the detailed system analysis are: (1) interviews; (2) questionnaires; (3) reviewing current system documentation; and (4) observing current procedures. During this phase of the system study, the analyst must develop a critical, questioning approach to each procedure within the current system to determine what is actually taking place. Often it is found that operations are being performed not because they are efficient or effective, but because "they have always been done this way."

Information gathered during this phase includes: (1) the output of the current system; (2) the procedures used to produce the output; and (3) the input to the current system.

An increasingly popular method for documenting this information is called structured analysis. **Structured analysis** is the use of analysis and design tools such as data flow diagrams, data dictionaries, structured English, and decision tables and trees to document the specifications of an information system.

Data Flow Diagrams One of the difficulties with the analysis of any system is documenting the results in a way that others can understand. Structured analysis addresses this problem by using graphics to represent the flow of data between processes and files. These graphics are represented by data flow diagrams.

Data flow diagrams (DFD) graphically show the flow of data through a system. The key elements of a DFD (Figure 10-6) are arrows or vectors called data flows, representing data; circles (also called "bubbles") representing processes, such as verifying an order or creating an invoice; parallel lines representing data files; and squares, called sources or sinks, that represent either

FIGURE 10-6

The symbols used to create data flow diagrams.

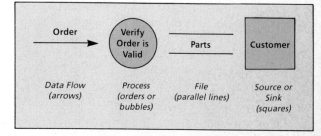

Order →	Verify Order is Valid	—— Parts ——	Customer
Data Flow (arrows)	Process (orders or bubbles)	File (parallel lines)	Source or Sink (squares)

FIGURE 10-7

Data flow diagrams (DFD) are used to graphically illustrate the flow of information through a system. The customer (box) both originates data and receives information (arrows). The circles indicate where actions take place on the data. Files are shown as parallel lines.

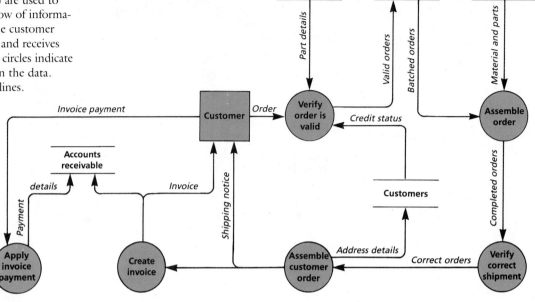

**CUSTOMER ORDER PROCESSING
DATA FLOW DIAGRAM**

or both an originator of data or a receiver of information such as a customer. Because they are visual, DFDs are particularly useful for reviewing the existing or proposed system with the user. (See Figure 10-7).

Data Dictionaries The **data dictionary** describes the elements that make up the data flow. Elements can be thought of as equivalent to fields in a record. The data dictionary (Figure 10-8) includes information about the attributes of an element, such as length; where the element is used (what files and data flows include the element); and any values or ranges the element might have, such as a value of 2 for a credit limit code to indicate a purchase limit of $1,000.00. The data dictionary is created in the analysis phase and is used in all subsequent phases.

Structured English **Process specifications** document what action is taken on the data flows. Referring to the DFD in Figure 10-7, process specifications will describe what goes on in each of the circles. One way of writing process specifications is to use **structured English**, a style of writing and presentation that highlights the alternatives and actions that are part of the process. Figure 10-9 shows an example of a structured English process specification describing a policy for order processing.

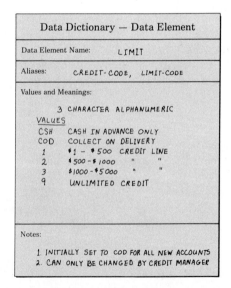

FIGURE 10-8

The data dictionary is used to document the elements that are included in the data flows. This illustration shows the information on length, type of data, and possible values that is recorded for each data element in the dictionary.

Decision Tables and Decision Trees   Another way of documenting the system during the analysis phase is with a decision table or decision tree. A **decision table** or **decision tree** identifies the actions that should be taken under different conditions. Figures 10-10 and 10-11 show a decision table and decision tree for the order processing policy described with structured English in Figure 10-9. Decision tables and trees are an excellent way of showing the desired action when the action depends on multiple conditions.

```
If the order amount exceeds $1,000,
    If customer has any unpaid invoices over 90 days old,
        Do not issue order confirmation,
        Write message on order reject report.
    Otherwise (account is in good standing),
        Issue order confirmation.
Otherwise (order is $1,000 or less),
    If customer has any unpaid invoices over 90 days old,
        Issue order confirmation,
        Write message on credit follow-up report.
    Otherwise (account is in good standing),
        Issue order confirmation.
```

FIGURE 10-9

Structured English is an organized way of describing what actions are taken on data. This structured English example describes an order processing policy.

	Rules			
	1	2	3	4
Conditions				
1. Order > $1,000	Y	Y	N	N
2. Unpaid invoices over 90 days old	Y	N	Y	N
Actions				
1. Issue confirmation	N	Y	Y	Y
2. Reject order	Y	N	N	N
3. Credit follow-up	N	N	Y	N

FIGURE 10-10

Decision tables help a user quickly determine the course of action based on two or more conditions. This decision table is based on the order processing policy described in Figure 10-9. For example, if an order is $1,000 or less and the customer has an unpaid invoice over 90 days old, the policy is to issue an order confirmation but to perform a credit follow-up on the past due invoice.

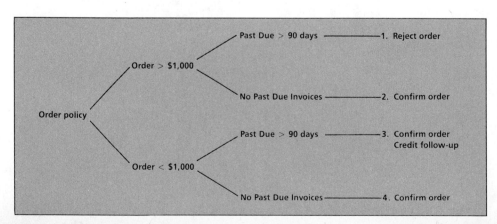

FIGURE 10-11

Like a decision table, a decision tree illustrates the action to be taken based on the given conditions, but presents it graphically. This decision tree is based on the order processing policy described in Figure 10-9.

Making the Decision on How To Proceed

Just as at the completion of the preliminary investigation, at the completion of the analysis phase, the user, systems analyst, and management face another decision on how to proceed. At this point the analyst should have completed a study of the current system and, using the same tools and methods, developed one or more proposed solutions to the current system's identified problems. Sometimes the systems analyst is asked to prepare a feasibility study and a cost/benefit analysis. These two reports are often used together. The **feasibility study** discusses whether the proposed solution is practical and capable of being accomplished. The **cost/benefit analysis** identifies the estimated costs of the proposed solution and the benefits (including potential cost savings) that are expected. If there are strong indications at the beginning of the project that some type of new system will be developed, the feasibility study and cost/benefit analysis are sometimes performed as part of the preliminary investigation.

   The results of the analyst's work are presented in a written report (Figure 10-12) to both user and information systems management who consider the alternatives and the resources, such as time, people, and money, of the organization. The end of the analysis phase is usually where organizations decide either to acquire commercial software from an outside source, contract outside the organization for system development, or develop the system internally. If a decision is made to proceed, the project enters the design phase.

DATE: April 1
TO: Management Review Committee
FROM: George Lacey, Corporate Systems Manager
SUBJECT: Detailed Investigation and Analysis of Order Entry System

Introduction

   A detailed system investigation and analysis of the order entry system was conducted as a result of approval given by the Management Review Committee on March 1. The findings of the investigation are presented below.

Objectives of Detailed Investigation and Analysis

   The study was conducted to investigate two major complaints of the wholesale auto parts order entry system. Complaints have been received that orders were not being shipped promptly, and customers were not notified of out-of-stock conditions for many days after sending in orders. In addition, billing invoices are running several days behind shipments. The objective of this study was to determine where the problems existed and to develop alternative solutions.

Findings of the Detailed Investigation and Analysis

   The following problems appear to exist within the order entry system:

2. Place the order entry and invoicing systems on the computer. Computer terminals would be installed in the sales department for order entry clerks. As orders are received, they would be entered into the computer. Orders could be immediately edited for proper customer and part numbers and a check could be made to determine if stock is available. Billing invoices could be mailed the same day as shipments. Estimated costs: (1) Systems analysis and design-$26,000; (2) Programming and implementation-$40,000; (3) Training, new forms, and maintenance-$7,000; (4) Equipment (four terminals)-$6,000.

Recommended Action

The systems department recommends the design of a computerized order entry and invoicing system utilizing alternative 2, which is believed to offer the most effective solution.

George Lacey

FIGURE 10-12

Written reports summarizing the analyst's work are an important part of the development project. This report was prepared at the end of the analysis phase and recommends the development of a computerized order entry and invoicing system.

Phase 2—Design

The proposed solution developed as part of the analysis phase usually consists of what is called a **logical design**, which means that the design was deliberately developed without regard to a specific computer or programming language and no attempt was made to identify which procedures should be automated and which procedures should be manual. This approach avoids early assumptions that may limit the possible solutions. During the **design** phase the logical design will be transformed into a **physical design** that will identify the procedures to be automated, choose the programming language, and specify the equipment needed for the system.

Structured Design Methods

The system design usually follows one of two methods, top-down design or bottom-up design.

Top-Down Design **Top-down design**, also called **structured design**, focuses on the major functions of the system, such as recording a sale or generating an invoice, and keeps breaking those functions down into smaller and smaller activities, sometimes called modules, that can eventually be programmed. Top-down design is an increasingly popular method because it focuses on the "big picture" and helps users and systems analysts reach an early agreement on what the major functions of the new system are.

Bottom-Up Design **Bottom-up design** focuses on the data, particularly the output of the system. The approach used is to determine what output is needed and move "up" to the processes needed to produce the output.

In practice, most system analysts use a combination of the two methods. Some information requirements like payroll checks, for example, have data elements that lend themselves to bottom-up design. Other requirements, such as management-oriented exception reports, are better suited to a top-down design.

Regardless of the structured design method used, the system analyst will eventually need to complete the design activities.

Design Activities

Design activities include a number of individual tasks that a system analyst performs to design an information system. These include designs for the output, input, database, processes, system controls, and testing.

Output Design The design of the output is critical to the successful implementation of the system because it is the output that provides the information to the users and that is the basis for the justification of most computerized systems. For example, most users don't know (or necessarily care) how the data will be processed, but they usually do have clear ideas on how they want the information output to look. Often requests for new or modified systems begin with a user-prepared draft of a report that the current system doesn't produce. During **output design**, the system analyst and the user document specific screen and report layouts that will be used for output to display or report information from the new system. The example in Figure 10-13 illustrates a report layout sheet.

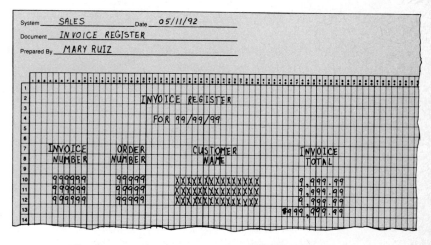

FIGURE 10-13

The report layout form is used to design printed output. Column titles, data width, and report totals are shown on the layout form.

Input Design   During **input design** the analyst and user identify what information needs to be entered into the system to produce the desired output and where and how the data will be entered. With interactive systems, the systems analyst and user must determine the sequence of inputs and computer responses, called a **dialogue**, that the user will encounter when entering data. Figure 10-14 shows a display screen layout sheet commonly used to document the format of a screen display.

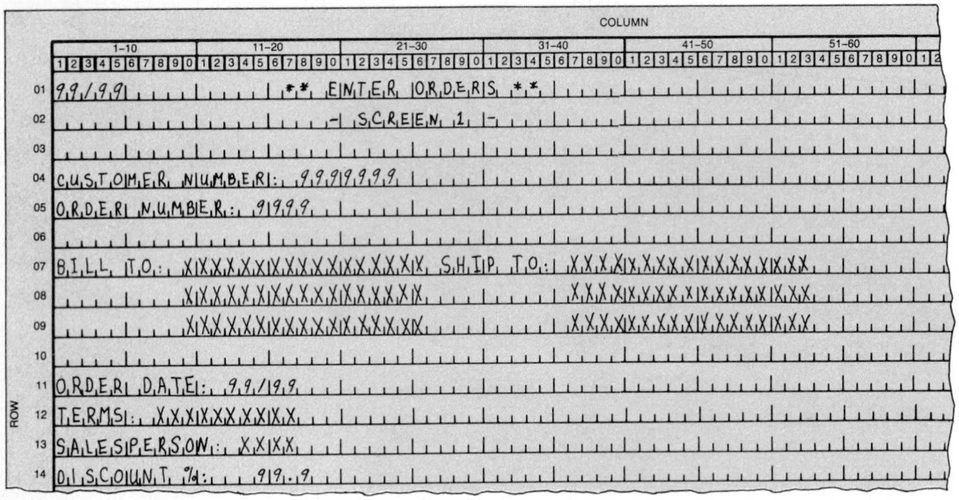

FIGURE 10-14

The display screen layout sheet is similar to the report layout form. Each row and column correspond to a row and column on the screen.

Database Design   During **database design** the systems analyst uses the data dictionary information developed during the analysis phase and merges it into new or existing system files. During this phase of the design, the analyst works closely with the database administrator to identify existing database elements that can be used to satisfy design requirements.

Efficient file design can be a challenging task, especially with relational database systems that stress minimum **data redundancy** (duplicate data). The volume of database activity must also be considered at this point. For example, large files that will be frequently accessed may need a separate index file (discussed in Chapter 7) to allow inquiries to be processed in an amount of time acceptable to the user.

Process Design   During **process design** the system analyst specifies exactly what actions will be taken on the input data to create output information. Decisions on the timing of actions are added to the logical processes identified in the analysis phase. For example, the analysis phase might have found that an exception report should be produced if inventory balances fall below a certain level. During the process design phase, the frequency of the report would be determined.

One way to document the relationship of different processes is with a **system flowchart** (Figure 10-15). The system flowchart shows the major processes (each of which may require one or more programs), reports (including their distribution), data files, and the types of input devices such as terminals or tape drives, that will provide data to the system. A template with the special symbols used in a system flowchart is shown in Figure 10-16.

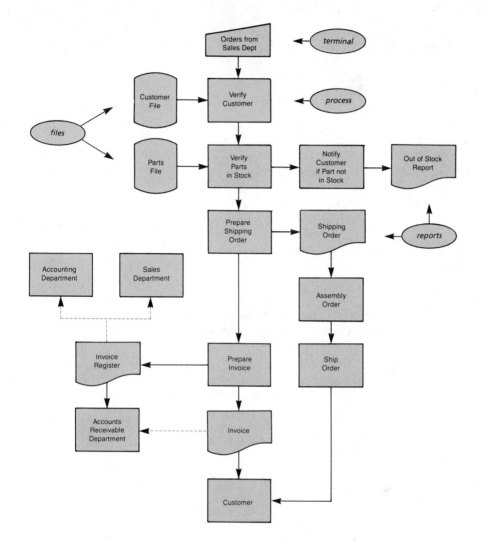

FIGURE 10-15

The system flowchart documents the equipment used to enter data, such as the terminals for the salespeople and the order department, the processes that will take place, such as "Verify Customer," the files that will be used, such as the Customer and Parts files, and the reports that will be produced, such as the shipping order. Dotted lines indicate additional copies of reports, such as the copy of the invoice that is sent to the accounts receivable department.

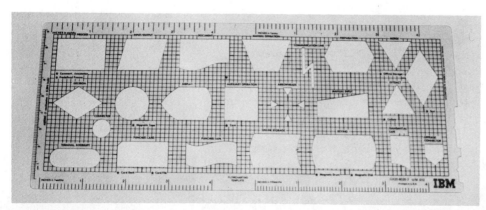

FIGURE 10-16

A template with the symbols used for preparing a system flowchart.

During process design the system analyst, the user, and other members of the development project sometimes meet to conduct a **structured walkthrough**, a step-by-step review of the process design. The purpose of these sessions is to identify any design logic errors and to continue the communication between the systems analyst and the user.

System Controls An important aspect of the design phase is the establishment of a comprehensive set of system controls. **System controls** ensure that only valid data is accepted and processed. Adequate controls must be established for two basic reasons: (1) to ensure the accuracy of the processing and the information generated from the system; and (2) to prevent computer-related fraud.

There are four basic types of controls that must be considered by the systems analyst. These controls are: (1) source document controls; (2) input controls; (3) processing controls; and (4) accounting controls.

Source document controls include serial numbering of input documents such as invoices and paychecks, document registers in which each input document is recorded and time-stamped as it is received, and batch totaling and balancing to predetermined totals to assure the accuracy of processing.

Input controls are established to assure the complete and accurate conversion of data from the source documents or other sources to a machine-processable form. Editing data as it enters the system is the most important form of input controls.

Processing controls refer to procedures that are established to determine the accuracy of information after it has been input to the system. For example, the accuracy of the total accounts receivable could be verified by taking the prior day's total, adding the current day's sales invoices, and subtracting the current day's payments.

Accounting controls provide assurance that the dollar amounts recorded in the accounting records are correct. An important accounting control is an audit trail. An **audit trail** is one or more reports that provide a history of how transactions have been summarized before they are recorded in the general ledger. For example, an audit trail for sales would include a daily sales register that shows each individual sale transaction, a monthly sales journal that shows the total sales for each day, and the general ledger that has an entry for total sales for the month. With an audit trail, a user can trace any summary entry in the general ledger back to the individual transactions that make it up.

Testing Design During the design phase, test specifications are developed. The exact tests to be performed should be specified by someone other than the user or the systems analyst, although both should be consulted. Users and systems analysts have a tendency to test only what has been designed. An impartial third party, who has not been actively involved in the design, is more likely to design a test for, and therefore discover, a procedure or type of data that may have been overlooked in the design. Sometimes organizations avoid test design and test their systems with actual transactions. While such "live" testing is valuable, it might not test all conditions that the system is designed to process. This is especially true of error or exception conditions that do not occur regularly. For example, payroll systems are usually designed to reject input for hours worked over some limit, say 60 hours in a week. If only actual data are used to test the system, this limit may not be tested. Thus it is important to design testing specifications that will test each system control that is part of the system.

Design Review

At the end of the design phase, management performs a **design review** and evaluates the work completed so far to determine whether or not to proceed (Figure 10-17). This is a critical point in any development project and all parties must take equal responsibility for the decision. Usually the design review will result only in requests for clarification of a few items. But sometimes an entire project may be terminated. Although canceling or restarting a project from the beginning is a difficult decision, in the long run it is less costly than implementing the wrong or an inadequate solution. If the decision is made to proceed, the project enters the development phase. Before discussing the development phase, we describe prototyping, a development method that can be used in several phases of a system development project.

FIGURE 10-17

The design review is a critical point in the development process. Representatives from the user and information systems departments and top management meet to determine if the system should be developed as designed or if additional design work is necessary.

Prototyping

Prototyping is building a working model of the new system. The advantage of prototyping is that it lets the user actually experience the system before it is completed. Some organizations use prototyping during the analysis phase, others use it during the design phase. Still other companies use prototyping to go directly from preliminary investigation to an implemented system. These companies just keep refining the prototype until the user says that it is acceptable. The disadvantage of such an accelerated approach is that key features of a new system, especially exception conditions, may be overlooked. Another disadvantage is that documentation, an important part of any system development effort, is usually not as well or as thoroughly prepared. When used as a tool to show the user how the system will operate, however, prototyping can be an important system development tool.

Phase 3—Development

Once the system design phase has been completed, the project enters the system development phase. There are two parts to **development**: program development and equipment acquisition.

Program Development

The process of developing the software, or programs, required for a system is called **program development** and includes the following steps: (1) reviewing the program specifications; (2) designing the program; (3) coding the program; (4) testing the program;

and (5) finalizing the program documentation. The primary responsibility for completing these tasks is assumed by computer programmers who work closely with the system analyst who designed the system. Chapter 11 explains program development in depth. The important concepts to understand now are that this process is a part of the development phase of the system development life cycle and that its purpose is to develop the software required by the system.

Equipment Acquisition

During the development phase, final decisions are made on what additional equipment, if any, will be required for the new system. A preliminary review of the equipment requirements is done during the analysis phase and included in the written report prepared by the systems analyst. Making the equipment acquisition prior to the development phase is premature because any equipment selected should be based on the requirements of the approved design from Phase 2. Equipment selection is affected by factors such as the number of users who will require terminals and the disk storage that will be required for new files and data elements. In some cases, even a new or upgraded CPU is required.

Phase 4—Implementation

Implementation is the phase of the system development process when people actually begin using the new system. This is a critical phase of the project that usually requires careful timing and the coordination of all project participants. Important parts of this phase that will contribute to the success of the new system are training and education, conversion, and postimplementation evaluation.

Training and Education

Someone once said, "If you think education is expensive, you should consider the cost without it." The point is that untrained users can prevent the estimated benefits of a new system from ever being obtained or worse, contribute to less efficiency and more costs than when the old system was operational. Training consists of showing people exactly how they will use the new system (Figure 10-18). This may include classroom-style lectures but should definitely include hands-on sessions with the equipment they will be using, such as terminals, and realistic sample data. Education consists of learning new principles or theories that help people to understand and use the system. For example, before implementing a modern manufacturing system, many companies now require their manufacturing personnel to attend classes on material requirements planning (MRP), shop floor control, and other essential manufacturing topics.

FIGURE 10-18

All users should be trained on the system before they have to use it to process actual transactions. Training could include both classroom and hands-on sessions.

Conversion

Conversion refers to the process of changing from the old system to the new system. A number of different methods of conversion may be used including direct, parallel, phased, and pilot.

With **direct conversion**, the user stops using the old system one day and begins using the new system the next. The advantage of this approach is that it is fast and efficient, if it works. The disadvantage is that it is risky and can seriously disrupt operations if the new system does not work correctly the first time.

Parallel conversion consists of continuing to process data on the old system while some or all of the data is also processed on the new system. Results from both systems are compared, and if they agree, all data is switched to the new system (Figure 10-19).

Phased conversion is used with larger systems that can be broken down into individual modules that can be implemented separately at different times. An example would be a complete business system that has accounts receivable, inventory, and accounts payable modules implemented separately in phases. Phased conversions can be direct, parallel, or a combination of both.

Pilot conversion means that the new system will be used first by only a portion of the organization, often at a separate location such as a plant or office.

FIGURE 10-19

During parallel conversion, the user compares results from both the old and the new system to determine if the new system is operating properly.

Postimplementation Evaluation

After a system is implemented, it is important to conduct a **postimplementation evaluation** to determine if the system is performing as designed, if operating costs are as anticipated, and if any modifications are necessary to make the system operate more effectively.

Phase 5—Maintenance

Maintenance is the process of supporting the system after it is implemented. Maintenance consists of three activities: performance monitoring, change management, and error correction.

Performance Monitoring

Performance monitoring is the ongoing process of comparing response times, file sizes, and other system performance measures against the estimates that were prepared during the analysis, design, and implementation phases. Variances from these estimates may indicate that the system requires additional equipment resources, such as more memory or faster disk drives.

Change Management

Change is an inevitable part of any system and should be provided for with methods and procedures that are made known to all users of the system. Sometimes changes are required because existing requirements were overlooked. Other times, new information requirements caused by external sources such as government regulations will force change. A key part of change management is documentation. The same documentation standards that were followed during the analysis and design phases should also be used to record changes. In fact, in many organizations, the same document that is used to request new systems (Figure 10-5) is used to request changes to an existing system (Figure 10-20). Thus the system development life cycle continues as Phase 1 (analysis) begins on the change request.

```
┌──────────────────────────────────────────────────────────┐
│                 REQUEST FOR SYSTEM SERVICES                │
│                                                            │
│                          ISD CONTROL #: 4703               │
│                                                            │
│  I.  To Be Completed By Person Requesting Services         │
│                                                            │
│  SUBMITTED BY: MIKE CHARLES DEPT AUTO PARTS SALES DATE: 2-1-93 │
│                                                            │
│  REQUEST TYPE:  ☑ MODIFICATION    ☐ NEW SYSTEM             │
│                                                            │
│  NEED:   ☑ ASAP    ☐ IMMEDIATE    ☐ LONG RANGE            │
│                                                            │
│  BRIEF STATEMENT OF REQUEST (attach additional material, if│
│  necessary)                                                │
│     SALES INVOICE PROGRAM NEEDS TO PROVIDE FOR 1%          │
│     COUNTY TAX THAT WILL GO INTO EFFECT JULY 1, 1993.      │
│  ─────────────────────────────────────────────────        │
│  ─────────────────────────────────────────────────        │
│                                                            │
│     ☑ ADDITIONAL MATERIAL ATTACHED COUNTY TAX RATE SCHEDULE│
│  ==========================================================│
│  II.  To Be Completed By Information Systems Department     │
│                                                            │
│  REQUEST INVESTIGATED BY:_____ DATE:_____  │
│                                                            │
│  COMMENTS:_____  │
│  _____  │
│  _____  │
│  _____  │
│                                                            │
│  ==========================================================│
│  III.  Disposition                                         │
│     ☐ REQUEST APPROVED FOR IMMEDIATE IMPLEMENTATION        │
│     ☐ Analyst assigned:_____       │
│     ☐ REQUEST APPROVED FOR IMPLEMENTATION AS SOON AS POSSIBLE │
│     ☐ REQUEST REJECTED                                     │
│  COMMENTS:_____  │
│  _____  │
│  _____  │
│                                                            │
│  SIGNED:_____ DATE:_____   │
└──────────────────────────────────────────────────────────┘
```

FIGURE 10-20

The same form that was used to request a new system (see Figure 10-5) is also used to request a modification to an existing system.

Error Correction

Error correction deals with problems that are caused by programming and design errors that are discovered after the system is implemented. Often these errors are minor problems, such as the zip code not appearing on a name and address report, that can be quickly fixed by a programmer. Other times, however, the error requires some level of investigation by the systems analyst before a correction can be determined.

Chapter Summary

Although the system development process may appear to be a straightforward series of steps, in practice it is a challenging activity that calls for the skills and cooperation of all involved. New development tools have made the process more efficient but the success of any project always depends on the commitment of the project participants. The understanding you have gained from this chapter will help you participate in information system development projects and give you an appreciation for the importance of each phase.

The following list summarizes the key topics discussed in this chapter.

1. An **information system** is a collection of six elements: equipment, software, data, personnel, users, and procedures that provide accurate, timely, and useful information (p. 10.2).
2. There are four types of information systems: (1) **operational systems**; (2) **management information systems**; (3) **decision support systems**; and (4) **expert systems** (p. 10.2–10.3).
3. The trend is to combine all of an organization's information needs into a single integrated information system (p. 10.4).
4. The **system development life cycle** is an organized approach to developing an information system and consists of five phases: analysis, design, development, implementation, and maintenance (p. 10.4).
5. Planning, scheduling, reporting, and controlling the individual activities that make up the information system development life cycle is called **project management**. These activities are usually recorded in a **project plan** (p. 10.5).
6. **Documentation** refers to written materials that are produced throughout the system development life cycle (p. 10.5).
7. All users and information system personnel who will be affected by the new system should have the opportunity to participate in its development (p. 10.5).
8. The systems analyst's job is a challenging one requiring good communication, analytical, and diplomatic skills to keep the development process on track and on schedule (p. 10.6).

9. The **analysis** phase is the separation of a system into its parts in order to determine how the system works. This phase consists of the preliminary investigation, detailed system analysis, and making the decision on how to proceed (p. 10.6).
10. The purpose of the **preliminary investigation** is to determine if a request warrants further detailed investigation. The most important aspect of this investigation is **problem definition** (p. 10.6).
11. **Detailed system analysis** involves both a thorough study of the current system and at least one proposed solution to any problems found (p. 10.7).
12. **Data flow diagrams** are a **structured analysis** tool that graphically show the flow of data through a system (p. 10.7).
13. Other tools that are used in the analysis phase include **data dictionaries, process specifications, structured English, decision tables**, and **decision trees** (p. 10.8–10.9).
14. A **feasibility study** and **cost/benefit analysis** are often prepared to show whether the proposed solution is practical and to show the estimated costs and benefits that are expected (p. 10.10).
15. During the **design** phase the **logical design** that was created in the analysis phase is transformed into a **physical design** (p. 10.10).
16. There are two major structured design methods: **top-down design** (or **structured design**) and **bottom-up design** (p. 10.11).
17. **Output design**, **input design**, and **database design** all occur during the design phase (p. 10.11–10.12).
18. When designing interactive systems, the systems analyst and user determine the sequence of inputs and computer responses, called a **dialogue** (p. 10.12).
19. During the **process design** the systems analyst specifies exactly what actions will be taken on the input data to create output information (p. 10.12).
20. One method of documenting the relationship of different processes is with a **system flowchart** (p. 10.12).
21. A **structured walkthrough**, or a step-by-step review, is sometimes performed on the process design (p. 10.14).

22. **System controls** ensure that only valid data is accepted and processed. Types of system controls include **source document controls**, **input controls**, **processing controls**, and **accounting controls**, including an **audit trail** (p. 10.14).

23. At the end of the design phase, a **design review** is performed to evaluate the work completed so far (p. 10.15).

24. **Prototyping** is building a working model of the new system (p. 10.15).

25. The **development** phase consists of program development and equipment acquisition (p. 10.15).

26. **Program development** includes: (1) reviewing the program specifications; (2) designing the program; (3) coding the program; (4) testing the program; and (5) finalizing the program documentation (p. 10.15–10.16).

27. The **implementation** phase is when people actually begin using the new system. This phase includes training and education, conversion, and the **postimplementation evaluation** (p. 10.16).

28. The process of changing from the old system to the new system is called a **conversion**. The conversion methods that may be used are **direct**, **parallel**, **phased**, and **pilot** (p. 10.17).

29. The **maintenance** phase is the process of supporting the information system after it is implemented. It consists of three activities: **performance monitoring**, **change management**, and **error correction** (p. 10.17–10.18).

Review Questions

1. List the six elements of an information system.
2. What are the four types of information systems? What is meant by integrated information systems?
3. List the five phases of the system development life cycle.
4. Describe project management and when it should be performed.
5. What is the preliminary investigation? What is the most important aspect of the preliminary investigation?
6. Briefly describe detailed system analysis. What are the fact-finding techniques used during detailed system analysis?
7. What are the symbols used in data flow diagrams? Why are data flow diagram useful?
8. Explain the difference between the logical and physical design of an information system.
9. What are the two methods of structured design? Briefly describe each method.
10. List and describe four basic types of system controls.
11. What is prototyping?
12. What are the steps in program development?
13. Write a description of the four types of conversion methods.
14. Describe the three major activities of system maintenance.

Program Development

11

Objectives

- Define the term computer program.
- Describe the five steps in program development: review of program specifications, program design, program coding, program testing, and finalizing program documentation.
- Explain the concepts of structured program design including modules, control structures, and single entry/single exit.
- Explain and illustrate the sequence, selection, and iteration control structures used in structured programming.
- Define the term programming language and discuss the various categories of programming languages.
- Briefly discuss the programming languages that are commonly used today, including BASIC, COBOL, C, FORTRAN, Pascal, Ada, and RPG.
- Explain and discuss application generators.
- Explain the factors that should be considered when choosing a programming language.

As we discussed in Chapter 10, the system development life cycle covers the entire process of taking a plan for processing information through various phases until it becomes a functioning information system. During the development phase of this cycle, computer programs are written. The purpose of these programs is to process data and produce output as specified in the system design. This chapter focuses on the steps taken to write a program and the available tools that make the program development process more efficient. In addition, this chapter discusses the different languages used to write programs.

Although you may never write a program yourself, it is likely that you will someday request information that will require a program to be written or modified. Therefore it is important for you to understand the process that takes place when a computer program is developed.

What Is a Computer Program?

A **computer program** is a detailed set of instructions that directs a computer to perform the tasks necessary to process data into information. These instructions, usually written by a computer programmer, can be coded (written) in a variety of programming languages that will be discussed later in this chapter. To create programs that are correct (produce accurate information) and maintainable (easy to modify), programmers follow a process called program development.

What Is Program Development?

In the early days of computing, programming was considered an "art" and the programming process was left to the "interpretation" of the programmer. While there is still room for creativity, **program development**, the process of producing one or more programs to perform one or more specific tasks on a computer, has evolved into a series of five steps that most experts agree should take place when any program is developed. These five steps (Figure 11-1) are:

1. Review of program specifications. The programmer reviews the specifications created by the system analyst during the system design phase.
2. Program design. The programmer determines the specific actions the program will take to accomplish the desired tasks.
3. Coding. The programmer writes the actual program instructions.
4. Testing. The written programs are tested to make sure they perform as intended.
5. Finalizing documentation. The documentation produced during the program development process is brought together and organized.

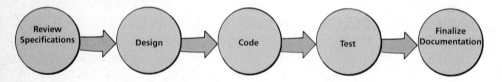

FIGURE 11-1

The five steps of program development.

Step 1—Review of Program Specifications

The first step in the program development cycle is a review of the program specifications. **Program specifications** can consist of data flow diagrams, system flowcharts, process specifications that indicate the action to be taken on the data, a data dictionary identifying the data elements that will be used, screen formats, and report layouts. These documents help the programmer understand the work that needs to be done by the program. Because it is important that the programmer understand the purpose of the program from the user's point of view, one or more meetings are usually held between the programmer, the user, and the systems analyst who designed the system.

If the programmer believes some aspect of the design should be changed, such as a screen layout, it is discussed with the analyst and the user. If the change is agreed on, the design specification is changed. However, the programmer should not change the specified system without the agreement of the analyst and user. If a change is authorized, it should be recorded in the system design. The analyst and user, through the system design, have specified *what* is to be done. It is the programmer's job to determine *how* to do it.

Large programming jobs are usually assigned to more than one programmer. In these situations, a good system design is essential so that each programmer can be given a logical portion of the system to be programmed.

Step 2—Program Design

After the program specifications have been carefully reviewed, program design begins. During **program design** a logical solution to the programming task is developed and documented. The logical solution or **logic** for a program is a step-by-step solution to a programming problem. Determining the logic for a computer program can be an extremely complex task. To aid in program design and development, a method called structured program design is commonly used.

Structured Program Design

Structured program design is a methodology that emphasizes three main program design concepts: modules, control structures, and single entry/single exit. Use of these concepts helps to create programs that are easy to write, read, understand, check for errors, and modify.

Modules   With structured design, programming problems are "decomposed" (separated) into smaller parts called modules. Each **module**, sometimes referred to as a **subroutine** in programming, performs a given task within the program. The major benefit of this technique is that it simplifies program development because each module of a program can be developed individually. When the modules are combined, they form a complete program that accomplishes the desired result.

Structure charts, also called **hierarchy charts**, are often used to decompose and represent the modules of a program. When the program decomposition is completed, the entire structure of a program is illustrated by the hierarchy chart and the relationship of the modules within the program (Figure 11-2).

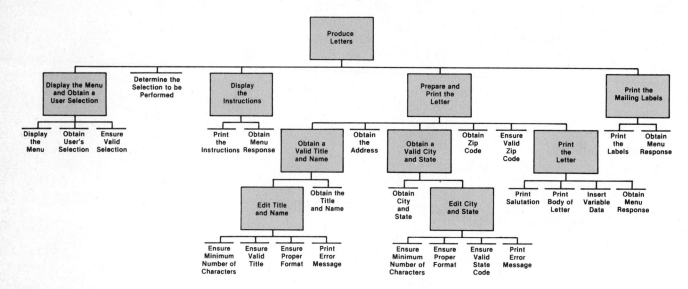

Control Structures In structured program design three basic **control structures** are used to form the logic of a program. All logic problems can be solved by a combination of these structures. The three basic control structures are: sequence, selection, and iteration.

In the **sequence structure**, one process occurs immediately after another. In Figure 11-3, each rectangular box represents a particular process that is to take place. For example, a process could be a computer instruction to move data from one location in main memory to another location. Each process takes place in the exact sequence specified, one process followed by the next.

The second control structure, called the **selection** or **if-then-else structure**, gives programmers a way to represent conditional program logic (Figure 11-4). Conditional program logic can be expressed in the following way: *If* the condition is true, *then* perform the true task, *else* perform the false task. When the if-then-else control structure is used, the "if" portion of the structure tests a given condition. The true task is executed if the condition tested is true and the false task is executed if the condition is false. For example, in a payroll program the number of hours worked might be tested to determine if an employee worked overtime. If the person did work overtime, the true task would be executed and overtime would be calculated. If the employee did not work overtime, then the false task would be executed and overtime would not be calculated. The selection or if-then-else structure is used by programmers to represent conditional logic problems.

FIGURE 11-2

A structure chart graphically illustrates the relationship of individual program modules.

SELECTION

SEQUENCE

FIGURE 11-3

Each box in the sequence control structure represents a process that takes place immediately after the preceding process.

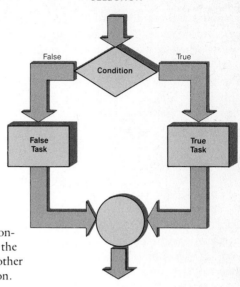

FIGURE 11-4

The selection or if-then-else control structure is used to direct the program to one process or another based on the test of a condition.

The third control structure, called **iteration** or **looping,** means that one or more processes continue to occur so long as a given condition remains true. There are two forms of this control structure: the **do-while structure** and the **do-until structure** (Figure 11-5). In the do-while structure a condition is tested. If the condition is true, the process is performed. The program then "loops" back and tests the condition again. If the condition is still true, the process is performed again. This looping continues until the condition being tested is false. At that time, the program exits the loop and performs some other processing. An example of this type of testing would be a check to see if all records have been processed. The do-until control structure is similar to the do-while except that the conditional test is at the end instead of the beginning of the loop. Processing continues "until" the condition is met.

FIGURE 11-5

The iteration control structure has two forms, do-while and do-until. In the do-while structure, the condition is tested before the process. In the do-until structure, the condition is tested after the process.

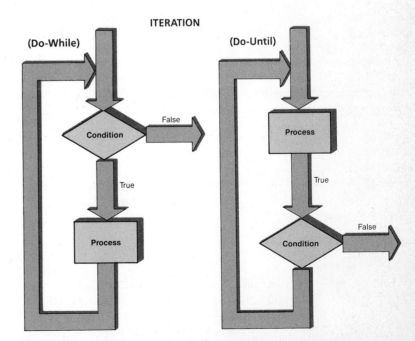

These three control structures, sequence, selection, and iteration, are combined by programmers to create program logic solutions. A structured program design rule that applies to these control structures and how they are combined is the single entry/single exit rule.

Single Entry/Single Exit   An important concept in structured programming is **single entry/single exit**, meaning that there is only one entry point and one exit point for each of the three control structures. An **entry point** is the point where a control structure is entered. An **exit point** is the point where the control structure is exited. For example, in Figure 11-6, when the if-then-else structure is used, the control structure is entered at the point where the condition is tested. When the condition is tested, one set of instructions will be executed if the condition is true and another set will be executed if the condition is false. Regardless of the result of the test, however, the structure is exited at the single exit point.

This feature substantially improves the understanding of a program because, when reading the program, the programmer can be assured that whatever happens within the if-then-else structure, the control structure will always be exited at a common point. Prior to the use of structured programming, many programmers would transfer control to other parts of a program without following the single entry/single exit rule. This practice led to poorly designed programs that were extremely difficult to read, check for errors, and modify.

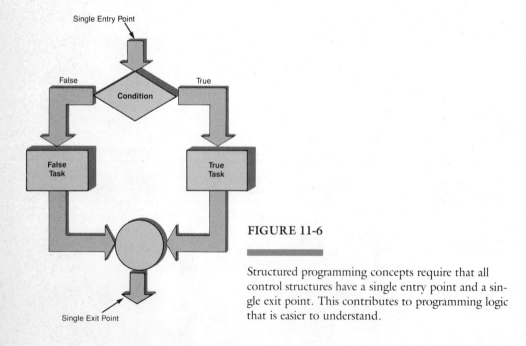

FIGURE 11-6

Structured programming concepts require that all control structures have a single entry point and a single exit point. This contributes to programming logic that is easier to understand.

Program Design Tools

There are several popular program design tools through which structured program design concepts can be applied. These design tools are used by computer programmers to develop and document the logical solutions to the problems they are programming. Two of the most commonly used design tools are program flowcharts and pseudocode.

Program Flowcharts Program flowcharts were one of the first program design tools. Figure 11-7 shows a flowchart drawn in the late 1940s by Dr. John von Neumann, a computer scientist and one of the first computer programmers. In a **program flowchart** all the logical steps of a program are represented by a combination of symbols and text.

A set of standards for program flowcharts was published in the early 1960s by the American National Standards Institute (ANSI). These standards, which are still used today, specify symbols, such as rectangles and diamonds, that are used to represent the various operations that can be performed on a computer (Figure 11-8).

Program flowcharts were used as the primary means of program design for many years prior to the introduction of structured program design. During these years, programmers designed programs by focusing on the detailed steps required for a program and creating logical solutions for each new combination of conditions as it was encountered. Developing programs in this manner led to programs that were poorly designed.

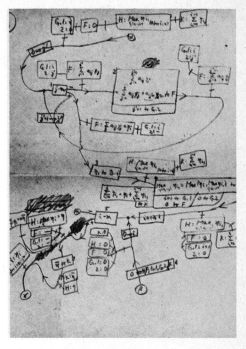

FIGURE 11-7

An example of an early flowchart developed by computer scientist Dr. John von Neumann in the 1940s to solve a problem involving game theory.

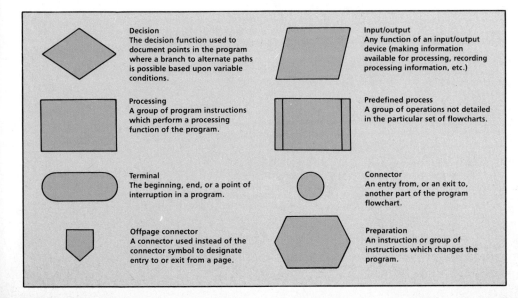

Decision
The decision function used to document points in the program where a branch to alternate paths is possible based upon variable conditions.

Processing
A group of program instructions which perform a processing function of the program.

Terminal
The beginning, end, or a point of interruption in a program.

Offpage connector
A connector used instead of the connector symbol to designate entry to or exit from a page.

Input/output
Any function of an input/output device (making information available for processing, recording processing information, etc.)

Predefined process
A group of operations not detailed in the particular set of flowcharts.

Connector
An entry from, or an exit to, another part of the program flowchart.

Preparation
An instruction or group of instructions which changes the program.

FIGURE 11-8

The standard symbols used to prepare program flowcharts.

FIGURE 11-9

This flowchart illustrates the use of standard flow-charting symbols and the three control structures used in structured programming. It displays the logic required to solve a payroll calculation task.

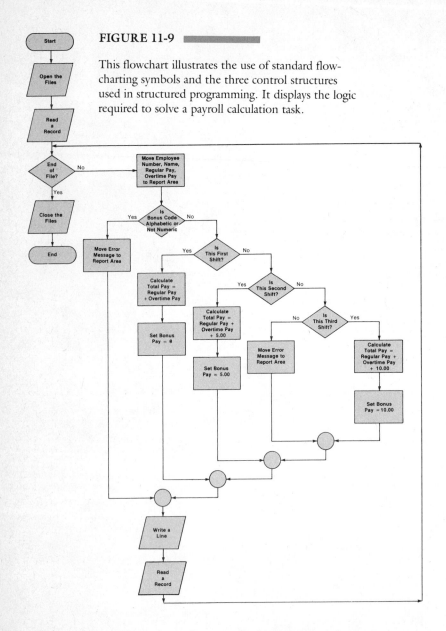

FIGURE 11-10

This pseudocode is another way of documenting the logic shown in the flowchart in Figure 11-9.

```
Open the files
Read a record
PERFORM UNTIL end of file
    Move employee number, name, regular pay, and
        overtime pay to the report area
    IF bonus code is alphabetic or not numeric
        Move error message to report area
    ELSE
        IF first shift
            Calculate total pay = regular pay +
                overtime pay
            Set bonus pay to zero
        ELSE
            IF second shift
                Calculate total pay = regular pay +
                    overtime pay + 5.00
                Set bonus pay to 5.00
            ELSE
                IF third shift
                    Calculate total pay = regular pay +
                        overtime pay + 10.00
                    Set bonus pay to 10.00
                ELSE
                    Move error message to report area
                ENDIF
            ENDIF
        ENDIF
    ENDIF
    Write a line
    Read a record
ENDPERFORM
Close the files
End the program
```

Today, programmers are taught to apply the structured design concepts when preparing program flowcharts (Figure 11-9). When the basic control structures are utilized, program flowcharts are a valuable program design tool.

Pseudocode Some experts in program design advocate the use of pseudocode when designing the logic for a program. In **pseudocode** the logical steps in the solution of a problem are written as English statements and indentations are used to represent the control structures (Figure 11-10). An advantage of pseudocode is that it eliminates the time spent with flowcharting to draw and arrange symbols while attempting to determine the program logic. The major disadvantage is that unlike flowcharting, pseudocode does not provide a graphic representation, which many people find useful and easier to interpret when examining programming logic.

Structured Walkthrough

After a program has been designed, the programmer schedules a structured walkthrough of the program. The programmer, other programmers in the department, and the systems analyst attend. During the walkthrough, the programmer who designs the program explains the program logic. The purpose of the design walkthrough is to review the logic of the program for errors, and if possible, improve it. It is much better to find errors and make needed changes to the program during the design step than to make them later in the program development process.

Once the program design is complete, the coding of the program begins.

Step 3—Program Coding

Coding the program refers to the process of writing the program instructions that will process the data and produce the output specified in the program design. As previously mentioned, programs are written in different languages that each have particular rules on how to instruct the computer to perform specific tasks, such as read a record or multiply two numbers. The differences in these languages will be discussed later in this chapter.

If a thorough program design has been produced, the coding process is greatly simplified and can sometimes be a one-for-one translation of a design step into a program step. Today, program code, or instructions, are usually entered directly into the computer via a terminal and stored on a disk drive. Using this approach, the programmer can partially enter a program at one time and finish entering it at a later time. Program instructions are added, deleted, and changed until the programmer believes the program design has been fully translated into program instructions and the program is ready for testing.

Step 4—Program Testing

Before a program is used to process "real" data and produce information that people rely on, it should be thoroughly tested to make sure it is functioning correctly. Several different types of tests can be performed.

Desk checking is the process of reading the program and mentally reviewing its logic. This process can be compared with proofreading a letter before you put it in the mail. The disadvantage of this method is that it is difficult to detect other than obvious errors.

Another type of testing identifies program **syntax errors**, violations of the grammar rules of the language in which the program was written. An example of a syntax error would be the program command READ being misspelled REED. Syntax errors missed by the programmer are discovered by the computer when it decodes the program instructions.

Logic testing is what most programmers think of when the term testing is used. During **logic testing**, the sequence of program instructions is tested to make sure they provide the correct result. Logic errors may be the result of a programming oversight, such as using the wrong data to perform a calculation, or a design error, such as forgetting to specify that some customers do not have to pay sales tax when they purchase merchandise.

Logic testing is performed with **test data**, data that simulates the type of input that the program will process when it is implemented. In order to obtain an independent and unbiased test of the program, test data and the review of test results should be the responsibility of someone other than the programmer who wrote the program. The test data should be developed by referring to the system design but should also try to "break" the program by including data outside the range of data that will be input during normal operations. For example, even though a payroll program should never have more than 60 hours per week input, the program should be designed, coded, and tested to properly process transactions in excess of 60 hours by displaying an error message or in some other way indicating that an invalid number of hours has been entered. Other similar tests should include alphabetic data when only numeric data is expected, and negative numbers when only positive numbers are normally input.

One of the more colorful terms of the computer industry is **debugging**, which refers to the process of locating and correcting program errors or **bugs** found during testing. The term was coined when the failure of one of the first computers was traced to a moth that had become lodged in the electronic components (Figure 11-11).

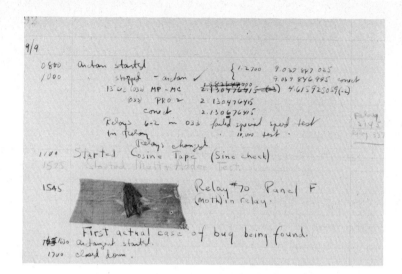

FIGURE 11-11

In 1945, the cause of the temporary failure of the world's first electromechanical computer, the Mark I, was traced to a dead moth caught in the electrical components. The term "bug," meaning a computer error, has been part of computer jargon ever since.

Step 5—Finalizing Program Documentation

Documentation is an essential but sometimes neglected part of the programming process. As reflected in the title of this section, documentation should be an ongoing part of developing a program and should only be finalized, meaning organized and brought together, after the program is successfully tested and ready for implementation. The difficulty in sometimes obtaining adequate documentation is that many programmers can and do develop programs without it; when the program is completed, they have little incentive to go back and complete the documentation "after the fact." In addition to helping programmers develop programs, documentation is valuable because it helps the next programmer who, six months or one year later, is asked to make a change to the program. Proper documentation can substantially reduce the amount of time the new programmer will have to spend learning enough about the program to know how best to make the change.

Documentation developed during the programming process should include a narrative description of the program, program flowcharts, pseudocode, program listings, and test results. Comments in the program itself are also an important part of program documentation (Figure 11-12).

FIGURE 11-12

Most programming languages allow explanatory comments to be placed directly in the program. This is an effective way of documenting the program.

```
100 REM TELLIST           SEPTEMBER 22        SHELLY/CASHMAN
110                                           REM
120 REM THIS PROGRAM DISPLAYS THE NAME, TELEPHONE AREA CODE
130 REM AND PHONE NUMBER OF INDIVIDUALS.
140                                           REM
150 REM VARIABLE NAMES:
160 REM    A.....AREA CODE
170 REM    T$....TELEPHONE NUMBER
180 REM    N$....NAME
190                                           REM
200 REM ***** DATA TO BE PROCESSED *****                    comments
210                                           REM
220 DATA 714, "749-2138", "SAM HORN"
230 DATA 213, "663-1271", "SUE NUNN"
240 DATA 212, "999-1193", "BOB PELE"
250 DATA 312, "979-4418", "ANN SITZ"
260 DATA 999, "999-9999", "END OF FILE"
270                                           REM
280 REM ***** PROCESSING *****
290                                           REM
300 READ A, T$, N$
310                                           REM
320 WHILE N$<> "END OF FILE"
330    PRINT N$, A, T$
340    READ A, T$, N$
350 WEND
360                                           REM
370 PRINT " "
380 PRINT "END OF TELEPHONE LISTING"
390 END
```

Program Maintenance

Program maintenance includes all changes to a program once it is implemented and processing real transactions. Sometimes maintenance is required to correct errors that were not found during the testing step. Other times, maintenance is required to make changes that are the result of the user's new information requirements. It may surprise you to learn that the majority of all business programming today consists of maintaining existing programs, not writing new programs.

Because so much time is spent on maintenance programming, it should be subject to the same policies and procedures, such as design, testing, and documentation, that are required for new programs. Unfortunately, this is not always the case. Because maintenance tasks are usually shorter than new programming efforts, they often aren't held to the same standards. The result is that over time, programs can become unrecognizable when compared with their original documentation. Maintaining high standards for program maintenance can not only lower overall programming costs, but also lengthen the useful life of a program.

Summary of Program Development

The key to developing quality programs for an information system is to follow the steps of the program development process. Program specifications must be carefully reviewed and understood. Structured concepts should be used to design programs that are modular, use the three control structures, and follow the single entry/single exit rule. The program should be carefully coded and tested. Documentation should be finalized. If each of these steps is followed, quality programs will be developed that are correct and that can be easily read, understood, and maintained.

What Is a Programming Language?

As mentioned at the beginning of this chapter, computer programs can be written in a variety of programming languages. People communicate with one another through language, established patterns of words and sounds. A similar definition can also be applied to a **programming language**, which is a set of written words and symbols that allow the programmer or user to communicate with the computer. Just like English, Spanish, Chinese, or other spoken languages, programming languages have rules, called syntax, that govern their use.

Categories of Programming Languages

There are hundreds of programming languages, each with its own syntax. Some languages were developed for specific computers and others, because of their success, have been standardized and adapted to a wide range of computers. Programming languages can be classified into one of four categories: machine language, assembly language, high-level languages, and fourth-generation languages.

Machine Language

A **machine language** is the fundamental language of the computer's processor. Programs written in all other categories of languages are eventually converted into machine language before they are executed. Individual machine language instructions exist for each of the commands in the computer's instruction set, the operations such as add, move, or read that are specific to each computer. Because the instruction set is unique for a particular processor, machine languages are different for computers that have different processors. The advantage of writing a program in machine language is that the programmer can control the computer directly and accomplish exactly what needs to be done. Therefore, well-written machine language programs are very efficient. The disadvantages of machine language programs are that they take a long time to write and they are difficult to review if the programmer is trying to find an error. In addition, because they are written using the instruction set of a particular processor, the programs will only run on computers with the same type of processor. Because they are written for specific processors, machine languages are also called **low-level languages**. Figure 11-13a shows an example of machine language instructions.

(a) Machine Language	(b) Assembly Language	(c) High-level Language
9b df 46 0c 9b d9 c0 9b db 7e f2 9b d9 46 04 9b d8 c9 9b d9 5e fc	fild WORD PTR [bp+12];qty fld ST(0) fstp TBYTE PTR [bp-14] fld DWORD PTR [bp+4];price fmul ST(0),ST(1) fstp DWORD PTR [bp-4];gross	gross = qty * price;

9b d9 c0
9b dc 16 ac 00
9b dd d8
9b dd 7e f0
90 9b
8a 66 f1
9e
9b dd c0
76 19
	fld ST(0)
	     fcom QWORD PTR $T20002
	fstp ST(0)
	     fstsw WORD PTR [bp-16]
	     fwait
	mov ah,BYTE PTR [bp-15]
	     sahf
	ffreeST(0)
	     jbe $I193
		if (qty > ceiling)

9b d9 46 fc
9b d9 46 fc
9b dc 0e b4 00
9b de e9
9b d9 5e 08
90 9b
 	
eb 0d
90
	fld DWORD PTR [bp-4];gross
	fld DWORD PTR [bp-4];gross
	fmul QWORD PTR $T20003
	fsub
	     fstp DWORD PTR [bp+8];net
	     fwait
	
	jmp SHORT $I194
	nop
	$I193:
		net = gross -
		    (gross * discount_rate);
		
		else

8b 46 fc 8b 56 fe 89 46 08 89 56 0a	mov ax,WORD PTR [bp-4];gross mov dx,WORD PTR [bp-2] mov WORD PTR [bp+8],ax ;net mov WORD PTR [bp+10],dx $I194:	net = gross;

FIGURE 11-13

This chart shows program instructions for: (a) machine language (printed in a hexadecimal form); (b) assembly language; and (c) a high-level language called C. The machine language and assembly language instructions shown in this example correspond to the high-level instructions and were generated when the high-level language statements were translated into machine language.

Assembly Language

To make it easier for programmers to remember the specific machine instruction codes, assembly languages were developed. An **assembly language** is similar to a machine language, but uses abbreviations called **mnemonics** or **symbolic operation code** to represent the machine operation code. Another difference is that assembly languages usually allow **symbolic addressing**, which means that a specific computer memory location can be referenced by a name or symbol, such as TOTAL, instead of by its actual address as it would have to be referenced in machine language. Assembly language programs can also include **macro instructions** that generate more than one machine language instruction. Assembly language programs are converted into machine language instructions by a special program called an **assembler**. Even though assembly languages are easier to use than machine languages, they are still considered a low-level language because they are so closely related to the specific design of the computer. Figure 11-13b shows an example of assembly language instructions.

High-Level Languages

The evolution of computer languages continued with the development of high-level languages in the late 1950s and 1960s. **High-level languages** more closely resemble what most people would think of as a language in that they contain nouns, verbs, and mathematical, relational, and logical operators that can be grouped together to form what appear to be sentences (Figure 11-13c). These sentences are called **program statements**. Because of these characteristics, high-level languages can be "read" by programmers and are thus easier to learn and use than machine or assembly languages. Another important advantage over low-level languages is that high-level languages are usually machine independent, which means they can run on different types of computers.

As mentioned previously, all languages must be translated into machine language before they can instruct the computer to perform processing. High-level languages are translated in one of two ways: with a compiler or an interpreter.

A **compiler** converts an entire program into machine language that is usually stored on a disk for later execution. The program to be converted is called the **source program** and the machine language produced is called the **object program** or **object code**. Compilers check the program syntax, perform limited logic checking, and make sure that data that is going to be used in comparisons or calculations, such as a discount rate, is properly defined somewhere in the program. An important feature of compilers is that they produce an error listing of all program statements that do not meet the program language rules. This listing helps the programmer make the necessary changes to correct the program. Figure 11-14 illustrates the process of compiling a program.

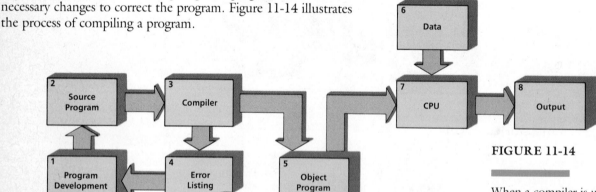

FIGURE 11-14

When a compiler is used, a source language program is compiled into a machine language object program. Usually, both the source and object programs are stored on disk. When the user wants to run the program, the object program is loaded into main memory and the program instructions begin executing.

Because machine language is unique to each processor, different computers require different compilers for the same language. For example, a mainframe, minicomputer, and personal computer each have different compilers that translate the same source language program into the specific machine language for each computer.

While a compiler translates an entire program, an **interpreter** translates one program statement at a time and then executes the resulting machine language before translating the next program statement. When using an interpreter, each time the program is run, the source program is interpreted into machine language and executed. No object program is produced. Figure 11-15 illustrates this process.

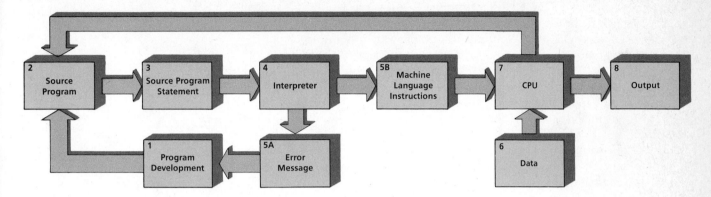

Interpreters are often used with personal computers that do not have the memory or computing power required by compilers. The advantage of interpreters is that the compiling process is not necessary before program changes can be tested. The disadvantage of interpreters is that interpreted programs do not run as fast as compiled programs because the translation to machine language occurs each time the program is run. Compilers for most high-level languages are now available for the newer and more powerful personal computers.

Fourth-Generation Languages

The evolution of computer languages is sometimes described in terms of "generations" with machine, assembly, and high-level languages considered the first, second, and third generations, respectively. Each generation offered significant improvements in ease of use and programming flexibility over the previous generation. Although a clear definition doesn't yet exist, **fourth-generation languages (4GLs)**, sometimes called **very high-level languages**, continue the programming language evolution by being even easier to use than high-level languages for both the programmer and the nonprogramming user.

A common term used to describe fourth-generation languages is **nonprocedural**, which means that the programmer does not specify the order of statement execution to be used to accomplish a task as is done with lower "procedural" language generations. Instead of telling the computer *how* to do the task, the programmer tells the computer *what* is to be done, usually by describing the desired output. A database query language (Figure 11-16) is an example of a nonprocedural fourth-generation language.

FIGURE 11-15

When an interpreter is used, one source language statement at a time is interpreted into machine language instructions that are executed immediately. Error messages indicating an invalid source language statement are produced as each source program statement is interpreted.

```
LIST CUSTOMERS CUSTOMER.NAME WITH BALANCE.DUE > '1000'
```

FIGURE 11-16

This database query is considered an example of a fourth-generation language because it tells the computer *what* the user wants, not *how* to perform the processing.

The advantage of fourth-generation languages is that they are "results" oriented and they can be used by nonprogramming personnel such as users. The disadvantage of fourth-generation languages is that they do not provide as many processing options to the programmer nor are they as efficient as other language generations. Most experts, however, believe that their ease of use far outweighs these disadvantages and predict that fourth-generation languages will continue to be more widely used.

An extension of fourth-generation languages, sometimes called the fifth generation, is a natural language. A **natural language** is a type of query language that allows the user to enter a question as if the user were speaking to another person. For example, a fourth-generation query might be stated as LIST SALESPERSON TOTAL-SALES BY REGION. A natural language version of that same query might be TELL ME THE NAME OF EACH SALESPERSON AND THE TOTAL SALES FOR EACH REGION. The natural language allows the user more flexibility in the structure of the query and can even ask the user a question if it does not understand what is meant by the initial query statement.

Programming Languages Used Today

Although there are hundreds of programming languages, only a few are used extensively enough to be recognized as industry standards. Most of these are high-level programming languages that can be used on a variety of computers. This section discusses the popular programming languages that are commonly used, their origins, and their primary purpose.

To help you understand the differences, we show program code for each of the most popular languages. The code is from programs that solve the same problem, the computation of the net sale price using a discount if the gross sale is over $100.00.

BASIC

BASIC, which stands for **B**eginner's **A**ll-purpose **S**ymbolic **I**nstruction **C**ode, was developed by John Kemeny and Thomas Kurtz in 1964 at Dartmouth College (Figure 11-17). Originally designed to be a simple, interactive programming language for college students to learn and use, BASIC has become one of the most commonly used programming languages on microcomputers and minicomputers.

```
5010 REM ****************P R O C E S S    A N D    D I S P L A Y********
5040 GROSS = QTY * SLSPR
5050 IF QTY > CEILING THEN NET = GROSS - (GROSS * DISC) ELSE NET = GROSS
5070 PRINT "THE NET SALES IS $";
5080 PRINT USING "$$#,###.##"; NET
5090 RETURN
```

FIGURE 11-17

An excerpt from a BASIC program.

COBOL

COBOL (**CO**mmon **B**usiness **O**riented **L**anguage) was introduced in 1960. Backed by the Department of Defense, COBOL was developed by a committee of representatives from both government and industry. Rear Admiral Grace M. Hopper was a key person on the committee and is recognized as one of the prime developers of the COBOL language. COBOL is one of the most widely used programming languages for business applications (Figure 11-18). Using an English-like format, COBOL instructions are arranged in ''sentences'' and grouped into ''paragraphs.'' The English format makes COBOL easy to write and read, but also makes it a wordy language that produces lengthy program code. COBOL is very good for processing large files and performing relatively simple business computations. Other languages are stronger at performing complex mathematical formulas and functions.

```
00100      016200 C010-PROCESS-AND-DISPLAY.
00101      016400*****************************************************
00102      016600* FUNCTION:              CALCULATE NET SALES AMOUNT    *
00103      016700*                        AND DISPLAY RESULTS           *
00104      016800* ENTRY/EXIT:            B000-LOOP-CONTROL             *
00105      016900* CALLS:                 NONE                         *
00106      017100*****************************************************
00107      017300     COMPUTE GROSS-SALES-WRK = QUANTITY-SOLD-WRK * SALES-PRICE-WRK.
00108      017500     IF QUANTITY-SOLD-WRK IS GREATER THAN CEILING
00109      017600        COMPUTE NET-SALES-WRK = GROSS-SALES-WRK -
00110      017700           (GROSS-SALES-WRK * DISCOUNT-RATE)
00111      017800     ELSE
00112      017900        MOVE GROSS-SALES-WRK TO NET-SALES-WRK.
00113      018100     MOVE NET-SALES-WRK TO NET-SALES-OUTPUT.
00114      018300     DISPLAY CLEAR-SCREEN.
00115      018500     WRITE PRINT-LINE FROM DETAIL-LINE
00116      018600        AFTER ADVANCING 2.
```

FIGURE 11-18

An excerpt from a COBOL program.

C

The **C** programming language was developed at Bell Laboratories in 1972 by Dennis Ritchie (Figure 11-19). Originally designed as a programming language for writing systems software, it is now considered a general-purpose programming language. C is a powerful programming language that requires professional programming skills to be used effectively. The use of C to develop various types of software on microcomputers and minicomputers is increasing.

```
float gross;
gross = qty * price;
if (qty > ceiling)
    net = gross - (gross * discount_rate);
else
    net = gross;
return(net);
```

FIGURE 11-19

An excerpt from a C program.

FORTRAN

FORTRAN (**FOR**mula **TRAN**slator), developed by IBM and released in 1957, was designed as a programming language to be used by scientists, engineers, and mathematicians (Figure 11-20). The language is noted for its ability to easily express and efficiently calculate mathematical equations.

```
 1    67.000        SUBROUTINE CALC(QTY,SALES,DISC,MAX,GROSS,NET)
 2    68.000        REAL SALES, DISC, MAX, GROSS, NET
 3    69.000        INTEGER QTY
 4    70.000        GROSS = QTY * SALES
 5    71.000        IF(QTY .GT. MAX) THEN
 6    72.000  1        NET = GROSS - (GROSS * DISC)
 7    73.000  1     ELSE
 8    74.000  1        NET = GROSS
 9    75.000  1     ENDIF
10    76.000        PRINT *, "   "
11    77.000        RETURN
```

FIGURE 11-20

An excerpt from a FORTRAN program.

Pascal

The **Pascal** language was developed by Niklaus Wirth, a computer scientist at the Institut fur Informatik in Zurich, Switzerland, in 1968. The name Pascal is not an abbreviation or acronym, but rather the name of a mathematician, Blaise Pascal (1623–1662), who developed one of the earliest calculating machines. Pascal, available for use on both personal and large computers, was one of the first programming languages that provided statements to encourage the use of structured program design (Figure 11-21).

```
BEGIN                           (* Begin procedure *)
    GROSS := SALES * QTY;
    IF QTY > CEILING
        THEN NET := GROSS - (GROSS * DISCOUNT_RATE)
        ELSE NET := GROSS;
    WRITELN('THE NET SALES IS $',NET:6:2);
END;                            (* End of procedure *)
```

FIGURE 11-21

An excerpt from a Pascal program.

Ada

The programming language **Ada** is named for Augusta Ada Byron, Countess of Lovelace, a mathematician in the 1800s, who is thought to have written the first program. Introduced in 1980, the development of Ada was supported by the Department of Defense. Ada was designed to facilitate the writing and maintenance of large programs that are used over a long period of time. The language encourages coding of readable programs that are also portable, allowing them to be transferred from computer to computer (Figure 11-22).

```
31     GROSS_SALES_PRICE := FLOAT(QUANTITY * SALES_PRICE);
32     if GROSS_SALES_PRICE > 100.0 then
33         GROSS_SALES_PRICE := GROSS_SALES_PRICE - (GROSS_SALES_PRICE * 0.05);
34     end if;
```

FIGURE 11-22

An excerpt from an Ada program.

RPG

RPG, which stands for **R**eport **P**rogram **G**enerator, was developed by IBM and introduced in 1964. As the name indicates, this language was primarily designed to allow reports to be generated quickly and easily. Instead of writing a set of instructions as in other languages, in RPG special forms are filled out that describe the desired report (Figure 11-23). With a minimum of training, a user can be taught to fill out the forms, enter the specifications into the computer, and produce the desired reports without having to design and develop a computer program.

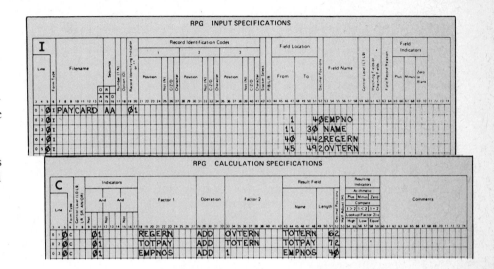

FIGURE 11-23

Special forms help the RPG programmer to quickly specify the input, calculation, and output requirements of a program. The input and calculation forms are shown in this illustration.

Other Popular Programming Languages

In addition to the commonly used programming languages just discussed, there are several other popular languages. Figure 11-24 lists some of these languages and their primary uses.

ALGOL	**ALGO**rithmetic **L**anguage. Structured programming language used for scientific and mathematical applications.
APL	**A P**rogramming **L**anguage. A powerful, easy to learn language that is good for processing data stored in a table (matrix) format.
FORTH	Similar to C. Creates fast and efficient program code. Originally developed to control astronomical telescopes.
LISP	**LIS**t **P**rocessing. Popular artificial intelligence language.
LOGO	Primarily known as an educational tool to teach problem-solving skills.
MODULA-2	Similar to Pascal. Used primarily for developing systems software.
PILOT	**P**rogrammed **I**nquiry **L**earning **O**r **T**eaching. Used by educators to write computer-aided instruction programs.
PL/I	**P**rogramming **L**anguage/**One**. Business and scientific language that combines many of the features of FORTRAN and COBOL.
PROLOG	**PRO**gramming in **LOG**ic. Used for artificial intelligence.

FIGURE 11-24

Other popular computer languages.

Application Generators

Application generators, also called **program generators**, are programs that produce source language programs, such as BASIC or COBOL, based on input, output, and processing specifications entered by the user. Application generators can greatly reduce the amount of time required to develop a program. They are based on the fact that most programs are comprised of standard processing modules, such as routines to read, write, or compare records, that can be combined together to create unique programs. These standard processing modules are stored in a library and are selected and grouped together based on user specifications. Application generators often use menu and screen generators to assist in developing an application.

A **menu generator** lets the user specify a menu (list) of processing options that can be selected. The resulting menu is automatically formatted with heading, footing, and prompt line text. A **screen generator**, sometimes called a **screen painter**, allows the user to design an input or output screen by entering the names and descriptions of the input and output data directly on the screen. The advantage is that the user enters the screen layout exactly as it will appear after the program is created. As each data name is entered, the screen generator asks the user to specify the length and type of data that will be entered and what processing, if any, should take place before or after the data is entered.

How to Choose a Programming Language

Although each programming language has its own unique characteristics, selecting a language for a programming task can be a difficult decision. Following are some of the factors that should be considered in making a choice:

- The programming standards of the organization. Many organizations have programming standards that specify that a particular language is used for all applications.
- The need to interface with other programs. If a program is going to work with other existing or future programs, ideally it should be programmed in the same language as the other programs.
- The suitability of a language to the application to be programmed. As we discussed, most languages are best suited to a particular type of application. For example, FORTRAN works well with applications requiring many calculations.
- The expertise of the available programmers. Unless another language is far superior, the language used by the programming staff should be chosen.
- The availability of the language. Not all languages are available on all computers.
- The need for the application to be portable. If the application will have to run on different computers, a common language should be chosen so the program only has to be written once.
- The anticipated maintenance requirements. If the user anticipates that the application will have to be modified frequently, a language that can be maintained easily and that supports structured programming concepts should be considered.

Chapter Summary

Although procedural languages such as COBOL and BASIC will continue to be used for many years, there is a clear trend toward the creation of programs using nonprocedural tools, such as fourth-generation and natural languages, that allow users to specify what they want accomplished. Your knowledge of programming languages will help you to better understand the process that takes place when the computer converts data into information and to obtain better results if you directly participate in the programming process.

The following list summarizes the key topics discussed in this chapter.

1. A **computer program** is a detailed set of instructions that directs a computer to perform the tasks necessary to process data into information (p. 11.2).
2. **Program development** is a series of five steps that take place when a computer program is developed (p. 11.2).
3. The five steps in program development are: (1) review the program specifications; (2) program design; (3) program coding; (4) program testing; and (5) finalizing the documentation (p. 11.2).
4. **Program specifications** can include many documents such as data flow diagrams, system flowcharts, process specifications, a data dictionary, screen formats, and report layouts (p. 11.2).
5. During **program design** a logical solution or **logic** for a program is developed and documented (p. 11.3).
6. **Structured program design** is methodology that emphasizes three main program design concepts: modules, control structures, and single entry/single exit (p. 11.3).
7. **Modules** or **subroutines**, which perform a given task within a program, can be developed individually and then combined to form a complete program (p. 11.3).
8. **Structure charts** or **hierarchy charts** are used to decompose the modules of a program (p. 11.4).
9. The three **control structures** are: **sequence** where one process occurs immediately after another; **selection** or **if-then-else**, which is used for conditional program logic; and **iteration** which is used for **looping** (p. 11.4–11.5).
10. The two forms of iteration are the **do-while structure** and the **do-until structure** (p. 11.5).
11. **Single entry/single exit** means that there is only one **entry point** and one **exit point** from each of the control structures (p. 11.6).
12. Two commonly used program design tools are **program flowcharts**, and **pseudocode** (p. 11.7–11.8).
13. Structured walkthroughs are used to review the design and logic of a program (p. 11.9).
14. **Coding** is the process of writing the program instructions (p. 11.9).
15. Before a program is used to process "real" data, it should be thoroughly tested to make sure it is functioning correctly. A simple type of testing is **desk checking** (p. 11.9).
16. Programs can be tested for **syntax errors** (grammar). **Logic testing** checks for incorrect results using **test data** (p. 11.10).
17. **Debugging** refers to the process of locating and correcting program errors or **bugs** found during testing (p. 11.10).
18. **Program maintenance** includes all changes to a program once it is implemented and processing real transactions (p. 11.11).
19. A **programming language** is a set of written words and symbols that allow a programmer or user to communicate with the computer (p. 11.12).
20. Programming languages fit into one of four categories: machine language, assembly language, high-level languages, and fourth-generation languages (p. 11.12).
21. Before they can be executed, all programs are converted into **machine language**, the fundamental language of computers, also called **low-level language** (p. 11.12).
22. **Assembly language** is a low-level language that is closely related to machine language. It uses **mnemonics** or **symbolic operation codes** (p. 11.13).
23. Assembly languages use **symbolic addressing** and include **macro instructions**. Assembly language programs are converted into machine language instructions by an **assembler** (p. 11.13).

24. **High-level languages** are easier to learn and use than low-level languages. They use sentences called **program statements** (p. 11.14).

25. **Compilers** and **interpreters** are used to translate high-level **source programs** into machine language **object code** or **object programs** (p. 11.14).

26. **Fourth-generation languages**, also called **very high-level languages**, are **nonprocedural**, which means that the user tells the computer *what* is to be done, not *how* to do it (p. 11.15).

27. A **natural language** allows the user to enter a question as if the user were speaking to another person (p. 11.16).

28. Commonly used programming languages include **BASIC, COBOL, C, FORTRAN, Pascal, Ada,** and **RPG** (p. 11.16–11.19).

29. **BASIC** is one of the most commonly used programming languages on microcomputers and minicomputers (p. 11.16).

30. **COBOL** is the most widely used programming language for business applications (p. 11.17).

31. **C** is an increasingly popular programming language that requires professional programming skills to be used effectively (p. 11.17).

32. **FORTRAN** is noted for its ability to easily express and efficiently calculate mathematical equations (p. 11.18).

33. **Pascal** contains programming statements that encourage the use of structured program design (p. 11.18).

34. **Ada**, developed and supported by the Department of Defense, was designed to facilitate the writing and maintenance of large programs used over a long period of time (p. 11.18).

35. **RPG** was primarily designed to generate reports quickly and easily (p. 11.19).

36. **Application generators** or **program generators** produce source language programs based on input, output, and processing specifications entered by the user (p. 11.20).

37. A **menu generator** lets the user specify a menu of options (p. 11.20).

38. A **screen generator** or **screen printer** allows the user to design screens (p. 11.20).

39. Some of the factors that should be considered when choosing a programming language are: the programming standards of the organization; the need to interface with other programs; the suitability of a language to the application to be programmed; the expertise of the available programmers; the availability of the language; the need for the application to be portable; and the anticipated maintenance requirements (p. 11.20).

Review Questions

1. What is a computer program?
2. List the five steps in program development and give a brief description of each step.
3. What is the purpose of reviewing the program specifications? List at least four types of documents that may be included in the program specifications.
4. Draw the three control structures used in structured program design.
5. Briefly describe two types of program design tools that are used by programmers.
6. What is the difference between a syntax error and a logic error?
7. Describe the four categories of programming languages.
8. Explain how a compiler and an interpreter work. What is a source program? What is an object program?
9. Why are high-level languages referred to as machine-independent languages?
10. List five commonly used programming languages and explain their primary uses.
11. How do application generators reduce the amount of time required to program?
12. List seven factors that should be considered when choosing a programming language.

Trends, Issues, and Opportunities

12

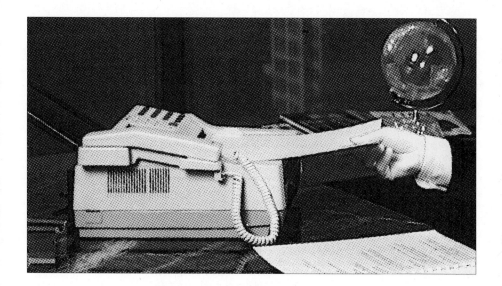

Objectives

- Discuss the electronic devices and applications that are part of the automated office.
- Describe the technologies that are developing for the automated factory, including CAD, CAE, CAM, and CIM.
- Discuss the use of personal computers in the home.
- List the steps for purchasing a personal computer.
- Discuss social issues related to computers.
- Discuss the three areas that provide the majority of computer-related jobs.
- Describe the career positions available in an information systems department.
- Describe career opportunities in sales, service and repair, consulting, and education.
- Discuss the compensation and growth trends for information processing careers.
- Discuss career development, including professional organizations, certification, and professional growth.

After reading the preceding chapters, you know what a computer is, what a computer does, how it does it, and why a computer is so powerful. You have learned about computer equipment and software, and how the system development process is used to combine these elements with data, personnel, users, and procedures to create a working information system.

In this chapter, we examine current and future trends in information systems, including changes occurring in the workplace. We also discuss how personal computers are used in business, as well as some of the social issues related to the computer industry, such as computer security, computer crime, and privacy.

This chapter concludes with a discussion about career opportunities in the computer industry and on how to prepare for a computer career. Even if you don't choose a career in the computer field, an understanding of computer careers is important, because any job you choose is likely to require your contact with computers or computer personnel.

Information Systems in Business

The largest single user of computers is business. Millions of systems ranging from mainframes to microcomputers are installed and used for applications such as inventory control, billing, and accounting. This section discusses how these traditional applications will be affected by changes in technology and methods. It also discusses two other areas of business applications, the automated office and the automated factory. Although the term automated can be applied to any process or machine that can operate without human intervention, the term is commonly used to describe computer-controlled functions.

How Will Existing Information Systems Change?

Existing business information systems will continue to undergo profound changes as new technology, software, and methods are applied to the huge installed base of traditional business system users. Important overall trends include more online, interactive systems and less batch processing. In addition, the increased use of relational database systems means that users have a wider variety of data and information available for decision making, and more flexibility, presenting information on reports and displays (Figure 12-1).

FIGURE 12-1

Trends that will affect information systems of tomorrow.

EQUIPMENT

- Increased use of personal computers networked to other personal computers and to central mini or mainframe computers.
- Increased storage capacity of disks using improved and new technologies such as laser disks.
- Terminals that can display 132 or more characters per line, as well as graphics and images.
- Faster, better quality printers.
- Reduced instruction set computers (RISC) and parallel processing that will greatly increase the number of instructions that can be processed at one time.

SOFTWARE

- Fourth-generation and natural languages that will enable the user to communicate with the computer in a more conversational manner.
- Computer-aided software engineering (CASE) that will shorten the system development time frame.
- Increased use of decision support and artificial intelligence systems to help users make decisions.
- Increased implementation of graphic interfaces using icons and symbols to represent information and processes.

DATA

- Automatic input of data at the source where it is created.
- Storage and use of non-text data such as voice and image.

INFORMATION SYSTEMS PERSONNEL

- Increased interface with users.
- Emphasis will shift from how to capture and process data to how to use the available data more effectively.

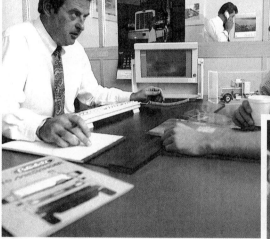

USERS

- Most people will be computer literate, with a basic understanding of how computers work and how they can use them in their jobs.

The Automated Office

The **automated office**, sometimes referred to as the **electronic office**, is the term that describes the use of electronic devices such as computers, facsimile machines, and computerized telephone systems to make office work more productive. As was the case with traditional business applications such as accounting, automated office applications such as word processing, electronic mail, voice mail, desktop publishing, facsimile, image processing, and teleconferencing started out as separate, stand-alone applications. In recent years, however, the trend has been to integrate these applications into a network of devices and services that can share information. The functions of word processing, desktop publishing, and electronic mail in the automated office were described in Chapter 2. A brief discussion of the capabilities of the other types of automated office applications follows.

Voice Mail **Voice mail** can be considered verbal electronic mail. Made possible by the latest computerized telephone systems, voice mail reduces the problem of "telephone tag," where two people trying to reach each other wind up leaving a series of messages to "please call back." With voice mail, the caller can leave a message, similar to leaving a message on an answering machine. The difference is that with a voice mail system, the caller's message is digitized (converted into binary ones and zeros) so that it can be stored on a disk like other computer data. This allows the party who was called to hear the message later (by reconverting it to an audio form) and also, if desired, add a reply or additional comments and forward the message to someone else who has access to the system.

Facsimile **Facsimile** or **Fax** machines are used to transmit a reproduced image of a document over standard phone lines (Figure 12-2). The document can be printed, hand written, or a photograph. Fax machines optically scan the document and convert the image into digitized data that can be transmitted, using a modem, over the phone. A compatible Fax machine at the receiving end converts the digitized data back into its original image. Besides the separate Fax machines, plug-in circuit boards are also available for personal computers. Using a modem, these boards can directly transmit computer-prepared documents or documents that have been digitized with the use of a scanner. Fax machines are having an increasing impact on the way businesses transmit documents.

Image Processing **Image processing** is the ability to store and retrieve a reproduced image of a document. Image processing is often used when an original document, such as an insurance claim, must be seen to verify data. Image processing and traditional applications will continue to be combined in many areas. For example, American Express recently began sending cardholders copies of the individual charge slips that were related to the charges on their statement. These charge slips were recorded by an image processing system and then merged with the customer statements.

FIGURE 12-2 ▬

This facsimile (Fax) machine can send and receive copies of documents to and from any location where there is phone service and a compatible Fax machine.

Teleconferencing Teleconferencing once meant three or more people sharing a phone conversation. Today, however, **teleconferencing** usually means **video conferencing**, the use of computers and television cameras to transmit video images and the sound of the conference participants to other participants with similar equipment at a remote location. Special software and equipment is used to digitize the video image so that it can be transmitted along with the audio over standard communication channels. Although the video image is not as clear for moving objects as is commercial television, it does contribute to the conference discussion and is adequate for nonmoving objects such as charts and graphs.

Summary of the Automated Office The trend toward integrated automated office capabilities will continue. Incompatible devices will be standardized or will be provided with software that will enable them to communicate and transfer data with other devices. The increased productivity provided by automated office devices will encourage more and more organizations to adopt them to help control costs and remain competitive.

The Automated Factory

As in the automated office, the goal of the **automated factory** is to increase productivity through the use of automated, and often computer-controlled, equipment. Technologies used in the automated factory include computer-aided design, computer-aided engineering, computer-aided manufacturing, and computer-integrated manufacturing.

Computer-Aided Design (CAD) Computer-aided design (CAD) uses a computer and special graphics software to aid in product design (Figure 12-3). The CAD software eliminates the laborious drafting that used to be required and allows the designer to dynamically change the size of some or all of the product and view the design from different angles. The ability to store the design electronically offers several advantages over traditional manual methods. For one thing, the designs can be changed more easily than before. For another, the design database can be reviewed more easily by other design engineers. This increases the likelihood that an existing part will be used in a product rather than a new part designed. For example, if a support bracket was required for a new product, the design engineer could review the design database to see if any existing products used a support bracket that would be appropriate for the new product. This not only decreases the overall design time but increases the reliability of the new product by using proven parts.

Computer-Aided Engineering (CAE) Computer-aided engineering (CAE) is the use of computers to test product designs. Using CAE, engineers can test the design of an airplane or a bridge before they are

FIGURE 12-3

Computer-aided design (CAD) is an efficient way to develop plans for new products.

built (Figure 12-4). Sophisticated programs are available to simulate the effects of wind, temperature, weight, and stress on product shapes and materials. Before the use of CAE, prototypes of products had to be built and subjected to testing that often destroyed the prototype.

FIGURE 12-4

Computer-aided engineering (CAE) allows the user to test product designs before they are built and without damaging the product.

Computer-Aided Manufacturing (CAM) Computer-aided manufacturing (CAM) is the use of computers to control production equipment. CAM production equipment includes software-controlled drilling, lathe, and milling machines as well as robots (Figure 12-5). The use of robots has aroused much interest, partially because of preconceived ideas of robots as intelligent, humanlike machines. In practice, most industrial robots rarely look like a human and can only perform preprogrammed tasks. Robots are often used for repetitive tasks in hazardous or disagreeable environments, such as welding or painting areas.

FIGURE 12-5

Computer-aided manufacturing (CAM) is used to control production equipment such as these welding robots on an automobile assembly line.

Computer-Integrated Manufacturing (CIM) Computer-integrated manufacturing (CIM) is the total integration of the manufacturing process using computers (Figure 12-6). Using CIM concepts, individual production processes are linked so that the production flow is balanced and optimized, and products flow smoothly through the factory. In a CIM factory, automated design processes are linked to automated machining processes that are linked to automated assembly processes that are linked to automated testing and packaging. Under ideal CIM conditions, a product will move through the entire production process under computer control. Because of its complexity, many companies may never fully implement CIM. But CIM's related concepts of minimum inventory and efficient demand-driven production are valid and will be incorporated into many manufacturers' business plans.

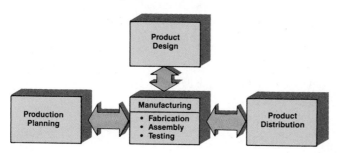

FIGURE 12-6

The concept of computer-integrated manufacturing (CIM) is to use computers to integrate all phases of the manufacturing process from planning and design to manufacturing and distribution.

Bringing the Information Age Home

Since personal computers became available in the mid-1970s, millions of personal computers have been purchased for home use. It is expected that the use of personal computers in the home will continue to increase. Just as the use of computers in the workplace will change how we work, the use of computers in our homes will change various aspects of our personal lives. The next two sections discuss how personal computers are used in the home, including some possible new applications, and things you should consider when purchasing a personal computer system.

The Use of Personal Computers in the Home

Personal computers can be used in many different ways in the home. Five general areas of use include: (1) personal services; (2) control of home systems; (3) telecommuting; (4) education; and (5) entertainment.

Personal Services In many ways running a home is similar to running a small business. The productivity tools that are used in the office, such as word processing, spreadsheet, and database, can also be used in the home to aid with creating documents, financial planning and analysis, and filing and organizing data. Personal computer software is also available to assist with home accounting applications such as balancing checkbooks, making household budgets, and preparing tax returns. In addition, using a personal computer to transmit and receive data over telephone lines allows home users to access a wealth of information and services. For example, teleshopping and electronic banking are two services that are becoming more popular, and information such as stock prices and airline schedules is available to home users who subscribe to database services such as CompuServe and The Source.

Control of Home Systems Another use of computers in the home is to control home systems. Personal computers used in this manner are usually linked to special devices such as alarms for security, thermostats for environmental control, and timing devices for lighting and landscape sprinkler systems. When the personal computer system has communication capabilities, a homeowner who is away can use a telephone or another computer to call home and change the operation of one of the control systems. For example, suppose a homeowner is on vacation in Texas and learns that heavy rains have been falling at home in Pennsylvania. It is possible for the homeowner to call home and use the keys of a touch-tone telephone to instruct the computer to turn off the landscape sprinkler system.

Telecommuting Telecommuting refers to the ability of individuals to work at home and communicate with their offices by using personal computers and communication lines. With a personal computer, an employee can access the main computer at the office. Electronic mail can be read and answered. Databases can be accessed and completed projects can be transmitted. It has been predicted that by the end of the 1990s 10% of the workforce will be telecommuters. Most of these people will probably arrange their business schedules so that they can telecommute two or three days a week. Telecommuting provides flexibility, allowing companies and employees to work out arrangements that can increase productivity and at the same time meet the needs of individual employees.

Education The use of personal computers for education, called **computer-assisted instruction (CAI)**, is another rapidly growing area. While CAI is frequently used to describe software that is developed and used in schools, much of the same software is available for home users. CAI software can be classified into three main types: drill and practice, tutorials, and simulations.

  Drill and practice software uses a ''flashcard'' approach to teaching by allowing users to practice skills in subjects such as math and language. A problem or word is displayed on the computer screen and the user enters the answer. The computer accepts the answer and responds by telling the student whether or not the answer was correct. Sometimes the user gets second and third chances to select the correct answer before the computer software will display the correct answer. With **tutorial software**, the computer software displays text and graphics and sometimes uses sound to teach a user concepts about subjects such as chemistry, music theory, or computer literacy. Following the instruction, tutorial software may quiz the user with true/false or multiple choice questions to help ensure that the concepts being taught are understood. The increased use of optical disk storage that provides high-quality graphics and direct access capability promises to greatly enhance this type of CAI.

The third type of CAI, **simulation software**, is designed to teach a user by creating a model. For example, many simulation packages are available to teach business concepts. One program designed for children simulates running a lemonade stand and another program for adults simulates the stock market. In the lemonade simulation, the user makes decisions about "How many quarts of lemonade to make" and "What price to charge customers for a glass of lemonade." The computer software accepts the user's decisions, performs computations using the software model, and then responds to the user with the amount of profit or loss for the day. Good CAI software is designed to be user friendly and motivate the user to succeed (Figure 12-7).

FIGURE 12-7

Computer-assisted instruction (CAI) software provides a structured yet motivating way to learn. This software package helps the user to develop deductive reasoning, reference, and research skills while learning geography, history, economics, government, and culture.

Entertainment   Entertainment software, or game playing, on home computers has always had a large following among the younger members of the family. However, many adults are surprised to find that entertainment software can also provide them with hours of enjoyment. Popular types of entertainment software include arcade games, board games, simulations, and interactive graphics programs. Most people are familiar with the arcade-type games (similar to video games such as Pac-Man) that are available for computers. A popular board game is computer chess. Simulations include games such as baseball and football and a variety of flight simulators that allow users to pretend they are controlling and navigating different types of aircraft (Figure 12-8). With entertainment software, the computer becomes a fun, skillful, and challenging game partner.

FIGURE 12-8

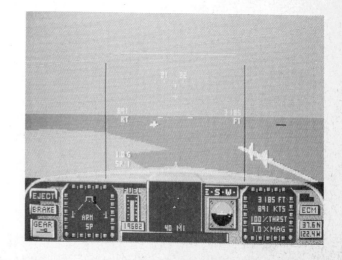

Flight simulators can be part fun and part educational. Some simulators offer realistic instrument consoles and flight patterns that help teach the user about flying.

A different type of entertainment available to users who have personal computers with communication capabilities is the access and use of electronic **bulletin board systems**, called **BBSs**, that allow users to communicate with one another and share information. While some bulletin boards provide specific services such as buying and selling used computer equipment, many bulletin boards function as electronic clubs for special interest groups and are used to share information about hobbies as diverse as stamp collecting, music, genealogy, and astronomy. Some BBSs are strictly social; users meet new friends and conduct conversations by entering messages through their keyboards.

In addition to sharing hobby information with other computer users on a BBS, some personal computer users use their home computer as a tool for personal hobbies. Computers are used by hobbyists to design quilt and stained glass patterns, run model trains, organize stamp, doll, and photography collections, and write, transpose, play, and print musical scores.

Summary of Bringing the Information Age Home

Personal computers are used in homes to aid in a variety of tasks such as personal services, control of home systems, telecommuting, education, and entertainment. Whether or not you now use a personal computer in your home, it is very probable that you will at some time in the near future. In fact, it is very possible that within the next decade you will have multiple computers in your home. Because computers can be used in so many different ways and also because computer technology is changing so rapidly, it is important that you carefully choose any computer system that you may purchase.

Today, many colleges offer seminars on how to purchase a personal computer system. Five general steps recommended for purchasing your own computer include:

1. Define and prioritize the type of tasks you want to perform on your computer.
2. Select the software packages that best meet your needs.
3. Select equipment that will run the software you have chosen.
4. Select the suppliers for the software and equipment.
5. Purchase the software and equipment.

The changes that accompany the information age raise many issues that are related to society as a whole. Some of these issues are discussed in the following section.

Social Issues

Significant inventions such as the automobile and television have always challenged existing values and caused society to think about the right and wrong ways to use the new invention. So too has the computer. This section discusses some of the social issues related to computers, including computer security, computer crime, and privacy.

Computer Security and Crime

Computer security and computer crime are closely related topics. **Computer security** refers to the safeguards established to prevent and detect unauthorized use and deliberate or accidental damage to computer systems and data. **Computer crime** is the use of a computer to commit an illegal act. This section discusses the types of crimes that can be committed and the security measures that can be taken to prevent and detect them.

Software Theft Software theft, often called **software piracy**, became a major problem with the increased use of personal computers. Some people have a hard time understanding why they should pay hundreds, perhaps thousands of dollars for what appears to be an inexpensive diskette or tape, and instead of paying for an authorized copy of the software they make an illegal copy. This leads software manufacturers to install elaborate copy protection schemes designed to prevent anyone from copying the software. However, the copy protection also prevents authorized users who have paid the license fee from making backup copies of the software for security purposes. Today, software piracy is still an issue. It is estimated that for every authorized copy of a commercial program, there is at least one illegal copy.

Unauthorized Access and Use **Unauthorized access** can be defined as computer trespassing, in other words, being logged on a system without permission. Many so-called computer hackers boast of the number of systems that they have been able to access by using a modem attached to their computer. These hackers usually don't do any damage and merely "wander around" the accessed system before logging off.

Unauthorized use is the use of a computer system or computer data for unapproved and possibly illegal activities. Unauthorized use may range from an employee using the company computer for keeping his or her child's soccer league scores to someone gaining access to a bank funds system and creating an unauthorized transfer. Unauthorized use could also include the theft of computerized information such as customer lists or product plans.

The key to preventing both unauthorized access and unauthorized use is an appropriate level of authorization. Authorization techniques range from simple passwords to advanced biometric devices that can identify individuals by their fingerprint, voice, or eye pattern. The level of authorization should match the degree of risk and should be regularly reviewed to determine if the level is still appropriate.

Malicious Damage Malicious or deliberate damage to the data in a computer system is often difficult to detect because the damaged data may not be used or carefully reviewed on a regular basis. A disgruntled employee or an outsider may gain access to the system and delete or alter individual records or an entire file. One of the most potentially dangerous types of malicious damage is done by a **virus**, a computer program designed to copy itself into other software and spread through multiple computer systems. Figure 12-9 on the next page shows how a virus can spread from one system to another. Although they have been known for a long time, it is only in recent years that viruses have become a serious problem. Besides developing specific programs called **vaccines** to locate and remove viruses, organizations are becoming more aggressive in prosecuting persons suspected of planting viruses. In what was described as the first computer virus trial, in 1988 a former programmer was convicted in Texas of planting a program in his employer's computer system that deleted 168,000 sales commission records.

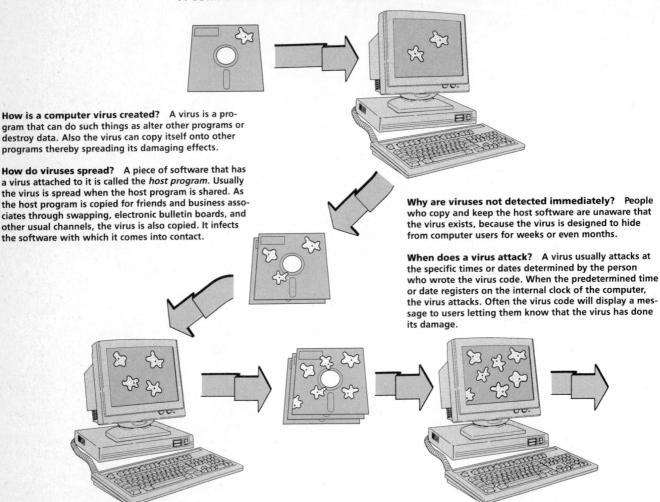

A COMPUTER VIRUS: WHAT IT IS AND HOW IT SPREADS

How is a computer virus created? A virus is a program that can do such things as alter other programs or destroy data. Also the virus can copy itself onto other programs thereby spreading its damaging effects.

How do viruses spread? A piece of software that has a virus attached to it is called the *host program*. Usually the virus is spread when the host program is shared. As the host program is copied for friends and business associates through swapping, electronic bulletin boards, and other usual channels, the virus is also copied. It infects the software with which it comes into contact.

Why are viruses not detected immediately? People who copy and keep the host software are unaware that the virus exists, because the virus is designed to hide from computer users for weeks or even months.

When does a virus attack? A virus usually attacks at the specific times or dates determined by the person who wrote the virus code. When the predetermined time or date registers on the internal clock of the computer, the virus attacks. Often the virus code will display a message to users letting them know that the virus has done its damage.

Single acts of malicious damage, especially when performed by employees with authorized access to the computer system, are very difficult to prevent. The best protection against this type of act remains adequate backup files that enable damaged data to be restored.

FIGURE 12-9

This illustration shows how a virus program can be transmitted from one computer system to another.

Privacy

In the past, one way to maintain privacy was to keep information in separate locations—individual stores had their own credit files, government agencies had separate records, doctors had separate files, and so on. However, it is now technically and economically feasible to store large amounts of related data about individuals in one database. Some people believe that the easier access to the data increases the possibility for misuse. Others worry that the increased storage capacity of computers may encourage the storage of unnecessary personal data.

The concern about information privacy has led to federal and state laws regarding the storage and disclosure of personal data. Common points in these laws include: (1) Information collected and stored about individuals should be limited to what is necessary to carry out the function of the business or governmental agency collecting the data. (2) Once collected, provisions should be made to restrict access to the data to those employees within the organization who need access to it to perform their job duties. (3) Personal information should be released outside the organization collecting the data only when the person has agreed to its disclosure. (4) When information is collected about an individual, the individual should know that data is being collected and have the opportunity to determine the accuracy of the data.

Summary of Social Issues

Based on current and planned developments, the impact of computers and the information age will be even greater in the future than it has been to date. However, as a society and as individuals, we have an obligation to use the computer responsibly and not abuse the power it provides. This presents constant challenges that sometimes weigh the rights of the individual against increased efficiency and productivity. The computer must be thought of as a tool whose effectiveness is determined by the skill and experience of the user. As a computer literate member of society, you will be better able to participate in decisions on how to best use computerized information systems.

The Information Processing Industry

The information processing industry is one of the largest industries in the world with annual sales of well over $100 billion. Job opportunities in the industry come primarily from three areas: the companies that provide the computer equipment; the companies that develop computer software; and the companies that hire information processing professionals to work with these products. As in any major industry, there is also a large group of service companies that support each of these three areas. An example would be a company that sells computer supplies such as printer paper and disks.

The Computer Equipment Industry

The computer equipment or hardware industry includes all manufacturers and distributors of computers and computer-related equipment such as disk and tape drives, terminals, printers, and communication equipment (Figure 12-10). The

FIGURE 12-10

This photo shows newly manufactured computer keyboards being tested before shipping.

five largest mini and mainframe computer manufacturers in the United States, IBM, Digital Equipment Corporation, UNISYS, Hewlett-Packard, and NCR, are huge organizations with tens of thousands of employees worldwide. Major microcomputer manufacturers include IBM, Apple, Compaq, and Tandy. The largest company, IBM, has had annual sales of over $60 billion. In addition to the major companies, the computer equipment industry is also known for the many new "start-up" companies that appear each year. These new companies take advantage of rapid changes in equipment technology, such as laser printers, video disks, and fiber optics, to create new products and new job opportunities. Besides the companies that make end user equipment, thousands of companies make components that most users never see. These companies manufacture chips (processor, memory, and so on), power supplies, wiring, and the hundreds of other parts that go into computer equipment.

The Computer Software Industry

The computer software industry includes all developers and distributors of application and system software. In the early days, computer software was almost exclusively produced by the computer manufacturers. Today, thousands of companies provide a wide range of software from operating systems to complete business systems. The personal computer boom in the early 1980s provided numerous opportunities in the software industry. Many individuals started by working out of their homes, developing their first software products on their own time while holding other jobs.

Today, software alone is a huge industry whose leaders include companies such as Microsoft, Lotus, and Ashton-Tate, with annual sales in the hundreds of millions of dollars.

Information Processing Professionals

Information processing professionals are the people that put the equipment and software to work to produce information for the end user. This includes people such as programmers and systems analysts who are hired by companies to work in an information systems department. These and other positions available in the information processing industry are discussed in the next section.

Career Opportunities in Information Processing

The use of computers in so many aspects of life has created thousands of new jobs. Some of these occupations, such as personal computer software sales representative, didn't even exist ten years ago. The following section describes some of the career opportunities that currently exist.

Working in an Information Systems Department

In Chapter 1 we discussed the various types of career positions that exist within an information systems department. These positions include: data entry personnel, computer operators, computer programmers, systems analysts, database administrator, manager of information systems, and vice president of information systems.

The people in these positions work together as a team to meet the information demands of their organizations. Throughout this book, the responsibilities associated with many of these positions were discussed, including the role of the systems analysts in the system development life cycle (Chapter 10) and the steps programmers perform in program development (Chapter 11). Another way to visualize the positions and their relationships is to look at an organization chart such as the one shown in Figure 12-11. In addition to management, the jobs in an information systems department can be classified into five categories:

1. Operations
2. Data administration
3. Systems analysis and design
4. Programming
5. Information center

Operations personnel are responsible for carrying out tasks such as operating the computer equipment that is located in the computer center. The primary responsibility of data administration is the maintenance and control of an organization's database. In systems analysis and design the various information systems needed by an organization are created and maintained. Programming develops the programs needed for the information systems, and the information center provides teaching and consulting services within an organization to help users meet their departmental and individual information processing needs. As you can see, an information systems department provides career opportunities for people with a variety of skills and talents.

FIGURE 12-11

This organization chart shows some of the positions available in an information systems department.

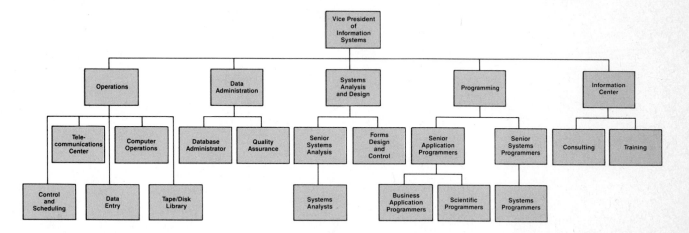

Sales

Sales representatives must have a general knowledge of computers and a specific understanding of the product they are selling. Strong interpersonal or "people" skills are important, including the ability to listen and the ability to communicate effectively both verbally and in writing. Sales representatives are usually paid based on the amount of product they sell, and top sales representatives are often the most highly compensated employees in a computer company.

Some sales representatives work directly for equipment and software manufacturers and others work for resellers. Most personal computer products are sold through dealers such as Computerland or Businessland (Figure 12-12). Some dealers, such as Egghead Discount Software, specialize in selling the most popular software products.

FIGURE 12-12

Computer retailers, such as Computerland, need salespeople who understand personal computers and have good "people" skills.

Service and Repair

Being a **service and repair technician** is a challenging job for persons who like to troubleshoot and solve problems and who have a strong background in electronics (Figure 12-13). In the early days of computers, repairs were often made at the site of the computer equipment. Today, however, malfunctioning components, such as circuit boards, are usually replaced and taken back to the service technician's office or sent to a special facility for repair. Many equipment manufacturers are now including special diagnostic software with their computer equipment that helps the service technician identify the problem. Using a modem, some advanced computer systems can automatically telephone a computer at the service technician's office and leave a message that a malfunction has been detected.

FIGURE 12-13

Computer service and repair is one of the fastest growing computer-related professions. A knowledge of electronics is essential for this occupation.

Consulting

After building experience in one or more areas, some individuals become **consultants**, people who draw upon their experience to give advice to others. Consultants must not only have strong technical skills in their area of expertise, but must also have the people skills to convince their clients to follow their advice. Qualified consultants are in high demand for such tasks as computer system selection, system design, and communication network design and installation.

Education and Training

The increased sophistication and complexity of today's computer products has opened wide opportunities in computer education and training. Qualified instructors are needed in schools, colleges, and universities and in private industry as well. In fact, the high demand for teachers has created a shortage at the university level, where many instructors have been lured into private industry because of higher pay. This shortage probably will not be filled in the near future; the supply of Ph.D.s, usually required at the university level, is not keeping up with the demand.

Compensation and Growth Trends for Information Processing Careers

Compensation is a function of experience and demand for a particular skill. Demand is influenced by geographic location, with metropolitan areas usually having higher pay than rural areas where, presumably, the cost of living is lower. Figure 12-14 shows the result of a salary survey of over 70,000 computer professionals across the United States and Canada. These amounts represent an average increase of approximately 7% over the prior year. According to the survey, the communications, utility, and aerospace industries paid the highest salaries. These industries have many challenging applications and are willing to pay the highest rate to obtain the best qualified employees.

PROGRAMMING:	YRS. EXP.	LOWER 20%	MEDIAN	UPPER 20%
Commercial	<2	20,000	24,000	28,000
	2–3	23,500	27,600	32,000
	4–6	27,000	32,000	36,800
	>6	31,500	37,700	45,000
Engineering/Scientific	<2	21,400	26,000	29,200
	2–3	25,000	30,000	34,000
	4–6	28,000	34,000	45,000
	<6	33,500	40,000	48,000
Microcomputer/ Minicomputer	<2	20,000	24,000	27,500
	2–3	22,000	27,000	32,000
	4–6	26,500	32,000	37,000
	>6	31,000	38,000	46,000
Software Engineer	<2	21,000	27,000	32,000
	2–3	26,500	32,000	35,000
	4–6	30,000	35,000	39,800
	>6	35,000	42,000	50,200
Systems Software	<2	N/A	N/A	N/A
	2–3	25,000	30,000	35,000
	4–6	29,000	34,900	39,000
	>6	33,800	39,000	46,600
MANAGEMENT:				
Data Center Operations		30,000	44,500	53,000
Programming Development		44.000	51,600	60,000
Systems Development		43,500	52,000	65,500
Technical Services		40,000	49,000	62,000
MIS Director/VP		49,200	60,000	76,800
BUSINESS SYSTEMS:				
Consultant		34,000	43,200	55,000
Project Leader/Sys. Analyst		34,000	40,700	49,500

SPECIALISTS:	YRS. EXP.	LOWER 20%	MEDIAN	UPPER 20%
Technical Data Center Analyst	<4	24,000	29,500	42,000
	4–6	27,000	33,500	42,000
	>6	34,000	43,000	51,000
Database Management Analyst	<4	25,000	29,100	34,000
	4–6	30,000	35,000	40,000
	>6	37,500	45,000	52,000
Information Center Analyst	<4	22,000	25,900	31,200
	4–6	25,800	31,000	36,000
	>6	30,000	37,000	45,000
Office Automation Analyst	<4	23,000	27,500	33,000
	4–6	27,000	32,000	36,600
	>6	32,000	40,000	48,000
SALES:				
Technical Support	<2	20,000	24,500	28,600
	2–3	23,000	28,000	31,500
	4–6	27,500	33,000	38,900
	>6	33,300	40,000	50,000
Management		45,000	65,000	85,000
OTHER:				
Computer Operator	<2	15,000	19,000	22,000
	2–3	17,500	21,000	24,300
	4–6	19,000	23,500	29,000
	>6	22,500	27,400	35,000
Edp Auditor	<4	N/A	N/A	N/A
	4–6	27,000	33,000	39,500
	>6	36,000	43,000	52,000
Technical Writer	<4	22,000	26,000	30,000
	4–6	27,000	31,500	35,000
	>6	30,000	35,900	42,000

FIGURE 12-14

This table shows salary levels for various computer industry positions based on the number of years of experience. (Source: Source Edp, 1989 Computer Salary Survey.)

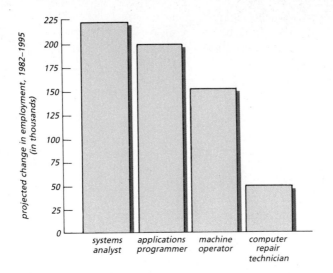

FIGURE 12-15

This chart shows computer careers with the highest projected growth, as compiled by the U.S. Bureau of Labor Statistics.

According to the U.S. Bureau of Labor Statistics, the fastest growing computer career positions between 1982 and 1995 will be systems analyst, applications programmer, machine operator, and computer repair technician (Figure 12-15).

Preparing for a Career in Information Processing

To prepare for a career in the information processing industry, individuals must decide what computer field they are interested in and obtain education in the chosen field. This section discusses the three major computer fields and some of the opportunities for obtaining education in those fields.

What Are the Fields in the Information Processing Industry?

While this book has primarily focused on the use of computers in business, there are actually three broad fields in the information processing industry (Figure 12-16): computer information systems, computer science, and computer engineering. **Computer information systems (CIS)** refers to the use of computers in areas relating to business. The field of **computer science** includes the technical aspects of computers such as hardware operation and systems software. **Computer engineering** deals with the

FIGURE 12-16

There are three broad fields of study in the information processing industry. Each field has specialized study requirements.

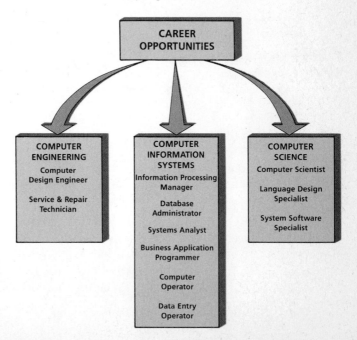

design and manufacturing of electronic computer components and computer hardware. Each field provides unique career opportunities and has specialized study requirements. Several avenues of study are available to persons interested in obtaining formal education in information processing.

Obtaining Education for Information Processing Careers

The expanded use of computers in today's world has increased the demand for properly trained computer professionals. Educational institutions have responded to this demand by providing a variety of options for students to study information systems. Trade schools, technical schools, community colleges, and colleges and universities offer formal education and certification or degree programs in computer-related fields. If you are evaluating a program offered by one of these institutions, it is important that you remember the three areas of information processing: computer information systems, computer science, and computer engineering. Frequently schools will have separate programs for each area. Understanding the differences among the three fields will help you to find the courses you want. For example, in a university, courses relating to computer information systems may be listed with the business courses, computer science courses may be with mathematics, and computer engineering may be with electronic technology or electrical engineering. Because schools list and organize their computer courses in different ways, you should carefully read individual course descriptions whenever you are selecting computer education classes.

Career Development in the Information Processing Industry

There are several ways for persons employed in the information processing industry to develop their skills and increase their recognition among their peers. These include professional organizations, certification, and professional growth and continuing education activities.

Professional Organizations

A number of computer-related organizations have been formed by people who have common interests and a desire to share their knowledge. Some of the organizations that have been influential in the industry include:

- **Association for Computing Machinery (ACM)**. An association composed of persons interested in computer science and computer science education. The association has many special interest groups such as computer graphics, database, and business.
- **Association of Information Systems Professionals**. This association was originally aimed at word processing professionals, but now includes a much broader interest area, including office automation.

- **Association of Systems Management (ASM)**. A group composed of individuals interested in the improvement of the systems analysis and design field.
- **Data Processing Management Association (DPMA)**. A professional association of programmers, systems analysts, and information processing managers.
- **Institute of Electrical and Electronic Engineers (IEEE)** and **IEEE Computer Society**. Organizations primarily composed of computer scientists and engineers.

Each of the above organizations has chapters throughout the United States (several throughout the world), offers monthly meetings, and sponsors periodic workshops, seminars, and conventions. Some organizations have student chapters or offer reduced membership fees for students. Attending professional meetings provide an excellent opportunity for students to learn about the information processing industry and to meet and talk with professionals in the field. In addition to these and other professional organizations, user groups exist for most makes of computers. Most metropolitan areas have one or more local computer societies that meet monthly to discuss topics of common interest about personal computers. For anyone employed or just interested in the computer industry, these groups can be an effective and rewarding way to learn and continue career development.

Certification

Many professions offer certification programs as a way of encouraging and recognizing the efforts of their members to attain a level of knowledge about their profession. The best known certification program in the information processing industry is the **Certificate in Data Processing (CDP)**, originated by DPMA but now administered by the **Institute for the Certification of Computer Professionals (ICCP)**. The CDP is awarded to persons who pass an examination that has five parts: (1) computer equipment; (2) computer programming and software; (3) principles of management; (4) accounting and quantitative methods; and (5) systems analysis and design. To be eligible to take the examination, a person must have a minimum of five years of experience in the information processing industry. People who pass the examination are authorized to place the initials CDP after their name.

Professional Growth and Continuing Education

Because of rapid changes in technology, staying aware of new products and services in the information processing industry can be a challenging task. One way of keeping up is by participating in professional growth and continuing education activities. This broad category includes events such as conferences, workshops, conventions, and trade shows that provide both general and specific information on equipment, software, services, and issues affecting the industry, such as computer security. Workshops and seminars usually last a day or two while conferences, conventions, and trade shows often last a week. Some of the larger trade shows, such as **COMDEX** (**COM**puter **D**ealer **EX**position), bring together over a thousand vendors to display their latest products and services.

Chapter Summary

The following list summarizes the key topics discussed in this chapter.

1. Existing business information systems will continue to undergo profound changes as new technology, software, and methods become available (p. 12.2).

2. Trends will include more online, interactive systems; less batch processing; and increased use of relational database systems (p. 12.2).

3. The **automated office**, sometimes referred to as the **electronic office**, is the term that describes the use of electronic devices such as computers, facsimile machines, and computerized telephone systems to make office work more productive (p. 12.3).

4. **Voice mail** can be considered verbal electronic mail (p. 12.4).

5. **Facsimile** or **Fax** machines are used to transmit a reproduced image of a document over standard phone lines (p. 12.4).

6. **Image processing** is the ability to store and retrieve a reproduced image of a document (p. 12.4).

7. **Teleconferencing** usually means **video conferencing**, the use of computers and television cameras to transmit video images and the sound of the conference participants to other participants with similar equipment at a remote location (p. 12.5).

8. The goal of the **automated factory** is to increase productivity through the use of automated, and often computer-controlled, equipment (p. 12.5).

9. **Computer-aided design (CAD)** uses a computer and special graphics software to aid in product design (p. 12.5).

10. **Computer-aided engineering (CAE)** is the use of computers to test product designs (p. 12.5).

11. **Computer-aided manufacturing (CAM)** is the use of computers to control production equipment (p. 12.6).

12. **Computer-integrated manufacturing (CIM)** is the total integration of the manufacturing process using computers (p. 12.7).

13. Personal computers are used in the home in many different ways, including: (1) personal services; (2) control of home systems; (3) telecommuting; (4) education; and (5) entertainment (p. 12.7–12.9).

14. The personal services provided by home computer use allow people to perform personal and business-related tasks quickly and conveniently in the comfort of their own homes (p. 12.7).

15. Another use of computers in the home is to control home systems such as security, environment control, lighting, and landscape sprinkler systems (p. 12.8).

16. **Telecommuting** refers to the ability of individuals to work at home and communicate with their offices by using personal computers and communication lines (p. 12.8).

17. The use of personal computers for education, called **computer-assisted instruction (CAI)**, is a rapidly growing area (p. 12.8).

18. CAI software can be classified into three main types: **drill and practice software**, **tutorial software**, and **simulation software** (p. 12.8–12.9).

19. Popular types of entertainment software include arcade games, board games, simulations, and interactive graphics programs (p. 12.9).

20. Electronic **bulletin board systems**, called **BBSs**, allow users to communicate with one another and share information (p. 12.10).

21. The guidelines for purchasing a personal computer recommend that you: (1) become computer literate; (2) select the software packages that best meet your needs; (3) select equipment that will run the software you have chosen; (4) select the suppliers for the software and equipment; and (5) purchase the software and equipment (p. 12.10).

22. **Computer security** refers to the safeguards established to prevent and detect unauthorized use and deliberate or accidental damage to computer systems and data (p. 12.10).

23. **Computer crime** is the use of a computer to commit an illegal act (p. 12.10–12.11).

24. Today, **software piracy** is still an issue and it is estimated that for every authorized copy of a commercial program, there is at least one illegal copy (p. 12.11).

25. **Unauthorized access** can be defined as computer trespassing, in other words, being logged on a system without permission (p. 12.11).

26. **Unauthorized use** is the use of a computer system or computer data for unapproved and possibly illegal activities (p. 12.11).

27. The key to preventing both unauthorized access and unauthorized use is an appropriate level of authorization (p. 12.11).
28. One of the most potentially dangerous types of malicious damage is done by a **virus**, a computer program designed to copy itself into other software and spread through multiple computer systems (p. 12.11).
29. The concern about information privacy has led to federal and state laws regarding the storage and disclosure of personal data (p. 12.12).
30. Job opportunities in the information processing industry come from three areas: computer equipment companies, computer software companies, and companies that hire information processing professionals (p. 12.13).
31. The computer equipment industry includes all manufacturers and distributors of computers and computer-related equipment (p. 12.13).
32. The computer software industry includes all developers and distributors of application and system software (p. 12.14).
33. Information processing professionals are the people that put the equipment and software to work to produce information for the end user (p. 12.14).
34. Career opportunities in information processing include: working in an information systems department; sales; service and repair; consulting; and education and training (p. 12.14–12.17).
35. The jobs in an information systems department can be classified into five categories: (1) operations; (2) data administration; (3) systems analysis and design; (4) programming; and (5) information center (p. 12.15).
36. **Sales representatives** are often the most highly compensated employees in a computer company (p. 12.16).
37. Being a **service and repair technician** is a challenging job for persons who like to solve problems and who have a strong background in electronics (p. 12.16).
38. **Consultants**, people who draw upon their experience to give advice to others, are in high demand for such tasks as computer system selection, system design, and communication network design and installation (p. 12.17).
39. According to the U.S. Bureau of Labor and Statistics, the fastest growing computer career positions between 1982 and 1995 will be systems analyst, applications programmer, machine operator, and computer repair technician (p. 12.18).
40. The three fields in information processing are computer information systems; computer science; and computer engineering (p. 12.19).
41. **Computer information systems** refers to the use of computers in areas relating to business (p. 12.19).
42. **Computer science** includes the technical aspects of computers such as hardware operation and systems software (p. 12.19).
43. **Computer engineering** deals with the design and manufacturing of electronic computer components and computer hardware (p. 12.19–12.20).
44. Trade schools, technical schools, community colleges, and college and universities offer formal education and certification or degree programs in computer related fields (p. 12.20).
45. Computer professionals may continue to develop their skills and increase their recognition among their peers through professional organizations, certification, and professional growth and continuing education activities (p. 12.20).
46. Professional organizations, such as the **Data Processing Management Association (DPMA)**, have been formed by people who have common interests and a desire to share their knowledge (p. 12.20–12.21).
47. The **Certificate in Data Processing (CDP)** is the best known certification program in the information processing industry (p. 12.21).
48. Computer professionals stay current by participating in professional growth and continuing education activities such as conferences, workshops, conventions, and trade shows (p. 12.21).

Review Questions

1. List three electronic devices that are used in an automated office. What is voice mail? How is a Fax machine used?

2. What is the goal of the automated factory? Briefly explain the four technologies that are used.

3. What are some of the personal services available to home computer users?

4. Describe the three general categories of educational software.

5. List the six guidelines for buying a personal computer. Why is it recommended that you select your software before your equipment?

6. What is software piracy?

7. What is unauthorized access and unauthorized use? How can they be prevented?

8. Explain why computer viruses are malicious. What is a ''vaccine'' program?

9. Discuss the four common points covered in the state and federal information privacy laws.

10. Briefly discuss the computer hardware and software industries.

11. The positions in an information systems department can be classified into what five categories?

12. List and discuss four information career opportunities other than working in an information systems department.

13. What are the four fastest growing computer career positions?

14. Describe the three fields in information processing.

15. List five computer-related professional organizations.

16. What are the five parts of the CDP exam?

Index

Photo Credits

Chapter 1

Page 1.1, 1-1, 1-2 International Business Machines Corp. / **1.7** (a) Compaq Computer Corp.; (b) NCR Corp.; (c) International Business Machines Corp.; (e, d) Cray Research, Inc. / **1-13** Intertec Diversified Systems / **1-14** Racal-Milgo / **1-15** Management Science America / **Page 1.23** Top: United Press International; Bottom: Carl Howard; (center) Iowa State University; (right) Princeton University / **Page 1-24** Top: U.S. Department of the Navy; Bottom: (both) International Business Machines Corp. / **Page 1-25** Top: (left) International Business Machines Corp.; (right both) Intel Corp.; Bottom: (left) Dartmouth College News Services; (right) Digital Equipment Corp. / **Page 1-26** Top: (left both) International Business Machines Corp.; Bottom: (left) The Computer Museum, Boston; (right) Apple Computer, Inc. / **Page 1-27** Top: (left) Microsoft Corp.; (right both) Lotus Development Corp.; Bottom: International Business Machines Corp. / **Page 1-28** Top: (left) International Business Machines Corp.; (right) Intel Corp.; Bottom: Compaq Computer Corp.

Chapter 2

Page 2.1, 2-1 (a, b) Curtis Fukuda / **2-28** Aldus Corp. / **2-29** T/Maker Co. / **2-30** Computer Associates / **2-32** Claris Corp.

Chapter 3

Page 3.1 Adage, Inc. / **3-2** Curtis Fukuda / **3-3** (left) Wyse Technology; (right) Apollo Computer Inc. / **3-4** International Business Machines Corp. / **3-5** Top: Logitech, Inc.; Bottom: Curtis Fukuda / **3-6** Diebold, Inc. / **3-7** Adage, Inc. / **3-8** Lear Siegler, Inc. / **3-9** Texas Instruments, Inc. / **3-11** NCR Corp. / **3-12** Soricon Corp. / **3-15** Caere Corp. / **3-16** (both) Spectra-Physics / **3-17** AST Research Inc. / **3-18** LXR Division of Electromagnetic Science Inc. / **3-19** Motorola, Inc. / **3-28** Acme Visible Records

Chapter 4

Page 4.1 Intel Corp. / **4-1** Micron Technology, Inc. / **4-18** Photo Network / Michael Manheim

Chapter 5

Page 5.1 Storage Technology Corp. / **5-7** (left) Atchison, Topeka & Santa Fe Railway Co.; (right) Storage Technology Corp. / **5-8** Epson America Inc. / **5-9** Data Products Corp. / **5-13** Beagle Bros. / **5-14** Radio Shack, A Division of Tandy Corp. / **5-16** International Business Machines, Corp. / **5-18** Hewlett-Packard Co. / **5-20** McDonnell Douglas Automation Co. / **5-21** Data Products Corp. / **5-22** Xerox Corp. / **5-25** Toshiba America, Inc. / **5-26** Radio Shack, A Division of Tandy Corp. / **5-27** Hewlett-Packard Co. / **5-28** (both) Calcomp

Chapter 6

Page 6.1 Storage Technology Corp. / **6-1, 6-2** Curtis Fukuda / **6-8** (both) Plus Development Corp. / **6-10** Seagate Technology / **6-11** Plus Development Corp. / **6-12** Curtis Fukuda / **6-14** Lockheed Corp. / **6-15** International Business Machines Corp. / **6-18** Hewlett-Packard Co. / **6-19** Curtis Fukuda / **6-20, 6-12** Hewlett-Packard Co. / **6-22** Curtis Fukuda / **6-26** (left) Hitachi America Ltd.; (right) Drexler Technology Corp. / **6-27, 6-28** Storage Technology Corp.

Chapter 7

Page 7.1, 7-16 Hewlett-Packard Co.

Chapter 8

Page 8.1 Panasonic Industrial Co. / **8-2** BR Intec Corp. / **8-3** Corning Glass Works / **8-4** Siecor Corp. of America / **8-6** Hewlett-Packard Co. / **8-13, 8-14** Hayes Microcomputer Products, Inc. / **8-15** Panasonic Industrial Co.

Chapter 9

Page 9.1 A.T. & T. Archives / **9-7** International Business Machines Corp. / **9-8** Apple Computer, Inc.

Chapter 10

Page 10.1 Management Science America / **10-1** Internal Revenue Service / **10-16** Curtis Fukuda / **10-17** American Software / **10-18** Walter Bibikow / Image Bank / **10-19** Curtis Fukuda

Chapter 11

Page 11.1 Curtis Fukuda / **11-11** U.S. Department of the Navy

Chapter 12

Page 12.2 Canon USA Inc. / **12-1** (top to bottom) Radio Shack, A Division of Tandy Corp.; Claris Corp.; Lotus Development Corp.; Compaq Computer Corp.; Hewlett-Packard Co. / **12-2** Canon USA Inc. / **12-3** Apollo Computer, Inc. / **12-4** NASA / **12-5** General Motors Corp. / **12-7** (both) Broderbund Software, Inc. / **12-8** Electronic Arts / **12-10** Radio Shack, A Division of Tandy Corp. / **12-12** Computerland / **12-13** Radio Shack, A Division of Tandy Corp.

Cover Photo: Tim Davis Photography